Who killed kurt cobain?

The Mysterious Death of an Icon

Who killed kurt cobain?

The Mysterious Death of an Icon

Ian Halperin and

Max Wallace

BLAKE

Published by Blake Publishing Ltd,
3 Bramber Court,2 Bramber Road,
London W14 9PB,England

First published in paperback in the UK in 2002

ISBN 1 85782 5101

British Library Cataloguing-in-Publication Data:
A catalogue record for this book is available
from the British Library.

Design by ENVY

Printed and bound in Great Britain by Bookmarque, Croydon, Surrey

5 7 9 10 8 6

To the memory of sixty-eight lost souls

Contents

Introduction

July 1994, Ian Halperin was on a West Coast tour with his band State of Emergency. As a longtime musician who played all over the world, Ian knew many figures from the Seattle music scene. During the nine days Ian spent in Seattle, he talked to several musicians who related their doubts over the suicide of Kurt Cobain three months earlier.

"Kurt was definitely not suicidal at the time of his death," said one friend, who boasted that he had used the same heroin dealer as Cobain. "Something else happened; he may have been killed."

By the end of the trip, Ian had heard a number of similar stories from people who had a nagging sense of unease about the official version.

Ian had worked as a journalist for more than ten years before becoming a full-time musician. At first the stories sounded like they had all the elements of a classic conspiracy theory. Rumours of Courtney Love's involvement made the story sound all the more far-fetched. Courtney-bashing, it seemed, had become a national sport. People were always willing to believe the worst about Courtney, much like her predecessor as America's most famous rock widow, Yoko Ono.

But among the myriad unsubstantiated rumours was a report that Courtney's own private detective believed Kurt was murdered. Ian's journalistic instincts immediately took over.

Ian had met Kurt in Montreal in 1990 when Nirvana played for about two hundred people at the small alternative music club Foufounes Electrique. Ian, like Kurt, frequently wrote lyrics about oppression and suicide.

"So you play sax," Kurt said during their conversation a few minutes before Nirvana's set. "Man, I've thought about using some horns in our band, but in a bit of a tweaked-out way."

"How's the band doing?" Ian asked. "It's tough, but things have been picking up lately," Kurt said. "We're starting to get more gigs.... Hey, man, ya know where I can score some smack?"

"Don't ask me, I'm not into it," Ian replied. "I have a couple of Bulgarian friends who are musicians. If they show, I'm sure they can help you."

Krist Novoselic then came up and told Kurt that there were only a couple of minutes to go before they would go on.

"See ya later," Kurt said.

Ian left midway through the set. He never talked to Kurt Cobain again.

After Ian returned from Seattle in the summer of 1994, he contacted his old writing partner Max Wallace. The two once shared a *Rolling Stone* magazine award for investigative journalism. Wallace was station manager of Ottawa's CKCU-FM – North America's oldest alternative radio station – and had good connections in alternative music circles. After Ian told him what he had heard in

Seattle, the two agreed it might be an interesting story and decided to do further research, which led to the publication of a somewhat skeptical article in the June 1995 issue of *Canadian Disk* magazine.

Halperin and Wallace were subsequently commissioned to turn the article into a video documentary, and in late 1995 they traveled to California and Seattle to investigate the case. They spent several months on the road and interviewed more than one hundred people who knew the Cobains or were familiar with the case. All of this led to the idea of a book after their investigation yielded better results than they had anticipated.

Two years later the world continues to believe Kurt Cobain put a gun to his head and ended his angst-ridden life. Courtney Love has emerged as one of the world's most celebrated figures, shedding tears at will for reporters and fans when she talks about her husband's death while she catapults from tragic rock widow to a full-fledged star in her own right.

But as she signs autographs and revels in her never-ending publicity, one man – L.A. private investigator Tom Grant – has vowed to reveal the truth about what really happened in early April of 1994, by proving Kurt Cobain was murdered and possibly rewriting the annals of music history.

Who Killed Kurt Cobain? sheds a critical light on Grant's investigation, brings forward new information about Cobain's life and death, reveals many unanswered questions, and argues that the case must be reopened so the world can learn the truth.

Acknowledgements

In acknowledging the many people who made this book possible, it is important to first note that not everybody who cooperated with our project was fully aware of the book's subject matter. In fact, many of the interviews were conducted before the idea of a book was even contemplated.

Before we thank those who assisted us on our two-year odyssey, we must acknowledge the many people who asked that their names not be used for personal reasons but who were nevertheless committed to the truth. These include friends of Kurt and Courtney; members of the music industry; mainstays of the Portland, Seattle, Olympia, and Los Angeles scene; and two brave members of the Seattle police force.

Special thanks to Toby Amirault, Neil Bakshi, Hillel Black, the *Boston Phoenix*, Al Bowman, Nick Broomfield, Alain Brunet, Dylan Carlson, Jacquie Charlton, Lance

Chilton and Much Music, CHOM-FM, Esmond Choueke, CKCU-FM, Peter Cleary, Lori Clermont, Mark Connelly, Diane Diamond, Julien Feldman, Greta Fenwick, Gillian Gaar, Cory Garfinkle, Rhonda Green, Julius Grey, Daniel Harris, Betty Hawkins, Jane Hawtin, Noah Lukeman, Diedtra Henderson and Duff Wilson of the *Seattle Times*, Andrew Halperin, Allan Katz, Neil Kushner, Santina Lucci, Ian MacLean, Joyce MacPhee, Bert McFarlane, Slim Moon, James Moreland, Much Music, David Nanasi, Albert Nerenberg, Stewart Nulman, the Opera House (Toronto), Positively 4th Street, Tim Perlich, Hillary Richrod, Shawn Scallen, Todd Shapiro, Steve Shein, Denise Sheppard, Victor Shiffman, Al Taylor, Jeremiah Wall, Marc Weisblott, Alice Wheeler, Bobby White, Anna Wolverston, and Morag York.

We would especially like to thank our parents and families for their unwavering support.

We're also indebted to several sources for biographical information about Kurt and Courtney. For details about Kurt's early years and Nirvana period, *Come As You Are* by Michael Azzerad was invaluable, as was *Wasted* by Christopher Sandford. For extra source material about Courtney Love, we drew on *Queen of Noise* by Melissa Rossi. For details about Courtney's trip to Ithaca, New York, we used "Kurt Cobain's Final Tour" from the March 1996 *Esquire* magazine.

1

Kurt: The Lost Boy

On a hot summer's day in 1994, Courtney Love lands at New York's Kennedy Airport after an overseas flight from Europe. On her back is a knapsack which resembles a teddy bear. As she goes through customs, an officer asks to inspect the knapsack. She removes it from her shoulder and hands it over. As he unzips the curiously shaped travel bag, a puff of ashes flies up toward the airport's ventilation system. "What's that?" asks the customs official.

"That's my husband," comes the reply.

Eight weeks earlier, at 9:40 a.m. on the morning of April 8, 1994, the phone rang in the studio of Seattle's KXRX radio. DJ Marty Reimer picked up the phone and was greeted by the words," You're going to owe me some pretty good Pink Floyd tickets for this one." It was the dispatcher for a local security firm with the news that his employee Gary Smith had just caught a glimpse through a window of the body of Kurt Cobain sprawled on the floor in a room at his Madrona, Washington, estate, where Smith was installing a security system. The dispatcher had phoned the radio station before notifying the police, and minutes later the world heard the news: the voice of a generation was dead. Thus was the world ushered into a world without Kurt Cobain. For millions, April 8, 1994, became a day as indelibly branded into their memories as November 22, 1963, August 16, 1977, and December 8, 1980 – the deathdates of JFK, Elvis, and John Lennon.

The body Smith found that day had come into the world twenty-seven years earlier, on February 20, 1967. Although Aberdeen, Washington, claims (not brags) to be the birthplace of Kurt Cobain, he was actually born to Donald Cobain and Wendy Fradenburg in the bleak logging town of Hoquiam, which is separated from Aberdeen by a street. While Wendy took care of the baby at their small rental house, Don supported the family as a mechanic at the Aberdeen Chevron station. When they had scraped up enough for a down payment, the Cobains bought a house on East First Street near Don's workplace, and little Kurt moved to the town he would later describe as "white-trash hell."

Much has been written about the depressed state of the little logging town which spawned the future rock legend; journalists have described the boarded-up storefronts; bumper stickers with recipes for cooking the spotted owl – the creature whose endangered status residents blame for the faltering logging industry; rampant alcoholism; and a suicide rate double the national average. It is said that because Kurt grew up in this setting, his eventual fate is no real surprise.

But in 1967, Aberdeen was a very different town than it is today. Its lifeblood, the logging industry, was still thriving, and unemployment was fairly low. Its legendary red-light district – at one point sporting more than fifty brothels servicing the sailors and loggers – had been shut down by a police crackdown during a wave of morality which had swept the town during the fifties. While the nation was caught up in the Summer of Love, Aberdeen was having none of it. You went off to Vietnam to fight for your country, you went to church, you kept your hair short, and you saluted the flag. If any of those hippie freaks from Seattle or Portland came through town, God help them, they'd get their ass kicked.

In later years, Kurt and his Aberdeen friends loved to tell horror stories about their hometown. Kurt's friend Dale Crover summed it up: "There was nothing to do there but smoke dope and worship Satan." As Kurt's onstage antics became more and more outrageous in later years, he would admit that most of his shock tactics were aimed at the Aberdeen rednecks of his youth. What he never talked about publicly was that some of those rednecks were related to him.

Every Christmas, Wendy's extended family gathered for a big dinner. Those dinners featured the usual laughter, arguments, and discussion which characterize any family dinner. Laced in the conversation, however, was a remarkable amount of good old-fashioned white supremacism. "Niggers and immigrants" were frequently lambasted because they were supposedly taking the jobs away from decent white folk. Says one family friend, "Not everybody in the family subscribed to that way of thinking, but nobody ever put up an argument. In those parts, that's the way people talked."

Wendy in particular liked to believe she had risen above her own white-trash surroundings. She refused to live in one of the many trailer parks which dotted the Aberdeen landscape, and scrimped and saved Don's earnings to ensure she could bring up her children in their own house – a badge of respectability signifying arrival into the middle class. Indeed, she wanted better things for her son and daughter, Kimberly, who was born when Kurt was three, and envisioned the day they would escape and make something out of themselves. In later interviews, Cobain would portray his early childhood years as fairly idyllic.

Lavished with attention by his many aunts and uncles, he was by all accounts an extrovert kid who would display his enthusiasm to anybody who paid attention. But there were several incidents that gave his parents cause for concern: when Kurt was only two, a seventy-eight-year-old man next door complained to Wendy that the little boy had tried to bite his ear off. A year later, an Aberdeen police officer came to the door informing the Cobains that a neighbour's cat had been tortured and their son was the prime suspect.

During the late sixties and early seventies, pharmaceutical companies spent millions of dollars distributing medical pamphlets urging pediatricians to liberally prescribe a drug called Ritalin – basically, speedæto children displaying signs of "hyperactivity" – the new medical buzzword. Any child who was a bit too raucous was considered a good candidate for the drug. The Cobains didn't argue when their pediatrician wrote a prescription for little Kurt. (Ironically, Courtney Love was also prescribed Ritalin as a child.)

Children on Ritalin would often become so keyed up that they couldn't sleep, necessitating another prescription for calming sedatives. Kurt was luckier than most. The sedatives were making him fall asleep in school, so he was taken off the drugs and subjected to another recent fad cure for hyperactivity, the elimination of sugar from the diet. It seemed to do the trick. There was probably nothing wrong with him in the first place, but from then on his family accepted his outgoing personality.

His cousin Beverly later claimed that she remembered the phrase "attention deficit" being chanted like a mantra to describe his condition, but this is fairly unlikely since attention deficit disorder (ADD) didn't become a recognized psychological condition until 1980, many years later. Today doctors indeed prescribe the drug for ADD rather than hyperactivity, although they are sometimes thought of as the same thing.

Attempts have been made by journalists and even family members to link his early Ritalin prescription to his later chronic drug use, but this seems to be stretching things, especially since he was taken off Ritalin less than three months after being started on the drug.

It was around this time in his early childhood that Kurt introduced the family to his invisible friend "Bodah." He liked to blame his own mischievous activities on his new friend, and he even had Wendy set an extra place at the table for him.

"I was an extremely happy child," Kurt told his official biographer, Michael Azerad. "I was constantly screaming and singing. I didn't know when to quit. I'd eventually get beaten up by kids because I'd get so excited about wanting to play. I took play very seriously. I was just really happy." In one of Kurt's typical contradictions, he would also tell the Los Angeles Times that he was a "seriously depressed kid," but that was probably just one of his many press-baiting remarks in which he took such great delight.

The constant singing may have had something to do with his much-discussed musical roots. Wendy's family had always been immersed in music. When she was growing up, her uncle Delbert had enjoyed some recording success in the style of the legendary tenor Mario Lanza after moving to California and changing his name to Dale Arden. Wendy's sister Mary had her own country band and played the local honky-tonks, even recording a self-financed single at one point.

Although accounts differ, it was probably Mary who first introduced Kurt to the guitar. She later said she tried to teach him but he didn't have the patience on account of his hyperactivity. Others say she never really made an effort but would occasionally hand him her guitar and he would fool around on the strings the way any child would. It was Mary, however, who, instilled in Kurt a lifelong love of pop music which he would never lose, even after pop music was decidedly uncool in the punk rock circles he travelled in.

When Kurt came over to visit, Mary would play records for him on her Hi-Fi – especially the Beatles, who were Kurt's favourites until his death. When he was seven, she gave him some of his favourite recordings, including the Beatles, the Mamas and the Papas, and the Monkees. Around that time, she also gave him his first musical instrument, a bass drum. His constant beating would drive his parents crazy and he would be banished outdoors to annoy the neighbours. Years later his drum-banging experience came in handy when he joined his junior high school band, playing the snare drum.

Walking through the streets of Aberdeen banging his drum, Kurt engaged in the first act in what would become his favorite hobby – pissing off Aberdonians. Even his grandmother acknowledged the boy's perverse joy at annoying the neighbours. As Kurt would later tell people, "It's hard to believe their necks could become a darker shade of red, but they did."

Kurt would stroll the streets of Aberdeen battling the townspeople with his sardonic tongue. "Hey, what the fuck are you looking at," he once yelled at a middle-aged man who was staring at Kurt on the sidewalk while stopped in his Chevy Impala at a red light. "Get a life, bastard. You got a staring problem or something?"

When the light changed to green and the car began to speed away, Kurt grabbed an empty Coke bottle from the ground and hurled it at the car. It hit the side of the Chevy and shattered into small pieces.

"Next time I'll throw it through your window, you fucker," Kurt yelled out.

Around 1973, family members started paying more attention to the little drawings Kurt would do whenever he ran out of energy. Although his artistic talent was still unrefined, his renderings displayed a definite flair (one of his drawings appeared on the front page of the school newspaper when he was six), and his parents began to seriously encourage his artistic side, signing him up for both art and music (drum) lessons.

Although he showed much more artistic ability, music was all that really mattered to him. He told everybody who would listen that he was going to be a "big rock star" one day – which would remain his goal until a couple of years later when he saw Evel Knievel on television and decided he was going to be a stuntman.

Cobain mythology attributes Kurt's sudden turnaround from happy child to disturbed pre-adolescent to his parents' divorce in 1975 when he was eight years old. His mother Wendy in particular paints family life as fairly rosy until she and Don split.

A number of incidents, however, would seem to suggest a downward spiral that began much earlier. Kurt was fond of telling the possibly apocryphal story of Christmas 1974, when he was seven and wanted a toy Starsky and Hutch gun. Early Christmas morning, Kurt and his sister raced downstairs to find their presents. Kurt was devastated to look in his stocking and discover only a large lump of coal.

Family members also recall Wendy constantly blowing up at Kurt for the littlest things and Kurt running up to his room in tears. Don was a less imposing figure in Kurt's life. Although he had a quick temper, he was rarely at home (Wendy later claimed Don once threw Kurt across a room, though Don and Kurt denied it). On weekends, he would try to play with Kurt, who showed little interest in sports but would sometimes play ball with his father because he knew it pleased Don, who was an avid jock and coached a number of neighbourhood teams.

Wendy was unquestionably the authority figure with the children and tried to be a good mother, nurturing Kurt's interests in art and music, but was often frustrated by his independent streak and manic tendencies.

Then there was Kimberly, whom Kurt regarded as the typical pesky sister, three years younger than her brother and seemingly always underfoot. Wendy had to be particularly adept to guard against the usual sibling rivalry ever since three-year-old Kurt ran away from home two days after Kim was born and was found crying under a nearby bridge.

At first Wendy seemed content to play mother and wife, but around 1974 she began to display an obvious unhappiness with her life. When she wasn't yelling at the kids, she was sounding off at Don, and when the divorce came, it was no surprise to anyone except, as Cobain lore goes, little Kurt.

Until Wendy moved out of her Aberdeen home in 1995, the wall of Kurt's old bedroom was covered in graffiti written in his childish scrawl. Among the rock band logos were these words: "I hate mom, I hate Dad. Dad hates mom, mom hates dad. It simply makes you want to feel so sad. Mom sucks. Dad sucks." Wendy liked to point to these words to illustrate the devastating effect the divorce had on young Kurt. In fact, Kurt wrote these sentiments months before the divorce, when he heard one of the many shouting matches his parents engaged in during those days.

Don finally moved his stuff out on March 1, 1976, a week after Kurt's ninth birthday, and took an apartment in Hoquiam. Wendy was allowed to keep the house and their 1968 Camaro, while Don got the Ford truck. Don received visitation rights and was ordered to pay $150 a month in child support to Wendy, who got full custody of the children.

Almost everything written about Kurt after his death – most of it using Wendy as a source – portrays the emotional devastation his parents breakup had on the nine-year-old boy. "It just destroyed his life," Wendy told Rolling Stone in 1992. "He changed completely. I think he was ashamed. And he became very inward – he just held everything. He became real shy." She believes the resulting trauma is what destroyed his life and set the stage for his eventual fate.

There is no question the divorce had an impact on Kurt. "I just remember all of a sudden not being the same person, feeling like I wasn't worthy anymore," he would recall.

But it was other events following the divorce that would prove to have a much stronger effect on his life.

Wendy's official version of why she divorced Don was that he was hardly ever around, that he was either working, playing sports, or coaching.

Wendy's new boyfriend moved in soon after Don moved out. Kurt still wasn't quite over the shock of his parents' split when this new man whom he would later call a "mean, huge wife-beater" – suddenly appeared on the scene. Almost right away the boyfriend took on the father role, with Wendy's full blessing. He would give Kurt orders and expect to be obeyed. Used to Don's rather laissez-faire attitude toward parenting, the boy wouldn't always react with enthusiasm. That usually earned him a smack. Kurt's protests to his mother almost always fell on deaf ears. (Years later Wendy admitted that the man was "nuts – a paranoid schizophrenic.")

Kurt began to withdraw into his own little world. He was terrified in the boyfriend's presence, never knowing when the man's powerful hand would be directed at his head. For the first time, he felt completely powerless and alone. Wendy attributed her son's morose behavior to jealousy. Kurt once told his friend Dylan Carlson that living with this man was much more psychologically damaging than the divorce itself.

Kurt began to get into trouble at school and at home. One night, in a scene reminiscent of the popular comic "Calvin and Hobbes," he locked his babysitter out of the house when she was taking out the garbage. And often, when his mother went out to a local bar with her new boyfriend, Kurt would call Don, begging his father to let him live with him. His mother's boyfriend was all too anxious to get rid of the young pest and convinced Wendy to let Kurt stay with his father. Although Wendy claims Kurt lived with her for a year after the divorce, in reality he remained with her for only a little more than three months.

By this time, Don had taken a job with a lumber company and moved to the nearby logging town Montesano, a twenty-minute drive east of Aberdeen.

Despite or because of her own origins, Wendy had always tried to protect Kurt from "white trash," specifically prohibiting him from playing with "poor kids." She must have had mixed feelings when Kurt moved into Don's new home, located in the middle of a Montesano trailer park.

Although Don had never been particularly close to his son as a young child, he was particularly touched that Kurt wanted to live with him, and resolved to be a good dad. The first thing he did was buy his son a new minibike – the envy of the neighborhood kids. He took him camping or on outings every weekend, and the two almost bonded. Kurt was beginning to come out of the shell he had built around himself after the divorce and return to his old self.

"He seemed pretty happy that year," recalls a trailer park neighbour, Shelley Renfrew. "You could tell Don really loved his son and was always showing him off to everybody."

Kurt's uncle Larry Smith later remembered a particular incident around that time when Kurt still seemed in good spirits: "A wonderful picture comes to mind of a rare, sunny day when I peeked out the window into the yard. There was Kurt with some kind of contraption on his head. It resembled a tinfoil hat. He was sneaking around the yard, followed by about half a dozen laughing toddlers. Kurt had the million-dollar grin on his face, and I could tell he was definitely in 'nirvana.' I guess you could say he was the pied piper of compassion."

In September, Kurt transferred to Beacon Elementary in Montesano and seemed to thrive that year, even getting involved in a number of school activities.

Things were going along well until just before Kurt's eleventh birthday, when Don announced he was remarrying. Kurt immediately displayed his displeasure at someone usurping his father's affections. To make matters worse, Kurt's stepmother came with two children of her own. The whole family moved to a real house in Montesano to begin their new life, but Kurt only went reluctantly. The trailer park was where he had been happy, and he didn't want to leave.

By all accounts, his new stepmother did everything she could to win Kurt's affection, but to no avail. At the same time, Don was anxious to win over his own new stepchildren, and Kurt was bitterly resentful at all the attention going to the newcomers.

It was around this time that Kurt first began to display the ugly side of his personality; the bully. He would mercilessly torment his new step-brother and stepsister and treat them much like his mother's boyfriend treated him.

He also liked to provoke some of the neighboring trailer park kids, recalling years later, "My mom thought that I was better than those kids, so I picked on them every once in a while – the scummy kids, the dirty kids. I just remember there were a couple of kids that stunk like pee all the time and I would bully them around and get in fights with them."

Although rarely reported, Kurt's dark side would manifest itself time and again throughout his life.

Increasingly frustrated by Kurt's behaviour, Don and his wife tried everything they could think of doing to placate the boy, but he refused to adjust to his new environment and became increasingly difficult, often resorting to full-scale tantrums over the smallest incidents. According to almost everybody who knew the family, Don's wife was no wicked stepmother. She bent over backwards to get Kurt to like her but was constantly rebuffed.

One Saturday afternoon the whole family went shopping at a nearby shopping mall. Kurt chose to forgo the outing and sulk alone in his basement room. When they returned a few hours later laden with new toys, Kurt took his stepsister's new doll and cut off her head – an act which presaged his later hobby of collecting dismembered doll figures.

Several months after Don remarried, Kurt demanded he be allowed to go back to live with Wendy. Don had no objections, but Wendy was still living with her boyfriend and refused to allow Kurt to come back. Pleading calls from Kurt couldn't persuade her to change her mind, although he frequently visited his mother.

On June 14, 1979 – when Kurt was twelve years old – Don filed a court petition to gain official custody of his son. At the time, he was at his wits' end trying to figure out a way to gain the acceptance of his son again. Technically, because of the divorce agreement, Wendy still had official custody of Kurt even though he hadn't lived with her for almost three years. "I did it to make him feel a part of the family," Don later said.

Kurt didn't take well to his father's gesture, screaming, "That bitch isn't my family," referring to his stepmother.

When he wasn't in school, Kurt spent all his time in his room drawing, watching television, and listening to his records, including his current favourites Queen and of course the Beatles. Across the ocean, a band called the Sex Pistols had begun a musical revolution which would one day change his life. But in Aberdeen, that music was still considered noise. Progressive rock and heavy metal ruled. That's what the cool kids listened to. Because of Kurt's reputation as a bully, a group of these teenagers took notice of twelve-year-old Kurt and invited him to hang out with them after school.

"They were way older than me," Kurt told his biographer. "They must have been in junior high. They were smoking pot and I just thought they were cooler than my geeky fourth-grade friends who watched Happy Days. I just let them come over to my house and eat my food, just to have friends."

Don, who was a big rock-'n'-roll fan, had recently sent away to Columbia Music House for one of their "Get twelve records for only one cent" offers. Kurt's new friends noticed all the great records – Kiss, Aerosmith, Black Sabbath – in Don's collection and insisted Kurt play them. This was Kurt's first introduction to a heavier sound than he had been used to. He liked it.

"After they turned me on to that music," Kurt recalled, "I started turning into this little stoner kid."

In fact, Kurt was at first reluctant to smoke pot with his new friends. They didn't really push it on him because of his age. He did acquire a taste for beer, however.

A thirty-one-year-old man who lived a couple of blocks away sparked his interest in the brew. Jim Randall concocted home brew in his basement and would regularly invite Kurt over for a pint or two. In exchange, Kurt would convince his friends to buy their beer from Randall whenever they had parties. Randall was unemployed and he sold brew to earn some cash. The Aberdeen teenage rebels were a perfect market for him because he treated them like adults, which gave them a more confident and less passive attitude at being regarded as the town's outcasts.

"Randall liked Kurt a lot," said Kevin Smiley, an old fried of Kurt's. "Sometimes he would give Kurt a special bottle if Kurt was able to sell a lot of beer for him." The special bottle, which Randall would always mark with the letters "PB" (the letters stood for Potent Brew) contained about 14 percent alcohol.

Then one weekend, one of his friends asked Kurt if he wanted to come to Seattle to a Sammy Hagar concert. They went with the friend's older sister. Don agreed to let his son go, pleased that Kurt seemed to be emerging from his cloud.

"On the way to the concert, Kurt recalled years later, "we drank a case of beer and we were stuck in traffic and I had to go so bad I peed in my pants. And when we got there, people were passing pipes of marijuana around and I'd never smoked pot before and I got really high. I had a Bic lighter in my shirt and I took it out for one of those lighter tributes at the end of the show and I was tripping out and the next thing I knew I had lit myself on fire."

Meanwhile, back home, the more attention he saw Don give to his new family, the more angry Kurt became. He was so anxious to win back his father's affection that he agreed to his father's suggestion that he join the school wrestling team despite his disgust at team sports. Don thought this would be the perfect release for his increasing aggression.

Indeed, Kurt seemed to have found a niche, showing a remarkable talent for lunging on other boys and pinning them to the mat for three seconds, although he later told people he had hated it, especially having to hang out with jocks.

Don never expected his son to show any athletic talent and was thrilled that Kurt seemed to excel at wrestling. He bragged to his friends and coworkers, especially when he received the news that Kurt had reached the finals in his school's wrestling championship for his weight category.

Don the proud father was sitting in the gym bleachers the day of the big match, certain his son would be bringing home the handsome trophy. Kurt, however, had other ideas. At last, he had seized upon the perfect way to pay his father back for the betrayal of marrying "that bitch."

As Kurt squared off with his opponent, he looked up at Don in the stands and gave him a sly grin. He kept the grin on his face as the whistle blew and he went limp, deliberately letting himself be pinned.

"You should have seen the look on his face," Kurt told Michael Azerad. "He actually walked out halfway through the match because I did it... four times in a row."

For Don, that was the final straw. Wendy refused to take him in, so he was sent to live with an aunt and uncle.

Between 1979 and 1981, Kurt was shuttled back and forth between relatives, with periodic returns to his father's house before he was thrown out again. According to Don, this period marked an almost friendless existence for Kurt, who spent most of his spare time in the library. Hilary Richrod was the reference librarian at Aberdeen's Timberland Library. She remembers Kurt sitting reading for hours at a time. "It was hard to miss him," she recalls. "He usually had multicoloured hair, and that kind of stuck out in a town like Aberdeen."

One of his junior high school classmates told writer Christopher Sandford that Kurt was "drowning in a tidal wave of self-hate" during this period. Kurt's uncle Larry Smith also remembers this bleak period of his nephew's life and the way the boy coped with his troubles, which he recalled in a letter to the editor of the local Aberdeen newspaper after Kurt died.

"My grandfather comprehended the intelligence and individuality in Kurt at a time when Kurt was being beaten down mentally and physically. 'Gramps' often told me of his respect for Kurt's tenacity and compassion even though he was in emotional pain. Shortly before Gramps died, he had been talking about Kurt. He looked at me and said words to the effect that he could see a nobility about Kurt that he had never seen in anyone in all his seventy years.

"One time, Gramps invited Kurt along on one of our steelhead fishing trips. We were spread out a few hundred feet apart along the Wynooche River. All of a sudden, we heard this horrendous combination of screaming, warbling, and yodeling from Kurt, who was upstream and out of sight. Gramps told me to run up there and help Kurt, who must have hooked a big fish. When I reached Kurt, he didn't even have his line in the water. When I asked him what was going on, he just looked at me with those piercing eyes and huge grin. He said, 'Oh, I'm just trying to thicken my vocal chords so I can scream better.'

"When I went back to Gramps to tell him, he just grinned and said, 'It figures. We'll just let him be. We can now say, Thank you, Kurt, for thickening your vocal chords!'"

Relatives from both sides of the family remember one thing in particular about this time – huge fights between Don and Wendy about their son whenever they saw each other. Wendy was becoming increasingly concerned about Kurt's deepening malaise, and she insisted he go to a psychiatrist, which he did for more than a year. But it didn't do much to change the boy, who continued to retreat inward.

At the end of 1980, Wendy finally broke up with her boyfriend after enduring years of physical and mental abuse. She had also just lost her job and she wasn't quite ready for the commitment of caring for Kurt, so she asked her brother Chuck Fradenburg to take him in for a while.

Uncle Chuck was one of the few relatives whom Kurt admired. A musician in the Aberdeen cover band

Fat Chance, Chuck knew every-thing there was to know about music, and Kurt loved listening to his giant record collection. Soon after Kurt moved in, Chuck reminded him that his fourteenth birthday was fast approaching and offered to buy him either a bicycle or a guitar. Kurt had fooled around with some of his stoner friends' guitars when he was younger, but he couldn't really play. He jumped at the chance to get a cool instrument so he could give up the decidedly uncool bass drum which he still played in his junior high school band.

Chuck asked his group's guitarist, Warren Mason, to find a guitar in time for Kurt's birthday in February. Warren obtained a six-string used Lindell from a local electrician friend – who later described it as a "piece of crap" – for $125. Kurt loved his new guitar and spent all his spare time playing it in his room. Chuck was so impressed by Kurt's passion for the instrument that he asked Mason to give his nephew lessons.

Cobain later described the effect of getting his first guitar: "It was definitely a good release. I thought of it as a job. It was my mission... as soon as I got the Lindell I just became obsessed with it."

Like most teenage guitarists of the early eighties, Kurt was determined to learn to play Led Zeppelin's "Stairway to Heaven" as well as his then guitar idol Jimmy Page. Although Kurt later denied ever liking Zeppelin, Mason later described his new student as playing the song with dazzling speed over and over.

"He wasn't the most technically gifted kid in the world," Mason remembers, "but he had a genuine feel for timing and phrasing. Kurt knew that the gaps between the notes are as important as the music. He had an intuitive grasp of what would and wouldn't work in a given song.

When Kurt was very young, his father noticed that he was left-handed. Although by the seventies this was no longer considered unacceptable, Don was determined his son would grow up right-handed, and he used some of the same methods his own father had used on him. These included slapping Kurt's wrist every time he used his left hand. This wasn't entirely effective but it did make Kurt ambidextrous. Although most guitars are made for right – handers and Kurt's Lindell was no exception – he chose to play it as a lefty, which presented a number of difficulties but gave him a distinctive style.

Wendy ordered Chuck to put a stop to Kurt's lessons only three months after they began them, which caused bitter resentment in young Kurt. He had finally found a sense of purpose and his mother had to go and interfere. This setback, however, didn't keep Kurt away from his guitar, which Mason described as his "best and only friend."

In downtown Aberdeen there was a music store called Rosevear's which sold instruments and had rooms upstairs which it rented out as rehearsal space. Unbeknownst to Wendy, Chuck gave Kurt money so he could rehearse whenever he wanted at Rosevear's, which became his home away from home.

Once again, Kurt revived his childhood dream of becoming a rock star. He began to devour music magazines like *Creem* and *Rolling Stone*.

Although his musical tastes still ran to mainstream rock – he had mastered Queen's "Another One Bites the Dust" and the Cars' "Best Friend's Girl" – he had seen the B-52s on Saturday Night Live and fell in love with the New Wave style. In fact, shortly after the broadcast he painted black and white squares on his sneakers in imitation of vocalist Fred Schneider's checkerboard Vans.

In *Creem* he constantly read about the exploits of Johnny Rotten and the Sex Pistols and loved the pictures of punk rockers, but he had no idea what punk sounded like and didn't know anybody with a punk record he could listen to.

Instead, he started to play his guitar the way he thought punk would sound. He described his music at the time as "really raunch riff rock... it was like Led Zeppelin but it was raunchy and I was trying to make it as aggressive and mean as I could." When he finally listened to his first punk record, the Clash's Sandinista, he was disappointed because it wasn't the way he had imagined punk would sound.

During one of his sojourns shuttling back and forth between relatives, he had stayed for a time with Don's parents, who were fairly religious and regularly attended church, bringing Kurt with them. He became enamoured of the church choir and decided to try out. The choirmaster was impressed by the boy's unique but untrained voice, which showed significantly more promise than his guitar playing.

Because he was constantly being praised for his vocal abilities and he thought he was a good guitarist, Kurt believed the time was right to start a band, although he later said he had abandoned the idea of becoming a rock star.

"I was so self-conscious at that time," he told Michael Azerad, "and I had such a small amount of self-esteem that I couldn't even think of actually becoming a rock star, never mind dealing with what they would expect a rock star to be. I couldn't imagine being on television or doing interviews or anything like that. Stuff like that didn't even seep into my mind at that time."

By the time he was fifteen, he had moved back in with Wendy, who had also taken in Rick Hansen, a local teenage boy whose mother had died. Rick also played guitar and the two would jam together for hours, sometimes with Rick's stoner friends, hatching plans to form a band but somehow never quite getting it together.

As usual when he would live with one parent, Kurt would become closer to the other parent. After several months with Wendy and her constant nagging,

Kurt was anxious to win Don's favour again in the hopes of maybe returning to live with his father one day. He even agreed to play on a Little League baseball team coached by Don, who, despite the wrestling incident years before, still harboured hopes for Kurt as a jock.

Kurt didn't take the team very seriously, deliberately striking out each time he came to bat, but it was during his brief baseball sojourn that he made a new friend named Matt Lukin.

Lukin played the bass for the Melvins, a local Aberdeen rock band. More than a year before, Kurt had actually attended a Melvins rehearsal with a friend of his who knew the drummer. At that time, when Kurt was in ninth grade, the band was still a cover band specializing in the Who and Jimi Hendrix. In awe at being in the presence of a real live band, Kurt – who later claimed he was drunk on wine – made a fool of himself telling the band members how great they were. After an hour of Kurt's effusive behavior, he and his friend were politely asked to leave.

But since that incident, the Melvins had discovered punk rock, and Kurt was excited to be friends with one of their members. While he and Lukin sat on the bench, they talked nonstop about music, although they weren't really friends outside the team that summer.

Kurt's real connection to the Melvins came during the previous school year, when he was in the same art class as Melvins leader Buzz Osbourne. He and Osbourne struck up a friendship and the two began to hang out. Osbourne was still heavily into the Who, but midway through the year he and the Melvins discovered punk and made plans to transform the band. He lent Kurt one of his new treasures, a photo book on the Sex Pistols, and passed on his newly acquired punk and New Wave tapes for Kurt to listen to.

These tapes were a revelation to fifteen-year-old Kurt, who began dressing punk and attending Melvins rehearsals. Everywhere he went, he would draw the Sex Pistols logo. According to Warren Mason and others, however, he was still listening to mainstream radio and to records by his favourite guitar influences, Jimmy Page and Jimi Hendrix. Mason believes Kurt's new image may have been contrived to fit in with his new friends.

Still, it is easy to imagine the appeal of punk – the music of rage and rebellionæto Kurt at that time. In their new incarnation, the Melvins began to attract a lot of attention, and they regularly played in Seattle and Olympia. Kurt began to tag along as a roadie, and he was in awe of their success.

Adhering to punk's do-it-yourself ethos, Kurt started recording some of his own music on a portable Toshiba tape recorder that he bought at Woolworth's for $14.99. "If you have something to say, pick up a guitar, write a song, and say it," Buzz Osbourne once told Kurt.

Kurt would record a few chords and improvise lyrics. When he played it back, he would usually think of a few more lyrics and then rerecord the song. The first time Kurt got the courage to play one of his tunes for Buzz, his friend was stoned and listened disinterestedly. "Not bad, needs a bit of work," he told Kurt of "Creation," a tune that had taken Kurt about an hour to write and record. Kurt knew, however, that Buzz was just being polite. He decided not to let anybody listen to his music again until it was more polished.

"That's all I ever wanted to do at that point," Kurt would later say. "I didn't have any high expectations of my music at all. I just wanted to have the chance to play in front of some people in Seattle. The thought of being in a band that was successful enough to go on tour was too much to ask at that time."

Aberdeen didn't have much of a punk rock club

scene, although the Ramones had passed through town when Kurt was ten and too young to care, but he was determined to experience the scene for himself. When Kurt heard that his favorite punk band, Black Flag, was coming to Seattle, he had to go. Wendy had forbidden Chuck to give Kurt any more money to indulge his music habit, so he sold his entire music collection to raise enough money for the ticket at Seattle's Mountaineer club and an ounce of pot for the road. Together with Buzz, Kurt spent the night slamdancing, and that night he made the fateful decision that he was going to be a punk rocker.

The day after the Black Flag show, Kurt got a punk haircut and embarked on what was to become his favorite endeavour, spray-painting cars with punk rock slogans.

Kurt's nearly three-year sojourn living with his mother came to an abrupt end when he was seventeen, in May 1984, when she married a longshoreman named Pat O'Connor, who Kurt later claimed was even worse than her previous psychotic boyfriend.

His new stepfather had no patience for the rebellious freak Kurt had become and made it clear he wasn't welcome under his roof. Once again Kurt was shuttled back and forth between relatives in Montesano, Aberdeen, and Hoquiam, most of whom also had no patience for the troublesome teenager.

Kurt's nomadic existence was miserable and he bitterly resented not being allowed to move back with his mother, with whom he had achieved a relatively peaceful coexistence in the days before she married Pat. Every night, Kurt would call up Wendy, sometimes in tears, begging to move back in. Finally, after being unceremoniously told by one of his aunts to vacate her house, Kurt phoned his mother to tell her he had run out of relatives willing to take him in. She convinced Pat he would stay only until he could find another place to live and told Kurt to come over.

This arrangement went fairly smoothly for a while as Kurt tried to be on his best behavior out of fear of another eviction. One day during this period, Pat returned home from one of his frequent drunken binges. From his room Kurt heard a vicious argument ensue, with Wendy accusing her husband of cheating on her. Moments later Wendy stormed out of the house to get drunk.

She returned several hours later with a determined look on her face. She headed for Pat's gun rack, which held a sizable collection of hunting rifles, and gathered up as many as she could. Unable to carry them all, she called for Kurt's sister, Kim, to take the rest along with a bag of ammunition and together they headed for the nearby Wishkah River, where they dumped the whole lot.

Watching his mother dump the guns, Kurt hatched a plan. Always on the lookout for ways to get dope money, Kurt brought a friend to the river that evening and they dredged the bottom until they had found nearly all the guns. They dragged the haul to town and sold them for enough money to buy Kurt a used amplifier. His friend used his share to buy an ounce of pot, and together they got very stoned to celebrate their good fortune.

Not long after this incident, Kurt returned home from practicing with the Melvins to find all his clothes and belongings packed in a box outside his room. Wendy had recently become pregnant and she didn't need the stress of her son's erratic behavior adding to her many existing problems.

Kurt moved into a small apartment with a friend, Jesse Reed, whose born-again-Christian parents had once taken him in, only to toss him out soon afterward because they thought he was a bad influence on their son.

Kurt was used to having other people clean up after him and wasn't particularly into domestic life. He liked to indulge in his hobby of dismembering dolls, covering them in fake blood, and hanging them in little nooses all over the apartment, which he later described as filled with "beer and puke and blood... garbage stacked up for months. I never did do the dishes. Jesse and I cooked food for about a week and then put all our greasy hamburger dishes in the sink and filled it up full of water and it sat there for the entire five months I was there."

2

Sex and Drugs and Rock'n'Roll

When he wasn't brooding in his room or at the library, Kurt was busy discovering girls. Cobain mythology has it that Kurt was a bisexual, actively pursuing relationships with both boys and girls. This misconception may have dated back to when Kurt was fifteen and befriended a boy named Myer Loftin, whom he met in one of his art classes. (Of course, Courtney's press-baiting comment that "Kurt fucked half the guys in Seattle" may have had something to do with it.) When Kurt first met Loftin, he was unaware his new friend was gay. When Kurt was informed this was so a few weeks later, his friend's homosexuality didn't bother him.

He and Loftin were almost inseparable. This didn't sit too well with the rednecks of Aberdeen, who didn't have a whole lot of tolerance for homosexuality.

"I started to realize that people were looking at me

even more peculiarly than usual," Kurt later recalled, describing countless incidents in school, especially after gym class, where he would be harassed and called "faggot." "They felt threatened because they were naked and I was supposedly gay so they either better cover up their penises or punch me. Or both."

At first, Kurt wore the distinction as a badge of honor and secretly delighted at pissing off these kids. "I started being proud of the fact that I was gay even though I wasn't. I really enjoyed the conflict. It was pretty exciting because I almost found my identity. I was a special geek. I wasn't quite the punk rocker I was looking for but at least it was better than being the average geek."

The fun soon wore off, however, as jocks started to turn from verbal to physical abuse, beating up Kurt almost every day after school. And then one day, in an act he would remember with shame for the rest of his life, he told Loftin that he couldn't hang around with him anymore. The abuse was too much to bear.

"He simply appeared one day and said he was getting too much grief for being the friend of a faggot," Loftin told Christopher Sandford. "He used the word 'faggot.' Then he gave me a stiff little hug, turned on his heel and walked away."

Kurt's uncle Larry later recalled what Kurt was going through. "Kurt didn't fit the general mold of society in a logging town, and so he was beaten up on by people who didn't understand him. One day I heard that he was in a fight a few blocks away. When I ran to the scene, the fight was over. However, I heard from a friend that Kurt was assaulted by a burly, 250-pound logger type. Evidently, Kurt did not even fight; he just presented the bully with the appropriate hand gesture every time he was knocked down until the bully gave up. To top it all off Kurt just had that usual grin on his face!"

Years later, after he was successful, Kurt would delight in dressing up in women's clothes in public or

French-kissing his fellow band members on live TV, confident that it would enrage his old neighbours in Aberdeen who were already talking about how they used to know Kurt in the old days.

In an attempt to redeem his reputation, he actively sought out girls, but he remained a virgin until he met a stoner girl named Jackie when he was seventeen. His first attempt at sex was thwarted when, just before consummation, Wendy burst into the room and shouted "Get that slut out of here."

He continued to have short flings, but by all accounts, he preferred pornography to live girls as an adolescent. While living in his first apartment with Jesse Reed, he had built up quite a collection – not the usual *Penthouse* and *Playboy* magazines but very hard-core titles with, amongst other things, women having sex with farm animals. He was also quite a voyeur.

One woman whom he and Reed had once hired to clean their apartment in exchange for drugs described Polaroids of women masturbating strewn around his bedroom. Much later Kurt would admit that he was never sexually normal.

When Kurt moved back to Aberdeen to live with Wendy, he also switched high schools from Montesano High to Aberdeen High. He had long since stopped hanging around with his old Melvins friends, who were back in Montesano, and he was anxious to join some crowd.

"I wanted to fit in somewhere, but not with the average kid, not with the popular kids at school. I wanted to fit in with the geeks, but the geeks were sub-geeks," he told Michael Azerad. "They weren't the average geek. They weren't the type of kid who would listen to Devo. They were just usually deformed."

There was one clique at the school with whom he was familiar – the stoners. Although he had long since rejected their mentality, he shared their taste in drugs and, secretly, in their music.

"Although I hated them, they were at least into rock 'n' roll," he said.

While he hung out with the stoners at the smokers' shed behind the school, Kurt struck up a friendship with Dale Crover, who had just joined the Melvins as their drummer. Crover, who lived in Aberdeen with his parents, had an attic room which he offered the Melvins as a rehearsal space. Kurt once again had an excuse to hang out with his old friends.

Kurt had long since decided that he was going to form a punk band, and spent long hours in the Aberdeen public library writing original material for the band he would someday have. Many of Kurt's new music friends were intrigued that he wrote his own stuff. Almost everybody at that time was content to play covers, but Kurt knew he would never be a rock star playing other people's material.

He convinced Crover and a friend named Greg Hokanson to start rehearsing some of his material, and the three were impressed by the results. When Buzz Osbourne heard the three rehearse one day, he invited them to open for the Melvins at an upcoming gig in nearby Moclips. Calling themselves Fecal Matter, the trio performed what Kurt would later call "a pretty lame effort."

Buoyed by their gig, the trio decided to take the next necessary step to rock stardom and record a demo tape. Kurt's aunt Mary offered to let them use her equipment.

Kurt began to circulate the results of this session to the assorted hangers-on who congregated at Melvins rehearsals. One of these regulars was a giant of a fellow named Krist Novoselic. A few years earlier, Krist had moved with his family – Croatian-born immigrants – from California to Aberdeen. Krist was a good friend of Dale Crover and would often bring his girlfriend Shelli to the rehearsals.

Describing his attraction to punk years later, Krist

said, "Punk rock kind of galvanized people in Aberdeen. It brought us together and we got our own little scene after a while and we all hung out. Punk rock had this cool, political personal message. It was a bit more cerebral than just stupid cock rock, you know."

When Krist heard Kurt's demo tape, he was blown away by the sound and right away knew this guy was going places.

Kurt had ditched Greg Hokanson from his band by this point and recruited Buzz Osbourne to play with him and Crover at assorted gigs under the name Brown Towel (misspelled on some posters as Brown Cow).

Krist was also a musician whose mother owned a beauty shop in Aberdeen. Above the shop was an empty room, perfect for a rehearsal space – a valuable commodity for musicians in those parts. Krist had once sung in a Melvins offshoot called the Stiff Woodies which played a few parties around town (Kurt even played drums with them once).

Krist offered the space to Kurt if he would form a band, and that winter the seeds of Nirvana began to take root. Every afternoon, Krist, Kurt, and Bob McFadden, a local jock they had recruited because he owned his own drums, would head up to the rehearsal space and jam. Their sessions soon began to attract the same kind of hangers-on as the Melvins rehearsals, until Krist one day posted a sign which read, "This is not a big crash pad. So just get out of here because we want to rehearse."

Meanwhile, Kurt had been evicted from his apartment. He was more than five months overdue on the rent. Wendy refused to take him in, because she had just read a book on a new way of dealing with problem kids, called "tough love." She was quite alarmed at his behaviour by this point and figured he had to do something to straighten himself out. This time Kurt was determined not to do the relative shuffle again, and instead he moved between friends' couches and even for a while to the back of Krist's van.

During this period, Kurt was living on a monthly ration of forty dollars' worth of food stamps. In later years, Kurt would tell people about the months he spent homeless living under the Wishkah Bridge. In fact, this was one of his favourite places to go and be alone to write poetry, but he never really lived there, according to his friend Rick Hansen, who said he really only spent one full night under the bridge.

In true punk rock fashion, Kurt loved to go out every night with a couple of friends and spray-paint slogans all over the town. Each morning the residents of Aberdeen would wake up to find "God Is Gay" or "Abort Christ" sprayed on their walls and pickup trucks.

One day, when Kurt was out on an excursion with Buzz and Krist, a police cruiser pulled up just as they had finished painting "Homosex Rules" on the side of a bank. The other two fled and hid in a garbage dumpster, leaving Kurt to take the rap. Ironically, when the cops brought him in and forced him to empty his pockets, out came a cassette of the punk group Millions of Dead Cops. Kurt was fined $180 and given a thirty-day suspended sentence.

Wendy had by this time abandoned her tough love experiment and rented a little shack, for one hundred dollars per month, where Kurt could live. He moved into the crude space with Matt Lukin of the Melvins.

He was still tight with the Melvins even though they had rejected his attempt to join the band a few months earlier. He had assembled his best material and was furiously rehearsing every day in hopes of joining his idols. But when the big audition came, Kurt was so nervous, he blew it. He forgot the words, forgot the chords, and just stood there, emitting feedback from his guitar. A fortuitous failure, as events turned out.

Although Seattle was still another world to Kurt's friends, Olympia was the happening place. Home of Evergreen College and a burgeoning alternative music scene, Olympia – the state capital – was a forty-five-minute drive from Aberdeen, and Kurt started making the trip with Krist almost every weekend, usually to see shows at Evergreen.

On one of these trips, they ran into Buzz Osbourne, who introduced Kurt to an Olympia woman named Tracy Marander. Tracy had once seen Fecal Matter perform and was impressed by Kurt's deep blue eyes and brooding personality.

From their first meeting, Kurt was hooked, and he began to spend every weekend in Olympia at Marander's apartment. During the week, he continued to practice with Novoselic and a new drummer, Aaron Burckhard. The mustachioed Burckhard was more of a metalhead than a punker, but Kurt and Krist needed a drummer and he was all they could find.

Kurt was starting to take his music more seriously and drove his fellow band members hard, insisting they practice constantly. Fueled by the compliments of their assorted friends and groupies, Kurt believed he was close to achieving his dream. The trio had yet to play live together and were anxious to get a gig. But this was easier said than done for a band that played original material.

"We just had to play a show," Kurt remembered. "God, if we could just play a show, it would be great."

Finally, a friend of Tracy's got them on the bill for a party in Olympia. An excited Kurt, Krist, and Aaron arrived ready to perform, only to discover that the party had been shut down by the police because of excessive noise.

A couple of weeks later, they finally got their chance when they were booked to play a house party in Raymond, Washington, opening for a metal band.

Their brand of showmanship, which included spreading fake vampire blood all over the house, didn't go over too well with the staid crowd of rich kids who Kurt later recalled "were so scared that they were in the kitchen hiding from us." They also weren't impressed by the original material, which included the first live performance of many future Nirvana staples, including "Floyd the Barber," "Beeswax," and "Hairspray Queen."

A few real gigs followed, and finally the band was hired one night to play the Community World Theatre in Tacoma, just outside Seattle. Until then, the band hadn't bothered giving themselves a name. When the promoter pressed Kurt for something to put up on the marquee, he came up with "Skid Row" on the spur of the moment.

People in the audience that night remember a fairly polished performance highlighted by Kurt's onstage antics, which included jumping five feet in the air and landing in a split.

As word spread and the band began to get more gigs, they seemed to constantly change their name, which went from Skid Row to Ted Ed Fred to Pen Cap Chew to Throat Oyster to Bliss to Windowpane.

During this period, Kurt was taking the money Wendy gave him for the rent on his shack and spending it on other things, usually drugs. Once again he was evicted for failing to pay the rent, but this time he had somewhere to go. Tracy had already invited him to move in with her in Olympia, and his eviction provided the perfect excuse. It was time to leave Aberdeen for good.

3
The Road to Nirvana

Kurt had mixed feelings about his new hometown. On the one hand, it was much more exciting than Aberdeen, with something to do almost every night and a thriving music scene. But Kurt kind of missed the rednecks and the feeling that he was different. In Olympia, his brand of angry rebel was a dime a dozen.

In Olympia, the main feeding ground for these rebels was the ultrahip Evergreen College, which was known for its mix of bohemians, progressive politics, alternative music, and feminists. Kurt had little patience for the latter group, and despite his later professions of sympathy toward women's issues, he would call feminists "angry bitches."

It was during his first few months in Olympia that Kurt first experienced the agonizing stomach pain which would haunt him for nearly the rest of his life. Years later he would describe the pain to *Details* magazine: "Imagine the worst stomach flu you've ever had, every single day. And it was worse when I ate, because once the meal would touch that red area, I would hyperventilate, my arms would turn numb, and I would vomit."

Doctor after doctor was puzzled by this ailment and couldn't diagnose what was causing it. Kurt had never been particularly healthy, suffering recurring bronchitis since he was a child. He also suffered from scoliosis (curvature of the spine) and a number of other minor ailments.

In later years, when Cobain's heroin addiction was first revealed, he and his publicists fell back on this stomach ailment as the source of his heroin use, claiming he did heroin only to ease the pain.

In fact, Kurt had first shot up nearly a year before, after he met a dealer named "Grunt" on one of his trips to Olympia. By this time, he was a regular user of pot, LSD, Percodans, and magic mushrooms.

"He was just about always high on something," says his friend Rick Hansen. "But that wasn't exactly uncommon in Aberdeen. The jocks did sports and the stoners did drugs, that's all there was to do."

His aunt Beverly Cobain says Kurt had an extremely addictive personality and would take large doses of aspirin or cough syrup whenever he wasn't feeling well. "From early childhood it was a religion for Kurt that everything could be cured by drugs," she told reporters after his death.

But the first time Kurt injected heroin into his arm, he knew he was taking his drug use to a different level. He had been offered the drug a number of times before and had always refused, but "Grunt" was always anxious to share the exhilaration he felt when he did smack, and told him what a great feeling it was. Kurt finally succumbed. That night Kurt sold his soul to what would become his own personal devil.

Kurt and Tracy were living in a tiny apartment at

114 North Pear Street. Visitors to the apartment were intrigued by the bizarre decor. On the refrigerator door was a collage Kurt made out of pictures of diseased vaginas he had found in a medical textbook. And on the shelves were nativity scenes he had constructed full of decayed bodies, skeletons, and demons. He had continued his fascination with dolls and had begun to make his own out of clay in all kinds of strange shapes. All over the walls were his most recent paintings, which often consisted of surreal landscapes peopled by fetuses or mangled animals. From the ceilings in every room hung fly strips covered with dead insects, which stemmed from an obsession of Kurt's.

"I have this weird magnetic attraction to flies," he would explain. "Or flies [are attracted] to me, actually. I'd wake up in the morning and these flies would keep me awake for hours, buzzing and bouncing off my face. They'd just attack me and this has happened over and over in my life." This is hardly surprising considering the squalor of his surroundings.

The band would still occasionally perform, bringing in a little income, but not enough to keep Kurt in drugs. Tracy had a decent job at the Boeing plant in Seattle, but she was reluctant to finance Kurt's habit and constantly nagged him to get a job, threatening to kick him out if he didn't. Only after he moved out and slept in the car for two nights did she stop criticizing him, afraid she would lose him. Kurt later included the line "I can't see you every night for free" in his song "About a Girl," in reference to Tracy's demands that he be responsible for his share. The only work he could find was for a janitorial company, earning four dollars an hour. He later recalled driving around town from job to job with "two coworkers from hell worse than your typical brain-dead Aberdonian." The job of travelling janitor did have its fringe benefits, however. Many of the company's clients were dentists, and Kurt learned how to inhale nitrous oxide (laughing gas), which became one of his favorite highs.

Although Kurt should have thrived in the bohemian atmosphere of Olympia, he detested the pretentiousness of the scene, which was dominated by the alternative music label K Records and its head, Calvin Johnson. Kurt contemptuously labeled Johnson's followers "Calvinists" but he thought the label was pretty cool, and one night in a drug-induced stupor, he went to a tattoo parlor with Dylan Carlson and had the K Records "K" logo tattooed on his forearm. Kurt had his sights set on his own record deal and began to save up his janitor money to record a demo. By this time the band had finally settled on a name Kurt liked, Nirvana.

"I wanted a name that was beautiful and nice and pretty instead of a mean, raunchy punk name like the Angry Samoans," he explained to Michael Azerad. "I wanted something different." Little did he know at the time that there were already two other groups named Nirvana – one a sixties psychedelic rock group from England, the other a Christian rock band. Both groups would surface after Kurt hit it big, and they had to be paid off not to sue.

Krist and Shelli had also moved to Olympia, staying with Kurt and Tracy in their cramped apartment for several weeks before getting their own place in Tacoma.

Burckhard wasn't taking the band very seriously. He was turned off by the punk rock crowd, recalling, "I'm not that much into that kind of scene where your hair is all different colours and whatnot." Kurt and Krist weren't amused when Burckhard frequently failed to show up for their nightly practices, preferring to party with his friends. He never believed the band was going anywhere, and for him it was all just for fun.

Kurt had other ideas and finally made the decision to invite his old Melvins buddy Dale Crover to practice with him and Krist as they prepared to record their demo. With a loan from Tracy, they finally had enough money to go into the recording studio, and chose Reciprocal Records because, according to Kurt, it was the most happening studio in Seattle. Actually, it was the cheapest, which is why it was so popular among fledgling bands.

The head of Reciprocal was a former Navy engineer named Jack Endino. The day Nirvana came in to lay down their tracks, he happened to be the only one around, so he ended up producing the group. Endino didn't believe in sophisticated production techniques. His philosophy was to record groups exactly the way they sounded on stage, which became Endino's trademark and earned him the title "father of the Seattle sound." Nirvana spent a little more than six hours in the studio that day, mixing a total of ten songs. The total bill was $152.44.

One thing in particular impressed Endino about this session – Kurt's distinctive vocals. Endino had seen just about every Seattle band come through his studio and usually didn't pay a lot of attention to the finished product after he delivered the master to the group. But that night Endino made himself a mix and dubbed a cassette, which he gave to his friend Jonathan Poneman of the new label Sub Pop records.

Poneman and Bruce Pavitt had founded the small indie music label three years earlier and it quickly built a reputation for its distinct sound, which would become better known as grunge. When Kurt himself heard the tape, he knew it was good and set out to get himself a record deal with any indie label which would accept him, sending out cassettes to a handful of his favourite labels. Enclosed with the demo was always some little gimmick to attract attention, such as a used condom filled with plastic ants. His secret ambition was to be signed to Chicago's Touch & Go records, home of Kurt's idols the Butthole Surfers. Ironically, he never sent one to Sub Pop because he didn't have their address, so he was surprised several days later when he got a call from Jonathan Poneman, who set up a meeting with the band at Seattle's Cafe Roma. At this meeting – attended by Kurt and a drunken Krist who was already showing signs of becoming an alcoholic – Poneman expressed interest in putting out a Nirvana single.

Soon after, Sub Pop arranged for Nirvana to play their first Seattle show at the Vogue club in a Sub Pop Sunday showcase. Most of the twenty people in attendance weren't very impressed by their lackluster performance, of which Kurt later said, "We sucked. We totally fucked it up." Nevertheless, the demo had been circulating around Seattle and was starting to cause a buzz.

Crover had left the band by this point, to be replaced by a number of drummers who didn't fit in very well with Kurt and Krist's ambitions. One brief replacement was their old drummer Aaron Burckhard, who was finally thrown out of the band for good. (Burckhard later compared himself to Pete Best, the Beatles' original drummer, who was thrown out of the band just before they made it big.)

Finally, Kurt recruited Chad Channing – a drummer he remembered from a band called Tick Dolly Row, who had once opened for Nirvana when they were called Bliss. This combination finally seemed to click.

Around this time, Nirvana received their first newspaper review in the free Seattle music fanzine *Backlash*. In this article, Kurt expressed the fear that people might think Nirvana was just a rip-off of the Melvins, who by then were a huge name in the burgeoning grunge scene. But the reviewer, Dawn Anderson, concluded her piece with the words, "With enough practice, Nirvana could become better than the Melvins." Kurt was ecstatic and soon his legendary ego began to manifest itself.

Music writer Christopher Sandford recalls an interview he did around that time in which Kurt called

Nirvana "the best fucking band since the Beatles."

Preparing for success, Kurt wrote a bio of the band which he gave to Sub Pop:

NIRVANA is a three-piece from the outskirts of Seattle, WA. Kurdt [sic] – guitar/voice and Chris – bass have struggled with too many undedicated drummers for the past 3 years... for the last 9 months we have had the pleasure to take Chad – drums under our wings and develop what we are now and always will be NIRVANA.

Willing to compromise our material (some of this shit is pretty old). Tour any time forever. Hopefully the music will speak for itself.

Kurt, Krist, and Chad went back into the studio with Endino to record the single. After recording a number of tracks, they finally settled on "Love Buzz," with "Big Cheese" (written about Jonathan Poneman) on the flip side. Kurt and the others were excited about the single which they thought was their big break. Months passed, however, and nothing happened. Kurt had been telling everybody he knew that he had a record and he was getting pretty pissed off at Sub Pop's inaction. What he didn't realize was the precarious financial situation of the then struggling label, which was deep in debt and operating from day to day. This hit home one day when Kurt received a call from Pavitt asking for a two-hundred-dollar loan so they could press the single. Kurt hung up on him, shattered. He had known it was too good to be true. For the next three weeks, Krist and Kurt went on a massive drug and alcohol binge, emerging only periodically to spray-paint "Sub Pop Sucks" all over town.

Just as the band decided to seek out another label, they got another call in November from Pavitt, informing them Sub Pop had scraped up the money and was releasing the single that month.

When he heard the news, Kurt went crazy, running out into the street screaming, "I'm going to be a rock star! Nirvana rules!"

When the single finally came out, his enthusiasm was dampened somewhat when he learned of Sub Pop's plans for it. Pavitt and Poneman had devised a marketing scheme called "Sub Pop Single of the Month", whereby subscribers would pay a fee to receive one of one thousand hand-numbered limited-édition singles. Nirvana's single was going to inaugurate the scheme, which didn't go over too well with the band members.

"We were really burned out about that," said Krist. "We put a single out and nobody could buy it."

The Sub Pop catalogue described the "Love Buzz" single as "heavy pop sludge from these untamed Olympia drop-ins."

The group was appeased somewhat when Sub Pop promised them it would be sent out to campus and community radio stations (which could make or break alternative music groups) with heavy promotion. Indeed, Kurt heard that Seattle's University of Washington station, KCMU, started the single on heavy rotation soon after they received it. When he heard the news, he drove with Tracy into the station's listening range and listened to the radio hoping he would hear the song. After they failed to play it, he went to a phone booth and called the station requesting the single. Twenty minutes later his unmistakable voice came out of the radio – an event which Kurt would call the happiest moment of his life.

"It was amazing," he told Michael Azerad. "I never thought I'd get to that point. I just thought I'd be in a band and maybe make a demo, but for them to play it on the radio was just too much to ask for at that time. It was really great. It was instant success and fame beyond my wildest dreams. More than I ever wanted. But once I got a taste of it, I really thought it was cool and I thought I would definitely like to hear my future recordings on the radio. And to be able to pay my rent with this band, it would be really great. It made us step up mentally to another level where it was a reality that we could actually live off of this. I didn't think anywhere past ever being able to afford more than a hundred-dollar apartment. That was going to be the rest of my life – to be in a band and tour and play clubs and hear my songs on the radio once in a while."

If the band had rehearsed hard before the single, their labour could not compare to the gruelling practices Kurt forced on them after its release. The buzz from "Love Buzz" was so positive that Sub Pop had mentioned the possibility of an album, although they said an EP was more realistic.

Kurt began to refine some of the songs he had written years before and even penned some new ones when he wasn't practicing. Sub Pop had booked the group into Endino's studio to record but, because of cash flow problems, told them they would have to pay for the studio time themselves.

Shortly before they went into the studio – on December 21, 1988, two months before Kurt's twenty-second birthday – Nirvana was booked for a show at the Hoquiam Eagles Lodge, the not quite prodigal son returning to his birthplace. In honour of the occasion that night, Krist played in his underwear and Kurt painted his neck red – the first of many onstage digs he would direct at his childhood roots.

On Christmas Eve, three days later, the band went into the studio to lay down the first tracks on the album which would become *Bleach* (named for the bleach junkies used to clean their needles). One month and thirty studio hours later, the album was finished. Endino calculated the time and sent out the most famous bill in music history – $606.17 – a price tag which the Nirvana publicity machine would tout repeatedly after they hit it big.

Kurt was spending all his spare money on drugs

and Krist was unemployed, so they didn't know how they could pay the bill, until Dylan Carlson introduced Kurt to a friend of his named Jason Everman, who had made a lot of money as a commercial fisherman in Alaska. Everman gave them a loan, and in gratitude the group listed him in the credits as a guitarist on *Bleach*, even though he never played on the album. He was a competent guitarist, which the band sorely needed so that Kurt could spend more time on his trademark vocals, and Everman was invited to join the group on their upcoming tour of the West Coast.

Around the time *Bleach* was released in 1989, alternative music was still a relatively fringe music movement, confined to college radio stations and church basements. Poneman and Pavitt knew their rock history and were acutely aware that many American musicians, including Seattle's Jimi Hendrix, had hit it big only after they created a buzz in the United Kingdom. A number of Seattle bands, including Mudhoney and Sound-garden, had already hit the U.K. indie charts, and Sub Pop was anxious to capitalize on this success.

The British saw in Seattle music a regional identity and flavour, explained Pavitt, likening it to the success of Motown in the sixties. "The history of rock music is broken down that way – it comes down to labels or scenes. We understood this from the beginning."

With this in mind, Poneman and Pavitt went deeper into debt to bring to the United States Everett True of the influential London music paper *Melody Maker*. Their investment worked. When True returned, he wrote a series of articles about the Seattle music scene.

The most important article True wrote as far as Nirvana's career went was titled "Seattle's New Generation of Thrash Metal Merchants." The article praised groups such as Green River and Beat Happening before focusing on Nirvana:

Basically, this is the real thing. No rock star contrivance, no intellectual perspective, no master plan for world domination. You're talking about four guys in their early twenties from rural Washington who wanna rock, who, if they weren't doing this, would be working in a supermarket or lumberyard, or fixing cars. Kurdt Kobain is a great tunesmith, although still a relatively young songwriter. He wields a riff with *passion*.

At the time, nobody could anticipate the effect these articles would have on Seattle, the world of music, or Kurt Cobain. What followed was nothing short of an invasion. First, the rest of the British rock press descended on the city to see for themselves what all the fuss was about, and soon the American music media picked up the theme, trumpeting the arrival of the "Seattle sound" and setting the stage for the eventual day that, as Veronika Kalmar of *The Rocket* described it, "grunge surpassed the status of a happening regional scene to become a worldwide fashion craze.

The American music press were not as unanimous in their enthusiasm for Nirvana and *Bleach* as the British. *Rolling Stone* labeled the album "undistinguished... relying on warmed over 70's riffs" (which may have accounted for Cobain's lifelong contempt for the magazine). *The Conflict* was even harsher, writing, "If you're going to be a simpleton rock band, then at least be more entertaining than this shit."

Sub Pop moved immediately to capitalize on the attention Nirvana was commanding, organizing a major tour of the United States and Europe. The U.S. leg consisted of twenty-six dates all over the country. Conditions were hardly ideal, as the band piled into a cramped Dodge van, played in small bars, and slept on floors if they were lucky. But most of the band had never been farther than Seattle, and they were thrilled to see all these new places. As the tour progressed, word of mouth started to spread about *Bleach* thanks to heavy college radio play, and attendance picked up significantly.

By the end of the tour, Krist's increasingly heavy drinking and the dissension between Jason and the other band members had taken their toll. At several shows, Kurt took to smashing his guitar on stage, which earned him several unfavourable comparisons to Pete Townshend by reviewers. Kurt would later say he didn't smash his guitar out of showmanship but to express his disgust with the way the show was going. If the band wasn't playing well or the sound was bad, down would come his guitar, splintering into a hundred pieces and often forcing a premature end to the show.

Kurt's stomach problems continued to plague him, and at one point early in the tour he even collapsed and had to be taken to the hospital.

At the end of the tour, Jason was asked to leave the band, never having been repaid the six-hundred-dollar loan which made *Bleach* possible. Kurt would claim he withheld the money for "mental damages."

As the year progressed, *Bleach* continued to sell steadily and Nirvana attracted more and more attention on the eve of their European tour. In September, they went into the studio to record an EP, which became *Blew*. Kurt was determined to record some catchy material in tribute to the pop music he still loved, telling Krist at one point, "Goddammit, I want something I can hum." When the EP was released, it was criticized by one reviewer who said it sounded too much like the Beatles.

Their arrival in Newcastle, England, that fall for their first show in a thirty-six-show/forty-two-day European tour signaled the first hint of the eventual Nirvanamania which would sweep the world a couple of years later. Unlike America, where they were lucky if the club was half full, in Europe almost every show was sold out and they were treated like celebrities. At first they reveled in the adulation, but the grueling tour schedule began to take its toll.

Once again Kurt started to smash his guitar after only a few songs and walk off the stage. Four songs into their Rome show, where the sound system was particularly bad, Kurt had what Bruce Pavitt called "a nervous breakdown on stage." He climbed onto a speaker stack high above the stage and hovered above the crowd. Then, just as it was about to collapse, he climbed up into the rafters and held up a chair, threatening to throw it down into the stunned crowd below. Finally, after he was subdued, he went backstage and broke two microphones before announcing in tears that he was quitting the band and going home. Poneman, who had flown in with Pavitt for the show, calmed him down and talked him out of it.

Kurt was already becoming disenchanted by Sub Pop. Theories abound about the roots of his unhappiness. Kurt and the others weren't particularly impressed when, midway through the European tour, the two label executives flew in first class and booked themselves into a nice hotel while the band had to suffer through what Kurt called "shitola surroundings."

The Sub Pop publicity machine, anxious to capitalize on Nirvana's humble beginnings, pushed the image of their white-trash roots on the British press. One profile read: "They're a little bit gross and they're a little bit awesome. What else would you be if you grew up in the backwoods redneck helltown of Aberdeen?"

Kurt found these kind of descriptions extremely condescending:

"To be thought of as this stump-dumb rocker dude. from Aberdeen who just blindly found his way up to Seattle and this hip label," he recalled. "It just felt kind of degrading to be thought of as someone like that when that was something I was fighting against all my life."

When the band returned from their European tour, they were almost immediately booked for another tour to take advantage of the increasing sales of *Bleach*, which was starting to create as much of a buzz in the

U.S. as in England. Yet, Sub Pop still didn't have much of a distribution network, and the record was hard to find outside big cities.

Nirvana was disenchanted and knew it was time to start shopping around for a real record deal. "When we went on tour," Kurt later explained, "kids would come up to us in flocks going, 'Where can we find the record? We can't find it.' That's the only reason we went with a major is just the assurance of getting our records into small towns like Aberdeen."

The group had already recorded some material for what was supposed to be their second Sub Pop album, but unbeknownst to Pavitt and Poneman, they started shopping this material as a demo tape to major labels.

Meanwhile, Kurt had become increasingly unhappy with the drumming of Chad Channing, whose bad timing and lack of power had never really impressed Kurt, who believed good drumming was essential to a group's sound. He later told Michael Azerad that Chad was the reason he smashed his instruments at shows.

"I got so pissed off at Chad that I'd jump into the drum set, then smash my guitar," he said.

Kurt had always put up with Chad in the band because the two got along so well, unlike Jason Everman, whom Kurt despised. Finally, he took the step he thought the band needed if it was going to move to the next level. He reluctantly told Chad he was through.

When Chad was fired, Kurt had nobody in mind to replace him and decided to cancel a planned U.K. tour so that he could find a new drummer. Dale Crover was temporarily recruited for a short West Coast tour after Kurt agreed to his only condition-not to jump into his drum set under any circumstances.

When the band returned from touring, Sub Pop requested another single, and Dan Peters of Mudhoney was asked to sit in on the session which became

"Sliver." Peters also played with the band at their biggest Seattle gig to date, the Motor Sports International, in front of 1,500 people. After the show, Buzz Osbourne introduced Kurt to his friend Dave Grohl, who had just played a gig in Olympia with his Washington, D.C., hard-core band Scream. Osbourne was impressed by Grohl's style and thought he would be perfect for Nirvana, who arranged an audition that week.

Dave passed the audition and the final edition of Nirvana was born. They knew they had finally found the drummer who was going to take them places.

"Kurt and Krist knew – and everybody else knew who saw them play – that they were only a hint of what they could be until Dave joined the band," says Slim Moon, Kurt's old neighbor in Olympia and head of Kill Rock Stars Records. "He just knew how to play drums and he understood their music."

Soon after Dave joined the band, Nirvana headed back to England to promote the new "Sliver" single, although it still hadn't been released.

This time the horrible conditions of their previous tour were just a bad memory. Their success warranted a complete entourage, including a soundman, a tour manager, and a monitor man, and, best of all, their own tour bus! They played thousand-seat venues instead of midsize clubs and attracted glowing reviews wherever they played.

This time there was no smashing of guitars and walking off the stage. Kurt was exhilarated by the group's success and the comfortable conditions, and he made sure to reward the crowds who came to see him.

When Kurt returned from touring, he headed back to his old apartment in Olympia, where he continued to live after breaking up with Tracy earlier that year. She could no longer tolerate his selfish behaviour, she would tell friends. Years later, Courtney Love was going through Kurt's belongings and found some old notes which Tracy liked to post around the house. They are a good example of Tracy's household style: "1. Good morning. 2. Will you fill up my car with unleaded gas? 3. Sweep kitchen floor. 4. Clean tub. 5. Go to K mart. 6. Get one dollar in quarters. Kurt never did any of those things.

He then dated Tobi Vail, an Olympia musician who was later credited with helping found the riot grrrl movement, a feminist offshoot of punk. While dating Tobi, Kurt first started to espouse the pro-woman sentiments which would become evident on some of his later songs like "Rape Me." But according to his friend Dylan Carlson, "Kurt could talk the talk, but in private he still referred to women as bitches and continued to collect some pretty sick porn." Years later, Courtney Love told journalist Kim Neely, "Kurt's one of the most liberal people I know, but he looked at me one day and said, 'I hate it when you read those fucking feminist books.'"

The band had finally told Sub Pop it was leaving to look for a major record deal. Poneman and Pavitt, who must have known the split was inevitable, felt betrayed but could do little.

Shortly after returning from the U.K. tour, Kurt received several phone calls from Danny Goldberg of Gold Mountain, an L.A. based management company keen on handling Nirvana's career. Goldberg assured Kurt he could make him a millionaire by securing the group a major deal. The dollar figures Goldberg was throwing around definitely piqued Kurt's attention, but he wasn't sure if he trusted this "slick corporate sleazebag," as Kurt described Goldberg to one friend. At first he figured he could negotiate his own deal with a major label without the middleman and their huge commissions. But Gold Mountain persisted. They assigned John Silva, who had indie rock connections, to convince the band. Silva assured Kurt he had connections with Geffen Records, which he knew was Kurt's first choice.

In November 1990, Gold Mountain flew the entire band to Los Angeles first-class to meet with Goldberg and Silva. After this meeting the band agreed to a management deal. It turned out to be a smart move. Within weeks virtually every major label was involved in a bidding war to see who could sign Nirvana, wining and dining the group in fancy restaurants while Kurt, Krist, and Dave savoured the attention.

Sonic Youth, whom Kurt revered, had already signed to Geffen, and the band's Kim Gordon was calling up Kurt every day, trying to persuade him that Geffen would allow them total artistic freedom, which belied the reputation of major labels for insisting on full creative control. Although the label wasn't offering as much as some of the other majors (rumoured to be dangling million-dollar offers), Kurt credited the sealing of the deal to Gordon's persuasive powers. The deal called for an advance of only $287,000. Even this figure was significantly reduced by taxes, management fees, and the money needed to buy out Nirvana's contract from Sub Pop. But more important than the money to Kurt was the artistic freedom the band insisted on.

"We have one of the best contracts any band has ever had," Kurt said at the time. "We have complete control over what we do, and what we release, which literally means that if we handed in a sixty-minute tape of us defecating, they would have to release and promote it."

Pavitt and Poneman didn't know how much leverage their contract with Nirvana gave them – a contract they had signed at the band's insistence two years earlier. They knew they were losing a gold mine, but they didn't have the heart or the resources for a lengthy legal battle. Geffen offered a $75,000 buyout fee plus 2 percent of sales on the next two Nirvana records. It was this percentage that single-handedly rescued the label from the verge of bankruptcy after the success of *Nevermind*, although reports later indicated Geffen would have gone as high as $1 million to buy out the contract.

Although the advance from Geffen was relatively low, Gold Mountain advised them to take it because it came with a very strong royalty package that would pay off if they succeeded, which, by then, few doubted. Kurt, Krist, and Dave signed their names on the dotted line on April 30, 1991, two months after Kurt's twenty-fourth birthday.

Signing with a major label was not part of the punk ethic, as Kurt was acutely aware. Already his old punk friends were referring to him as a sell-out, and Kurt seemed to step up his drug use as his fits of guilt intensified.

In attempting to rationalize his decision, Kurt later made up a story for Michael Azerad's authorized biography, *Come as You Are*, about how he originally planned what he called a "great rock 'n' roll swindle." He claimed that he had contemplated signing with Geffen, taking the money, and then breaking up and signing with the small Olympia punk label K Records. According to Dylan Carlson, Kurt never thought of any such thing. "He was anxious to sign with Geffen," he recalls. "He knew there would be a lot of resentment by his old friends and he felt a bit guilty but he basically said, 'Fuck 'em, they're just jealous.'"

A few months earlier, Krist and Dave had begun to realize that Kurt was doing heroin fairly regularly – a fact he had tried to keep secret from his bandmates. When Dave asked him what it was like, Kurt replied, "It sucked, it's stupid. It makes you feel gross and bad. I just wanted to try it." He told them he wouldn't do it again, but Krist didn't believe him. He was hardly in a position to lecture Kurt, as he himself was an obvious alcoholic.

Soon after the band signed, Nirvana toured Canada, where almost every show was completely sold out, before returning to Seattle, where they played one date in which they debuted a new song called "Smells Like Teen Spirit." At the time, nobody thought the song was anything special.

Geffen brought them to Sound City studios in Los Angeles to record their first album, which the label wanted out as soon as possible. For six weeks the group rehearsed the material and perfected the sound that their new producer, Butch Vig, was searching for. Finally they laid down the tracks and everybody knew they had something big – but nobody could have anticipated just how big.

Everybody seems to have a theory about why *Nevermind* was so successful. Beatlemania had hit America just three months after JFK was assassinated, and sociologists believe it was no coincidence. With Nirvanamania, the theory goes, it was the end of the Gulf War, which readied a generation for the angry rebellion of alternative music.

The album's music dealt with a wide range of topics, from the rape of a teenage girl in "Polly" to an attack on religious zealotry in "Lithium" to the mindless jocks of his youth in "In Bloom." There was nothing particularly groundbreaking in the lyrics when compared to those of other alternative bands, but the catchy mix of pop and punk with brilliant guitar riffs helped reach a brand-new audience – most of whom were previously accustomed to the bland cliche's of commercial rock – and something seemed to strike a chord.

"*Nevermind* came along at exactly the right time," wrote Michael Azerad. "This was music by, for and about a whole new group of young people who had been overlooked, ignored or condescended to."

Kurt was less analytical: "We got more attention [than other alternative bands] because our songs have hooks and they kind of stick in people's minds."

Whatever the reasons, *Nevermind* took off almost from the moment it was first sent to radio stations in

August 1991. The single "Smells like Teen Spirit" (named for a teenage girl's deodorant) was an almost instant hit. One community radio station in Massachusetts spun the song sixty-seven times in a single week. But the real break came when MTV placed the song in their "Buzz bin," guaranteeing it heavy rotation. Meanwhile the album was flying out of record stores at a pace faster than Geffen could ship it. In December the album hit number one on the Billboard charts, replacing Michael Jackson's *Dangerous*, an unheard-of accomplishment for an alternative group. Within four months of the album's release, it had already sold 3 million copies in the U.S. alone, and there was no end in sight.

Kurt relished his new superstardom at first, telling friends he would "leave the Beatles in our dust." Around this time, people started to notice a strange-looking bleached blond tagging along wherever the group went.

4
Endless Love

Courtney Love represents a tale rarely included in rock's official history. It's the story of a shady corner occupied by someone who has loved, slept with, supported, and suffered at the hands of the music industry in search of fame and fortune. Her life story reads like a Hollywood script, filled with tales of screwed-up parents, countless lovers, heavy drug and alcohol abuse, and plenty of stories about rock's liveliest unofficial conceptual art project, groupiedom.

From her first days on this planet, Courtney was getting into trouble, recalls her father, Hank Harrison. But he says he also remembers her "getting away with murder" all the time because "she's Courtney and she has an IQ of about 145. People who she steps on always wind up having a soft spot for her because they say, 'Oh, it's just Courtney.'"

It's easy to trace her chaotic existence as far back

as the day she was born. Her mother went into labour while her father was tripping out on LSD. After more than ten hours, Linda Carroll gave birth to Courtney Michelle Harrison on July 9, 1964. (Courtney claims her given name is Love.)

Her parents were typical sixties hippies. They lived in San Francisco and were experimenting with all kinds of hallucinogenic drugs. "We were doing tons of acid, changing sex partners, and tripping out on Dylan and the Beatles," her father remembers.

Harrison was managing a small local band called the Warlocks, which would later become better known as the Grateful Dead. In fact, the Dead's Phil Lesh is Courtney's godfather. Harrison is today often referred to as a Dead hanger-on or a Dead roadie, but he was in fact the band's first manager and in 1971 wrote the first book ever on the band, *The Dead, Volume 1*, still considered by many Deadheads to be the definitive account. The band later turned against him after he revealed in a subsequent book that some of them dealt drugs to finance their tours in the early days.

Courtney's mother, Linda Carroll, was a university student from a very affluent family whose money was made in eyeglass manufacturing. She became a psychologist and later made headlines in 1993 for counseling Katherine Anne Powers, a member of the terrorist Weather Underground, to come out of hiding after twenty-five years and face up to murder charges stemming from a Vietnam war protest bombing.

"Courtney is not the rags-to-riches rock-'n'-roll story," says Hank Harrison.

Hank and Linda's marriage lasted less than two years. A custody battle ensued and Harrison was no match for Linda Carroll's vast array of expensive family lawyers. According to the divorce papers filed in San Francisco Superior Court, Carroll claimed her husband had threatened to abduct Courtney and take her to another country. The court granted her custody, with only limited visitation rights to Harrison. Hank was shattered. He says he felt like "a loser" and took out his frustration by indulging in drugs and promiscuous sex more than he ever had before. Meanwhile, Linda married her former garbageman, Frank Rodriguez, and Courtney moved with her mom, stepfather, and her half sisters to Eugene, Oregon.

Carroll lived it up off the huge inheritance her adoptive parents left her. She attended college in Eugene and, according to Courtney, "gathered disciples wherever she went. My mother had ties to a lot of the women around the San Francisco hippie scene, like Ken Kesey's wife, and the Magic Bus people." Linda introduced all these people to her young daughter. She would even smoke pot and talk about sex around little Courtney.

In 1971, Rodriguez took legal steps to adopt Courtney – a move which Harrison contested. "They were afraid I would somehow get access to her trust fund," he contends. Things got messy. Carroll's lawyers dredged up all the dirty details of Harrison's past, including arrests for pot possession and petty theft while he was in college. The adoption was granted.

Linda's second marriage crumbled quickly and within a year she was again divorced. While on a rafting trip in Colorado, she met husband number three, David Manely. The family settled in nearby Marcola in a huge home.

"There were all these hairy, wangly-ass hippies in our house," Courtney said in a 1994 *Spin* magazine interview. "All these hippies were there doing Gestalt Therapy, running around the swimming pool naked, screaming. My mom was also adamant about a gender-free household: no dresses, no patent leather shoes, no canopy beds, nothing."

Despite her now obvious high intelligence, Courtney had the scholastic disadvantage of being diagnosed autistic. "At an early age I would not speak.

Then I simply bloomed," she recalled. "My first visit to a psychiatrist was when I was like three. Observational therapy. TM for kids... you name it. I've been there."

From first grade on, Courtney began a pattern of attending and getting kicked out of schools. She was also arrested for shoplifting several times.

Meanwhile, Carroll and her new husband decided to leave the Northwest and get a fresh start. In 1972 they moved to New Zealand and started a sheep farm. They left their troublesome daughter behind with a friend of Linda's in Eugene. Courtney became a nightmare to Carroll's friend, who was also her therapist. She would steal money from her wallet and use it to buy pot. She would also skip school most of the time and hang out at the mall. "There was nothing I could do," says Hank Harrison. "Linda had already brainwashed the kid not to listen to me, and Courtney just wanted to do everything that she wasn't supposed to."

Finally, Courtney was kicked out of her surrogate home and was ordered to join Carroll on the farm in New Zealand. Shortly after Courtney arrived, her mother arranged for her to live with a nearby friend named Shirley. "Shirley was great," says Love. "She had this incredible library and garden. I changed my name to Michelle – my middle name, which is a really decent, normal name – and I was really popular in school for a year. I thought Shirley and I were doing really well. Then my mother tells me that Shirley doesn't like me anymore and I can't continue to live with her. Which was really fucked."

Courtney was again sent packing, first to a Catholic school in Australia, from which she was soon expelled, and then back to Oregon, where she was shuttled from one of her mother's friends to another.

This period of her life seems to be characterized by a lot of insecurity about her looks. "I was really quite pretty until I was 12," she told *Spin*. "I sort of looked like Eddie Vedder. I was the last girl on the planet with tits. I was the girl that would never hit puberty. I forever looked like I was seven. And then I got ugly; I was ugly until I was 25. Still, I knew what I had and I worked the fuck out of it. And so when it was gone I really missed it. I really missed it. I really resented puberty for that. It took away my beauty."

To attract attention, she started to dress and behave more outrageously. It was in the seventh grade that Courtney started to live and look more like a rocker. She had a David Bowie hairdo and would always wear torn, faded jeans. She idolized the Bay City Rollers and would usually be the first to wait in the schoolyard to see if anybody was game for a good old streetfight or excursion to the mall to shoplift or play pinball in the arcade.

In the next couple of years, Courtney would have more run-ins with the law. She would shoplift compulsively and sometimes sneak into clubs that required a minimum age of twenty-one. When she was twelve, she was caught shoplifting a lipstick from a Woolworth's and, when the police called her mother to come get her, Linda instead told them she couldn't take it anymore. Courtney was put on probation. It didn't take long for her to violate the terms of her sentence. She ran away from home for several days, which was not unusual for the young teenager. This time, however, her mother told the police to take her away to Hillcrest Reform School in Salem, Oregon. She would later tell her biographer Melissa Rossi about arriving at the school in a police car, in handcuffs and with her ankles shackled, which seems unlikely for a girl so young whose only offense was shoplifting.

Courtney was quickly accepted by the tough, foulmouthed girls doing their stay at Hillcrest. In one letter she wrote to her father when she was fourteen, she described her experiences in great detail. She discussed attending group therapy sessions, dyeing her hair red, and bragged about the fact that she read in her files that she's the "most shrewd, cunning, devious person" her caseworker had ever seen. In another letter, written in 1979, she describes her ambition to become an actress, her goal of getting rich, her favourite book, *Lord of the Flies*, her favorite movie, *The Warriors*, her crush on actor Kurt Russell, and her relations with the other girls at the reform school. At one point she wrote, "I went out and knifed a girl because I didn't like her looks."

As she promised, Courtney started sending her father poems, all of which he still has. One of the most telling is a poem she wrote called "Future Date." Among the lines are these:

I'll destroy anyone in my way
I'll kill every lousy lay – Coz I got my eye on a Future Date

There's no official record of the stabbing incident, but there's no question Courtney was a problem inmate, since she was shuttled to a number of increasingly tougher reform schools during the next few years, including stints in schools reserved for violent offenders and teenage killers. Occasionally she would be released, only to get into trouble again and be sent right back.

During one of her stays in reform school after being caught shoplifting, she was exposed to punk rock for the first time. An intern who was working for school credit came back from England and noticed Courtney's resemblance to British punk rockers. He gave her several albums to listen to, including the Pretenders, Squeeze, and the Sex Pistols' *Never Mind the Bollocks*. Courtney claims that it was at this point that she decided that she would become a rock star.

Eventually, Hank Harrison – who hadn't seen his daughter in more than eight years – succeeded in convincing the State of Oregon to allow Courtney to come live with him, which she did for almost a year.

Harrison was scheduled to spend two years in Ireland researching a book on ancient Irish stones and the Holy Grail. By this time, he had already published two bestselling books on the Grateful Dead (*The Dead, Volume 1*, and *The Dead, Volume 2*), which chronicled the rise of the band as well as the social currents of the Haight-Ashbury scene. Harrison had been called the "Jane Goodall of Rock and Roll" by Professor Tom McNerney of San Jose State University and was receiving a lot of attention in academic as well as music circles. Courtney was excited that her father would be living near all that great music in Ireland and wanted him to take her along. He told her she could come to Ireland after he had settled down there. In the meantime, she was placed in a series of foster homes, mostly in Portland.

It is during this period that Courtney, then fifteen years old, claims she was approached by a representative of the Japanese underworld with an offer to fly her to Japan to work as a stripper. Courtney immediately accepted and disappeared for six months until she was deported back to the States, where she told her friends she had been part of the white slave trade.

"At the time, she wasn't good enough to travel and support herself with music or any other art," says Harrison. "So she took off her clothes and danced on men's laps. She did it all over the world and sometimes got into serious trouble."

But her world was about to become even more bizarre, if that is possible. Once back on the Portland scene, Courtney used her newly acquired sex trade experience to land a job cavorting naked through the audience of a strip club which didn't serve alcohol and thereby escaped the scrutiny of the state authorities. This gig lasted until the police raided the place one night and she was back in trouble once again.

After arriving at yet another reform school, the now sixteen-year-old Courtney mentioned to her social worker that she was an heiress. The social worker suggested she sue for legal and financial emancipation from her mother. The court granted this request and, upon her release, Courtney was given an income of eight hundred dollars a month from her trust fund. With her new financial freedom, Courtney decided it was time to hook up with her father in Dublin.

At first, Courtney seemed to find her niche, but after a while their relationship became very acrimonious. Hank recalls Courtney made fun of his weight and would frequently taunt him about his looks.

"She had this knack for making me feel worthless and ugly," he says. "She's so good at putting people down. She used to write me letters and call me her 'fat, fucking father.' Courtney would always make fun of me. Maybe she hated me for splitting up the family when she was so young. Sometimes, though, we would have a lot of fun because she's much more like me than Linda. But her mood changes so rapidly and then she starts chewing me out."

Courtney later claimed that she moved out of her father's house in Dublin after only three days because "he beat me up so badly I had to call the police." But Dublin police authorities have no record of such a complaint, and one of their neighbours, Mary Reilly, remembers Courtney being there for "several months." Harrison has a note that Courtney wrote him after this stay which she concludes with the words, "Thank you for letting me walk on the ice of the thickness of my own choosing."

While she was in Dublin, Courtney also claims to have studied humanities at Trinity College. University records, however, contradict this claim. She has also claimed that she was employed to take photos for the British music magazine *Hot Press* and that two of her sessions involved U2 and the Pretenders.

But *Hot Press* editor Niall Stokes denies all knowledge of Love's employment, claiming that he would definitely have remembered some-one as loud and brassy as Love.

According to a 1995 *Hot Press* story on her, "It's fairly typical Courtney behaviour to lie or exaggerate anyway. Throughout her career she has continually proffered colourful stories – often with several conflicting versions – about her past life to the media in order to increase her mystique and enhance her punk credibility."

Courtney stayed with Hank for four months before venturing off to England to become a groupie of Julian Cope's Teardrop Explodes in Liverpool, which was undergoing a musical renaissance at the time. Courtney brought along one thousand hits of LSD she had secured in the States and used them to insert herself into the local scene, crashing parties and rock shows to meet the local music royalty. She claims to this day that she had an affair with Cope, the eccentric British rocker. For his part, Cope claims Courtney was trouble from the day he met her and that nothing happened between them.

After Kurt and Courtney became an item and Cope started a comeback a few years ago, he took out an ad in the British press saying, "Free us from Nancy Spungen-fixated heroin A-holes who cling to our greatest rock groups and suck out their brains." He was also later quoted as saying, "She needs shooting and I'll shoot her." Courtney claimed to not understand what triggered Cope's attack on her. But Hank Harrison has an idea.

"Cope obviously used Courtney for something and then dumped her," he says. "But Courtney didn't want to leave and tried to drive him crazy. If Courtney can't have her way she can be a bigger nuisance than the plague. She'll keep hammering away at you until you either have a nervous breakdown or just do something to appease her so she'll think you're her friend and will leave you alone."

Courtney told writer Amy Raphael, "He [Cope]

portrays me as a demon sixteen-year-old, which I was."

It was around this time that she lost her virginity, she claims, to Michael Mooney, the former Psychedelic Furs guitarist, a claim he vehemently denies. But Courtney even contradicts her own claim in several interviews that quote her as saying she lost her virginity to Julian Cope.

Not everybody in Liverpool was enamoured of the in-your-face groupie. Something happened in Liverpool to force an abrupt departure, and in late 1982, Courtney moved back to Portland and continued to live off her trust fund.

She started to get deep into the Oregon punk scene, hanging out with musicians and junkies. Her stories about the Liverpool scene and all the famous British musicians she had met and bedded gave Courtney a badge of punk respectability, which she readily exploited.

Courtney's apartment became a regular hangout for Portland's underground characters, including the drag queens, drug dealers, and guys clad in tight leather pants whom she met at Metropolis, Portland's well-known gay dance club, where she worked for a time as a DJ.

Todd Curran remembers Courtney from the Metropolis scene. "She was totally outrageous," he recalls. "She was always causing some kind of a scene. The Metropolis wasn't exactly a likely setting for barroom brawls, but when Courtney was around, it was chaos. She was always bragging about all these famous musicians she had partied with in England. Nobody really believed her stories but people loved to hear them."

Her drug of choice was pills.

"She'd always be popping huge amounts of pills," Curran says. "Barbiturates, speed, whatever she could get her hands on. If she had extra, she'd distribute them around as if they were candy."

Today the most commonly told story about

Courtney is that she liked to burn down houses. Everybody's heard the story but nobody can give any examples. The stories may stem from the night one Portlander, one of many who hated Courtney with a passion, set fire to a house Courtney lived in. Other elements of her reputation may be more deserved, according to her biographer Melissa Rossi, who writes in *Queen of Noise*, "People had to be careful with their clothes, drugs and boyfriends when Courtney appeared; around her, they had a tendency to vanish."

Courtney often tells the story of the night a group of neo-Nazi skinhead girls kidnapped her, drove her to Bellingham, Washington, and dumped her out on the highway naked.

She later described those days to *Spin* magazine, saying, "Years ago in a certain town, my reputation had gotten so bad that every time I went to a party, I was expected to burn the place down and knock out every window."

Among the weird artists, hippies, and punks of the Portland subculture, the gods were musicians. Until that point, Courtney had only infiltrated the musical scene as a groupie. Now she decided she wanted the groupies to adore her. "I just made myself think I will not covet what the boys have," she told Rossi. "I'll just create it myself."

Through a punk fanzine called *Maximum Rock N Roll*, she began corresponding with Jennifer Finch, an L.A.-based punk rocker. Soon after, Courtney befriended a brash young stripper named Kat Bjelland. The two popped pills, dumpster-dived, and shared a passion for vintage antique clothes. The beginning of a lifelong love/hate relationship was born. They smoked pot all day, partied all night, and listened to the hottest albums in Courtney's apartment. One night the two went with Jennifer Finch to see a band called Frightwig. That night they decided to start a band together, which they called Sugar Babylon, later renamed Sugar Baby

Doll. Courtney still couldn't play an instrument, so she was chosen as lead singer. Kat played guitar, with Jennifer on bass. Courtney hadn't yet become interested in playing punk rock, only hanging out with punks, and she wanted the band to play melodic New Wave music, while her bandmates preferred a much harder edge. Although outnumbered, Courtney tried to impose her will on the others and demanded they come around to her way of thinking. But she had finally met her match. Kat and Jennifer weren't easily intimidated, since their personalities were equally as brash as Courtney's. One night, Kat couldn't take Courtney's tantrums anymore and kicked her out of the band, which soon disbanded. Although Sugar Babylon only lasted a few months, it would turn out to be the genesis of the riot grrrl movement of the nineties, with the three musicians heading some of the era's most influential bands. Courtney, of course, founded Hole, Kat headed Babes in Toyland, and Jennifer fronted L7.

"She would not be able to hold a band member for more than a year if she weren't famous," says one of Courtney's ex-muscians. "The bands should have been called Courtney Love, because that's all she ever cared about, having her name in front."

"It was a disaster," says Kat. "It wasn't a punk band – Sugar Baby Doll was softer, sweeter. Jennifer and I were not into it. We wanted to play punk rock. Courtney thought we were crazy. She hated punk then."

After the breakup, Courtney followed Kat to Minneapolis and played briefly with Kat's new band, Babes in Toyland, before Kat threw her out once again.

This time Courtney joined her father, who had returned to San Francisco. It was during this period that Courtney soon discovered her magic elixir, heroin, which filled her with a contentment that pills could never match.

"When I realized my daughter was a junkie," says Harrison, "I was stunned. I had done a lot of drug intervention work during the sixties and I tried to help her, but she told me to mind my own business and kept up her habit. She was stealing from me to buy more smack, so I finally threw her out."

Harrison's common-law wife, Trina, remembers Courtney during this period. "She could be really sweet one moment and then just turn into a monster," she recalls. "Once she started doing heroin, she was unbearable. I remember once she threatened to burn our house down. We just couldn't take it anymore.

Courtney turned once again to a surefire moneymaker, nude dancing. This time she was legal and the money was better. Part of her act consisted of slicing her skin with a razor blade and drawing blood, which she had taken to doing offstage as well whenever she was depressed. One day she got a call from her old bandmate Jennifer Finch, who was working as an actress in Los Angeles. Courtney had always dreamed of becoming a movie star, so she followed Jennifer to L.A.

Finch specialized in playing punk roles as an extra on TV dramas such as *CHiPs* and *Quincy* (on which Courtney claims to have appeared in one episode), and one day brought Courtney along to witness the filming of a TV show. Courtney was excited about meeting important people in the business, especially producers, actors, and directors. Around this time, she met Alex Cox, who had been hired to direct *Sid and Nancy*, the upcoming bio of legendary punk couple Sid Vicious and Nancy Spungen. Cox, who had already directed the cult classic *Repo Man*, found Courtney and her background fascinating and invited her to an audition. With no acting experience behind her, Courtney chose to audition for Nancy, the lead role opposite Gary Oldman's Sid.

"Courtney has guts," says Harrison. "She'll always try to go straight to the top even though she might know nothing or have not a shred of experience in what's involved. But she always wants to be at the top."

Courtney didn't get the part but was offered a bit

role as Nancy's best friend. Most people on the set unfairly believed Courtney had no talent, but rumours abounded that she was having an affair with Cox.

The rumors seemed to be confirmed when Courtney was seen frequently around town with Cox and was soon given one of the lead roles in Cox's next film, *Straight to Hell*, which is on some critics' lists as one of the worst films of all time and which was a huge bomb at the box office. Adored and abandoned, liberated yet still seeking the someone to take care of her, Courtney became a groupie of the Pogues, Elvis Costello, and Joe Strummer while *Straight to Hell* was shot in Spain.

"While she hung out with them, she frequently volunteered for menial jobs like carrying their guitars or amps and flirted with them to make them feel bigger and more wanted," says Peter Florio, a member of the Pogues' entourage at the time.

Around this period, Courtney became aware of the sexual engine that drives rock 'n' roll. The spectre of being a rock groupie helped Courtney understand rock's misogyny. The road to success, she soon learned, was not going to be smooth.

Courtney decided that image would be very important in her quest for rock stardom. She took the $20,000 she made off *Straight to Hell* and blew it on expensive clothes like black leather boots, a pink Chanel suit, and fancy silk lingerie, not to mention a $3,000 nose job to correct the part of her body she had always hated most. Indeed, the noticeable bump which had long marred her facial features was no longer evident. Courtney, by now almost twenty, must have been the most fashionable person using Portland public transportation that summer. Despite having lived in L.A., where a car is almost essential, Courtney never got her driver's license.

She trimmed down, sometimes eating only a slice of bread a day because she didn't want to wind up like her heavyset father, and wore heavy makeup to cover the collage of zits that covered her face. But Courtney was not bothered. She believed that you could have acne and still be a rock star.

Courtney started jamming with bands, including Faith No More. She would keep journals of poems and letters. She liked Leonard Cohen and dreamed of becoming the female version of the singer-poet.

"Courtney has no real musical talent but she's definitely a good poet," says her father. "She started to write poems as early as six years old. And she likes good poets like Dylan and Leonard Cohen. The only thing she never realized was that she couldn't put words to music the way they do."

Something disruptive happened when Courtney Love entered a room; barometric pressure changed; things accelerated. She wasn't a diva, there was no hysteria, but she was demanding, superior, self-possessed, and very abrasive. Bandmates found it impossible to play with her because, aside from her suspect talent, she drove everyone crazy. Faith No More kicked her out and again she went searching for a band that would put up with her.

Soon after, Courtney noticed an ad recruiting women to strip in Alaska. She landed the job and was on the road once again, dancing in small clubs catering to the pipeline workers. She made some cash up north and returned to Portland a few months later. A year later, in 1989, she was back in L.A., this time working at a swanky strip club, Star Strip. Courtney still visits Star Strip when she's on tour or recording in L.A. In December 1995, she went back and, according to the manager, got up and danced and tucked crisp new one-hundred-dollar bills in the bras of the strippers. "Even when Courtney goes to see a show she just can't sit around and watch," says Harrison. "She has to do something to become part of the show. She always needs to be in the spotlight."

In between Portland and L.A., Courtney moved to New York. She was determined to support herself by acting and wasn't afraid to schmooze with directors and producers to increase her chances for a role. "Court-ney's a great psychologist," explains Harrison. "That's how she became so successful. She wasn't afraid to mix with the top dogs in the business. And she read them well and was able to ingratiate herself to them. Courtney's easy to fall in love with when she puts on her charm."

She came close to getting a part in the film *Last Exit to Brooklyn* but did not survive the final cut. She did, however, land a role in an off-Broadway fringe play produced by Michael McLure called *The Beard*. She played Jean Harlow.

Courtney became a regular in the New York music scene. She was very taken by Sonic Youth's industrial sound and was a fan of its bassist and vocalist, Kim Gordon, who was one of the leaders of the future riot grrrl movement. Ironically, Gordon would be one of her biggest sparring partners when the two appeared on the same Lollapalooza tour years later. Back in L.A., Courtney was doing all right taking off her clothes at the Star Strip. The money was good, but again, she was insecure about her weight. She decided to go on one of her frequent binge diets. She also restructured her whole look, this time with another nose job to streamline her face and a bit of bleach in her already dyed hair.

This was the first time in a while that Courtney felt good about herself. After having an abortion the year before, she had gone into an emotional abyss. She would eat junk food all day and drown her sorrows with whatever alcoholic beverages she came in contact with. She had also increased her already heavy smoking habit to three packs a day.

"Courtney's always been obsessive with whatever she did in life," says Harrison. "She'll do everything to a very big extreme, whether its eating, music, or sex."

Courtney's interest in being a rock star resurfaced in Los Angeles. She decided to learn a little guitar so she wouldn't have to be dependent on other musicians. She placed an ad in *The Recycler*, a paper that specializes in ads bringing together musicians. *The Recycler* is renowned for having helped form some of the West Coast's hottest bands, including Guns 'N Roses. Courtney's ad read, "I want to start a band. My influences are Big Black, Sonic Youth, and Fleetwood Mac."

She received numerous phone calls. Some of them were curiosity seekers. Others turned out to be lonely men who just wanted a woman to talk to. Courtney was more than happy to oblige. She would ramble on and on about music and drugs and then usually turn the conversation into phone sex.

"Courtney loves to talk on the phone," says Tom Grant, the private investigator who worked for her. "She could ramble on for hours. But she goes from one subject to the next so quickly that it's hard to keep up with her."

Courtney auditioned nearly a dozen musicians. She loved the power of having people at her mercy. Courtney kept stressing how well known she was (she wasn't at the time), and that she was offering the chance of a lifetime to be in a band that she said would go places quickly.

She finally settled on a tall, lanky, dirty-blond guitarist named Eric Erlandson. She was impressed with Eric from the first time she met him at the audition in her apartment, but she didn't contact him for weeks, which led him to assume that he hadn't been chosen.

"After I called her, she didn't call me for two weeks," Erlandson was quoted as saying by writer Nick Wise. "Then she called me back at three in the morning and talked my ear off."

After that phone call, Courtney was convinced she had her man.

"He had a Thurston [Moore] quality about him," Courtney would say. "He was tall, skinny, blond. He dressed pretty cool, and he knew who Sonic Youth were. Eric's gotten pushed aside so much because of my persona that he doesn't get nearly enough credit. He's an intensely weird, good guitarist, and he's the glue that's kept me together."

Eric was impressed by Courtney's self-evident rightness and the clarity of her view of what direction the band would take, but he was still skeptical, telling Option magazine, "I met her and thought this isn't going to work. She didn't know how to play, and she had a really crazy lifestyle. I didn't think she would get her shit together."

Courtney realized the time was ripe to make a move up the music industry ladder. She had plenty of life experience and could play different roles to manipulate her way into the suites of the music industry. She could be sweet and fit stereotypical images of femininity, for which the men in the music business have always had a soft spot. But she refused to be submissive.

"Courtney was not the starving, naive kid that just wants to get their name on a contract," says Hank Harrison. "She would challenge the record industry. People were at first scared to sign her because they knew that they couldn't rip her off like they do to most new artists."

With Eric, Caroline Rue on drums, and Jill Emery on bass, Courtney started to make waves in the L.A. underground rock scene. She was notorious for her wild mannerisms on stage and would yell at the crowd to get them riled up. Courtney named the band Hole, which to this day she claims has no link to female genitalia. She usually claims she got the name from the Euripides play *Medea* and that it pertained to an abyss mentioned in the play.

The band started to tour with mixed results. Few

took the brash Courtney seriously.

"Without me this band is zero," she once told the other members of Hole, and proceeded to storm out of a jam the night before a gig. "Everybody talks behind my back. You all think you're better than me. But where were you before you met me? Nowhere. You were all, and actually still are, a bunch of losers."

The other members of Hole knew that Courtney was just having another bad day and decided, as usual, to let her use them as her punching bag. After Courtney left, Eric, Caroline, and Jill lit up a fat joint and launched into a jam session, which lasted more than five hours.

"We should tape the session and send it to the bitch," Jill said. "If she has any ears she'll realize that we sound twenty times better without her."

Hole started to command decent money for an underground band. And A&R reps from record companies were turning out regularly to their shows. When a major label approached Courtney after a show and told her that they needed a more "full sound," Courtney told him to "fuck off."

She added, "I'll bet you won't have a job in six months because we'll be signed and famous, and you'll be the one known for not signing us."

A lot of musicians in the L.A. scene were intent on sleeping with Courtney. Her promiscuous reputation spread quickly and she would usually live up to it. Most nights she would leave a gig with a member from another band on the same card as Hole. She would sleep with him for one night and then, usually, dump him.

"She seemed to always leave a gig with a different man," said Hank Harrison. "I guess it's in the family genes. I also had my share of affairs with women. Sometimes I made love to a different woman every day of the week. But that was in the free-loving sixties."

Courtney was a fan of macho L.A. punk rockers

the Leaving Trains. She was determined to sleep with their lead singer, the cross-dressing James Moreland, whose stage name was Falling James. Despite his penchant for wearing women's clothes, James was very much a heterosexual. Women usually rushed the stage when he and his band were playing. Moreland was instantly attracted to Courtney. After meeting her back-stage at one of his gigs, he invited her to his place and she accepted without hesitation. The two got stoned and had sex all night. Courtney told friends she felt great because she had got the man that all the other women at the gig wanted.

When Moreland said jokingly that he would like to marry her as they lay in bed smoking a postcoital cigarette, Courtney thought he was serious and she said yes. Moreland decided to go along with it and a day later the two drove to Las Vegas, where they were married. According to Courtney's version, the two soon realized they couldn't stand each other and quickly separated. But Moreland tells a different story.

"Our relationship wasn't exactly a bed of roses," he said in Los Angeles, where he still performs. "We would have these huge fights and split up for weeks at a time and then get back together. She was really fucked up on drugs most of the time and she could get uncontrollably violent."

Moreland said he doesn't know whether she was capable of having Kurt killed, but he remembers one of her more bizarre habits from the time when they lived in L.A.

"If somebody pissed her off a lot, she would pay this guy she knew fifty or a hundred dollars to beat them up. It was pretty scary."

In a conversation with his former father-in-law Hank Harrison – a conversation which Harrison played for us – Moreland bitterly recalled that Courtney got pregnant and continued to use heavy drugs, which eventually forced her to have an abortion. "It was a nightmare," he said. "I'll never forgive her for that."

Meanwhile, the grunge movement was picking up steam and Hole was getting more attention for its unique sound. Courtney knew her big chance was around the corner. Courtney hooked up with an indie music producer named Long Gone John, who had started up a small record label in Los Angeles called Sympathy for the Record Industry. John was intrigued by Courtney's unique personality and music. He fronted Hole $500 to record their first single, "Retard Girl," at Rudy's Rising Star Studio in Los Angeles.

The single was released in March 1990 and sold well enough for John to offer the band a contract to record an entire album.

But Courtney was never known for her loyalty and, without telling John, she had already signed an indie contract with the small but respected Caroline label, which had been impressed with the single. Hole went into the studio and started working on their debut album, *Pretty on the Inside*. Courtney was determined to have final say on everything in terms of album cover designer, order of musicians' credits in the liner notes, and even the spot where the price code went on the back.

"She was on a total power trip," said one band member. "But she didn't boss the musicians because she didn't have the knowledge to tell them how to change a solo or a riff. It's like we were just there to make some noise, almost any noise that Courtney could just put lyrics to and sing over.

Courtney was starting to gain a lot of attention in fanzines and college radio. Hole was headed to the top of the class of the riot grrrl movement, which included bands like Bikini Kill, Seven Year Bitch, Calamity Jane, L7, Babes in Toyland, and Bratmobile.

"We just don't look for all-girl bands for the novelty," says Slim Moon of Kill Rock Star Records,

Bikini Kill's label. "I remember Courtney in Hole's early days because I was also good friends with Kurt. She was good but definitely not anywhere near the most talented of the riot grrrl musicians."

Ambitious, driven, and self-interested, Courtney was close to the top. Stomping up and down rock clubs' small stages, slamming stage doors, and yelling at her growing coterie of fans, the bad girl of punk started attracting serious music industry attention.

In 1991, Hole ventured to England to capitalize on the overseas popularity of the burgeoning American alternative scene. Looking like a twisted Shirley Temple with her baby doll dresses and dark, melancholy attitude, she became the darling of the U.K. alternative press and was photographed repeatedly.

When *Pretty on the Inside* was released in 1991, the album soon became a staple in the collections of many alternative record buyers. It was recorded at Music Box Studios in Los Angeles and was coproduced by Don Fleming and Sonic Youth's Kim Gordon. Fleming was a guitarist and songwriter for underground band Gumball. Gordon was one woman Courtney had always admired.

To many, Hole's music comes across as nothing but a lot of screeching and noise but those with the patience to really listen often notice something else. A 1991 review of the album in *Spin* magazine captures its essence:

"Hole's first album, *Pretty on the Inside*, revolves around a fascination with the repulsive aspects of L.A. – superficiality, sexism, violence, and drugs. Love is the embodiment of what drives the band: the dichotomy of pretty/ugly.... The pretty/ugly dynamic also comes across in Hole's music. A song like 'Teenage Whore' at first comes across like a ranting noisy rage, but underneath is a surprisingly lush melody."

Courtney was starting to enjoy the recognition

and being sought by young teenage girls for her autograph. She started dating Smashing Pumpkins leader Billy Corgan and the two were backstage regulars at all the big alternative shows in England and L.A.

But Corgan was still relatively unknown and Courtney had already made up her mind to cast for bigger fish.

5
Kurt and Courtney

It's September 1992, the MTV awards have just ended and Kurt and Courtney are backstage, embellishing the rock tradition of postconcert debauchery. Kurt looks tired and stressed and shows no signs of the deadpan sense of humour that was part of his persona during Nirvana's early days. Dave Grohl and Krist Novoselic are mingling with the other artists, exchanging pleasantries and updates on tours and Seattle. It's been a long day. After nearly boycotting the ceremony because MTV tried to dictate what Nirvana should play, the band decided at the last minute to open the show. Courtney is holding Frances Bean in one hand and delving into a huge spread of food with the other. "She looks just like Kurt," one member of Soundgarden tells Courtney. "But she has your disposition," he adds.

Courtney does not look like a rock star. She looks like she was plucked from the crowd by a roadie at the band's behest and is trying to attract everybody's attention backstage.

"I can't wait till we get the fuck out of here," Kurt tells Courtney, loud enough to be heard by anyone within earshot. "Let's split. This is fucking bullshit."

But Courtney pretends she doesn't hear him. She is too busy star-gazing.

"Axl, Axl, come over here," she yells across the room after noticing Guns 'n Roses leader Axl Rose a few feet away. "Will you be the godfather to our child?" she asks. Rose was not a big admirer of Courtney, whom he had frequently run into on the L.A. music scene, and had told friends that she was a "phony bitch." He was no fan either of Kurt, who frequently attacked the sexism and homophobia of Guns 'n Roses, calling the band "pathetic and untalented." Nevertheless, Axl had once asked Nirvana to tour with his band and was rudely rebuffed.

Rose saunters over to Kurt, with several of his entourage and handlers beside him, and looks ready for a fight. "You shut your bitch up, or I'm taking you down to the pavement," he tells an amused Kurt.

Kurt turns to Courtney and says, "Shut up, bitch!" A crowd of musicians and record industry reps have gathered around the Cobains and Rose. Laughter erupts from the crowd of onlookers. Courtney seems happy that everybody is finally paying attention to her. Rose looks satisfied and he leaves the scene with his entourage.

"I guess I did what he wanted me to do – be a man," Kurt later said. "He just wanted to see me stand up to Courtney."

Flash back to 1990 and Nirvana is on stage in front of a crowd of about two hundred people at the Satyricon Club in Portland. One of the people in the crowd that night is a woman wearing black sunglasses and a white mini-dress – Courtney Love. As she watches the rising band onstage open for the Dharma Bums, her eyes grow fixed to its thin, blond singer, Kurt Cobain.

"He's got Dave Pirner damage," she thought. "But way cuter... hot in a Sub Pop rock god sort of way."

Kurt had heard of Courtney through his friend Calvin Johnson of K Records and through reports in the fanzines. He knew she was at the show and he sauntered over to her table and helped himself to a glass of beer, which he poured from her pitcher. Normally shy, Kurt was just curious to meet the woman about whom he heard all those rumours.

"I thought she looked like Nancy Spungen", Kurt later said. "She looked like a classic punk rock chick. I did feel kind of attracted to her. Probably wanted to fuck her that night, but she left."

But although Courtney pretended to be cold and disinterested, she was attracted to Kurt from the moment she set eyes on him. She was also curious because he didn't make a pass at her and she was anxious to see if she could land him. The two didn't bump into each other again for more than a year. But Courtney started keeping tabs on Kurt. She contacted her old bandmate Jennifer Finch. Finch was good friends with Nirvana drummer Dave Grohl and agreed to hook Courtney up with Kurt's drummer. Grohl told Courtney that Kurt had talked about their first meeting and was attracted to her. Courtney decided to give Dave something to give to Kurt.

Courtney liked to create miniatures in the shape of unusual figures. Most of her friends agree that she had more talent at drawing or painting than she did with music. She made Kurt a creation of shells and dollhouse furniture placed in a small, heart-shaped box. Dave passed it on to Kurt, who never called Courtney to thank her for the gift. Courtney later said if he had, she wouldn't have been as interested in him.

"When Courtney first started dating, she would

always try to get the guy that every girl wanted," says Hank Harrison. "And if the guy showed signs of liking her, she would try for the next guy. She always wants what she can't get in anything she does."

Meanwhile, Courtney continued seeing Billy Corgan and Kurt was still deep into his relationship with Bikini Kill drummer Tobi Vail.

In May 1991, Kurt and Courtney crossed paths again. This time they had gone to see a triple-band blowout in Los Angeles featuring the Butthole Surfers, Red Kross, and L7. They spotted each other and quickly struck up a conversation.

"We bonded over pharmaceuticals," Courtney later told Hot Press. "I had Vicodin extra-strength, which was pills, and he had Hycomine cough syrup. I said, 'You're a pussy, you shouldn't drink that syrup because it's bad for your stomach."' They went home together and got wasted before having sex the rest of the night.

"She had a completely planned way of seducing me and it worked," Kurt would recall. "Courtney was into sex and she pleased me that night like no other woman had in a while."

"Kurt was happy because he finally met a woman who liked doing drugs and also enjoyed getting laid," says Kurt's best friend, Dylan Carlson, who didn't meet Courtney until much later. "They were inseparable in the early stages of their relationship."

Kurt found Courtney to be sympathetic, brash, self-effacingly funny, and supportive. She soon became a regular at Nirvana's jam space, and she would party with the band constantly. She liked to order pizza and Chinese food and pick up the tab so that Kurt's bandmates would welcome her presence.

"She tried to ingratiate herself to everybody and at first they fell for it," Kurt would later explain. "But I was just getting out of another relationship that I didn't even want to be in, and I found Courtney was becoming too possessive."

Some of Courtney's friends claim that she was solely interested in the potential of Nirvana's success and wanted to be first in line when it happened. But Courtney has a totally different view.

"I thought I was going to be more famous than him," she told writer Nick Wise. "That was pretty obvious to me."

The couple separated for a few months because Kurt said he was confused. He told her he needed space to concentrate on making the *Nevermind* album. At first Courtney did whatever she could to make him change his mind. She even offered to treat him to a Caribbean holiday so that they could work things out in a place not surrounded by their friends and drug dealers. But Kurt insisted she give him some time and that if it was meant to be, they would get back together.

In the 1991 documentary *The Year Punk Broke* by Dave Markey, an obviously stoned Courtney looks straight into the camera and says, "Kurt Cobain makes my heart stop. But he's a shit." Courtney would say similar things about Kurt to the press throughout their tumultuous relationship.

Kurt and Courtney finally reunited at an L.A. nightclub after *Nevermind* hit it big a few months later.

From that point, Courtney was reluctant to let Kurt out of her sight. For a time, she vowed to be monogamous. She knew she had to be faithful to the world's biggest rock star and was determined to do everything she could to please him.

The new couple shared something in common which helped them bond, a penchant for large amounts of heroin.

"She let him do heroin," said Dylan Carlson. "Actually, Courtney's very smart. She knew that the more drugs Kurt did, the less trouble he would cause her." (Carlson admits, however, that most of his information about Courtney at this time came from Kurt and other friends and that he didn't actually meet Courtney until the day before their wedding.)

Publicly, Kurt would tell a different story. Although it is clear his heroin use increased significantly after Courtney came into his life, he said it only became a habit after his 1991 European tour while Courtney was still in Europe with Hole.

The way Kurt told the story to his biographer Michael Azerad, he and Courtney had done heroin together in Amsterdam around Thanksgiving 1991, but "It was my idea," he said. "I was the one who instigated it. But I didn't really know how to get it, so Courtney was the one who would be able to somehow get it. She would be the one who would take me to the place where we might be able to have a chance of being able to find it. We only did it twice the whole tour."

When Kurt returned from Europe, with Courtney remaining behind to tour with Hole, he said his stomach pain had become so bad, it made him want to kill himself. He said he met a dealer who was soon getting him heroin every day.

"It started with three days in a row of doing heroin and I don't have a stomach pain," he said. "This was such a relief, I decided, 'Fuck, I'm going to do this for a whole year.' I was determined to get a habit. This was the only thing keeping me from blowing my head off right now." (This, along with a number of other similar references in the next three years, would be cited after his death as proof that he had always been suicidal.)

On December 31, 1991, Kurt and Courtney attended a New Year's Eve party in the company of some of Hollywood's top stars. Keanu Reeves, a big grunge fan at the time, was trying to make conversation with Kurt. But Kurt acted disinterested. He was totally wasted on heroin and he barely knew where he was.

"There were a bunch of fucking Ashley Hamilton rich kids in their rooms and they were all fucking wasted," Courtney later recalled. "We were too."

Keanu invited Kurt to go deep-sea fishing, but Kurt said no. He thought Keanu was just interested in him for his Nirvana success. "I bet you wouldn't even give me the time of day if I wasn't a fucking rock star," Kurt told him. "Just leave me alone, man. Courtney, let's get the fuck outta here, now."

When they arrived back at their hotel room, Kurt scrawled a note on a piece of hotel stationery and taped it to the front door. "No famous people please – We're fucking!" it read.

The release of *Nevermind* turned Nirvana into superstars overnight, and Kurt was labeled the voice of the nineties. The band was booked to play NBC's Saturday Night Live on January 11, 1992. Kurt and Courtney showed up at the NBC studios in New York looking fragile and on heroin.

"Before that show, they both did heroin in their hotel room," says Dylan Carlson. "Kurt told me Courtney initiated it. She was insecure and jealous of the attention Kurt was receiving. But that's just Courtney for you."

Dave and Krist noticed Kurt was totally out of it. They discussed the problem because they said they were concerned about his health and about what would happen if millions of viewers and fans realized that Kurt was a junkie.

Kurt got through the *SNL* show but backstage he almost collapsed. When the band finished playing "Smells Like Teen Spirit," Kurt went backstage and fell into Courtney's arms.

"His bandmates were concerned because they had never seen him in this bad a state," says Carlson. "It was at this point that they realized that Courtney was the one who was responsible. That's when they first started comparing Courtney to Yoko Ono."

It was about this time that Courtney found out she was pregnant. She was more than anxious to tell Kurt.

"This was what gave her the security she wanted with Kurt," says Hank Harrison. "Courtney knew it would only be a matter of time before Kurt left her, so she needed something to put a stranglehold on him."

At first Kurt didn't believe Courtney because she had joked about being pregnant in the past. But when he realized she was serious, he proposed they get married. At first Courtney used reverse psychology. "Don't feel like you have to marry me because I'm carrying your child," she told Kurt. "I'll still be a good mother, you can bet your fucking life on that."

But Courtney has admitted she knew that Kurt would persist and convince her to get married, which she told friends she wanted for a long time.

The couple split their time between Seattle and their rented home in the Fairfax area of Los Angeles. The rest of the time, they spent on the road touring.

Kurt and Courtney decided on a wedding far away from family and friends. "Kurt's family wasn't happy," says Carlson, who was Kurt's best man at the wedding. "But it was Courtney's idea. First of all, she was worried that her family wouldn't show up to the wedding and the press would jump all over it. And she also didn't want to be photographed constantly by the world's media corps when she was pregnant."

Before they got married, Courtney insisted on a prenuptial agreement. Kurt was well known but he had yet to see the millions he would receive less than a year later. Courtney was still convinced she would be much more famous than Kurt.

"I didn't want Kurt running away with all my money," she joked at the time.

The couple flew off to Hawaii with a small group of friends and were married on February 24, 1992, in Waikiki. Courtney found a non-denominational female minister through the Hawaiian wedding bureau.

Kurt and Courtney started partying even before their flight took off. By the time they boarded the plane, they were both "high as a kite," according to Carlson, who took heroin with them before and after the ceremony. "We didn't even eat that day," he explains. "Something was weird. Kurt felt like he had to be wasted before he got married."

Kurt and Courtney both picked out the flowers they would hold at their wedding. Kurt decided to wear green pajamas. Courtney wore a lace dress that had once belonged to one of their mutual heroes, Hollywood actress Frances Farmer.

"Being from Aberdeen and raised with some sense of family values, Kurt thought he had no choice but to marry Courtney," said Carlson. "I know he liked Courtney a lot, but he would say many times that he was not even sure if he was in love. But Kurt said he was convinced that you didn't have to be in love to get married. Later, I think he really loved her."

The couple's wedding received a lot of media attention. MTV carried updates and even a tribute to Kurt. Krist Novoselic refused to attend the wedding because Courtney refused to invite his wife, Shelli, who made no secret of her distaste for Kurt's new bride. Carlson made the trip after Kurt asked him to be best man.

"Kurt told me I was his only choice and he said he needed me to go to Hawaii," Carlson said in a 1995 interview at the home of one of his friends in Seattle's University District. "Courtney didn't object. Actually, I always got along pretty well with Courtney. I still like her."

Kurt and Courtney enjoyed the next few months in Seattle and L.A. They became almost inseparable, except when Kurt insisted on hanging out with his junkie friends.

"Sometimes it was really an excuse for him to get a chance to get away from his wife," says Carlson. "Kurt hung around a lot of heroin dealers and junkies, but he wasn't always doing drugs."

Meanwhile, the increasing success of Hole's Pretty on the Inside was creating a huge buzz about Courtney and Hole within the music industry. The band's European tour several months before had resulted in much speculation that they were heading for a major record deal. Courtney was excited at the prospect and could talk of little else except who she would like to sign with.

Ironically, the person who Courtney talked about most was the first to approach her with a serious contract offer. Courtney was in awe of Madonna's fame and power in the music business. She wanted nothing short of the same clout that the "Material Girl" wielded.

"Madonna and Barbara Walters are the two people that Courtney followed religiously," says her father. "She always wanted to be bigger than Madonna and to be interviewed by Barbara Walters."

Courtney later had her dream fulfilled by making Walters's "10 most fascinating people" of 1995 list. Her relationship with Madonna, however, was not quite so cozy.

In late 1991, Gus Oseary was working for Madonna's new company, Maverick, and talked to Madonna and her manager, Freddy De Mann about signing Hole. He was told by De Mann to contact Courtney's lawyer, who happened to be Rosemary Carroll, the wife of record industry mogul Danny Goldberg. But Courtney didn't want to share the spotlight with Madonna or anybody else and she told people Madonna was only interested in having control over her so that she doesn't get too big.

"Madonna's interest in me was kind of like Dracula's interest in his latest victim," Courtney later said. "She wanted to buy not only us but all those underground bands she didn't have a clue about."

But Madonna has told an entirely different version of that episode and others with Courtney over the years.

First, Madonna was not amused at how Courtney exploited the confidentiality of the offer to the British tabloids who had a field day quoting Courtney about Madonna, who at this point she hadn't even met. Guy Oseary couldn't believe the monster in Courtney. "The stories in the English press went, 'Madonna doesn't have Aids and she wants to sign Hole"' he recalled. "From then on, it was 'Madonna's Hole,' suddenly we're just one of the bidders. At Hole's next show, thirteen A&R people were there."

In a 1995 interview with Britain's *New Musical Express*, Madonna talked about her attempt to sign Hole. Asked if she was irritated about Courtney's "vampire" comments, she replied, "Absolutely! Because she was the one calling me up at three a.m. going off on all these tangents about how women have to stick together and how she really admired and respected me for all I'd been through. Then she turns around and says all these things and I'm like, 'My god! This woman is completely insane.'"

She said she got the impression at the time that Courtney was "a miserable person" who was completely self-obsessed.

"When I met her, when I was trying to sign her, she spent the whole time slagging off her husband. She was saying, 'Oh, Hole are so much better than Nirvana' and just going off on a tangent. She just loves to hear herself talk. She doesn't even mean half the things she says, she's just incredibly competitive with people and anybody who's successful she's going to slag off. That's all there is to it."

News of Madonna's interest set off a bidding war among major labels to sign Hole. Arista boss Clive Davis reportedly offered the band more than a million dollars to sign. Rick Rubin of Def American and Jeff Ayeroff at Virgin were also seriously interested but they clashed heavily with Courtney's temperament.

Gary Gersh at Geffen was the person to ink Hole to its first major record deal. At the time, Courtney was already married to Kurt. "We didn't make the deal because she is married to Kurt Cobain," said Geffen boss Ed Rosenblatt. "But it is a little weird. Hole is a band who we happen to believe in and, oh, by the way, she's married to...."

Before Courtney agreed to the Geffen deal, she had her entertainment lawyer Rosemary Carroll carefully check every clause. The streetwise Courtney was no stranger to horror stories of bands signing contracts without going over the fine points. In fact, she even insisted that Geffen produce Nirvana's contract for her inspection. After reviewing it, she was adamant on receiving a similar deal but with more control of publishing rights.

Courtney finally walked away with a million-dollar deal, and about half a million for her publishing rights. There's no question that it was a more favorable arrangement than Kurt's deal, which is not surprising since Kurt was by comparison a novice when he signed his first major contract. "If those sexist assholes want to think that me and Kurt write songs together, they can come forward with a little more," she said at the time. "No matter what label I'm on, I'm going to be his wife. I'm enough of a person to transcend that."

As Courtney's pregnancy progressed, Kurt became increasingly excited about the prospect of fatherhood. Friends say he was obviously deeply in love with Courtney by this time and was always doting on her. But it took one slip of the tongue to a reporter to turn their life into the nightmare from which they would never recover.

Gold Mountain had arranged a cover story on Courtney in *Vanity Fair* magazine, which for her was the big time. Being married to Kurt was already paying off, but she was worried the piece would focus on her role as his wife rather than a celebrity in her own right. As she often said, "I want to be a rock star, not fuck a rock star."

After writer Lynn Hirschberg conducted the interview, Courtney posed for a six-hour photo session with photographer Michael Conte. She thought the interview went well and anxiously awaited its publication.

But almost from the day the issue hit the stands,

the controversy began. It was obvious Hirschberg hadn't been impressed with her subject, who she described as a "train wreck personality who isn't particularly interested in the consequences of her action... raising fears for the health of her unborn child."

A few unflattering words weren't the end of the world, but it was Courtney's own words which would set the train rolling.

Courtney describes a visit she and Kurt made to score heroin from a Lower East Side dealer in New York after his *Saturday Night Live* appearance in January 1992.

"We went on a binge," she said. "We did a lot of drugs. We got pills and then we went down to Alphabet City and Kurt wore a hat, I wore a hat, and we copped some dope. Then we got high and we went to *SNL*..."

Then Courtney uttered the words which would forever haunt her, "After that I did heroin for a couple of months." If this was true, it meant she was still doing heroin after she knew she was pregnant.

She went on to talk about her pregnancy, announcing they knew it was a girl and that they'd already picked out a name for her: Frances Bean Cobain.

"Kurt's the right person to have a baby with," Courtney explained. "We have money. I can have a nanny. The whole feminine experience of pregnancy and birth – I'm not into it on that level. But it was a bad time to get pregnant and that appealed to me.... Besides, we need new friends."

Lost in the subsequent uproar over Courtney's heroin admission were some telling quotes from her on-again, off-again best friend Kat Bjelland, leader of Babes in Toyland.

"Only about a quarter of what Courtney says is true," Bjelland told Hirschberg. "But nobody usually bothers to decipher which are the lies. She's all about image. And that's interesting. Irritating, but interesting ....Courtney's delusional. I called her a while ago because I was worried about her baby and her sanity, but I never heard back from her. In the past, I always forgave her, but I can't anymore. Last night I had a dream that I killed her. I was really happy."

It is Courtney's prophetic last quote which, in retrospect, would serve as the ultimate irony. "Things are really good," she concluded. "It's all coming true. Although it could fuck up any time. You never know."

She obviously hadn't known that her admission to using drugs while pregnant would set off a wave of revulsion worldwide, igniting a hatred for Courtney which stretched from people who had never heard of her before to members of Kurt's band who had already been heard to refer to her as "Yoko" but now had their mistrust confirmed. The day before the issue hit the stands, Kurt and Courtney – who had been tipped off about the contents – issued a press release claiming the profile "contains many inaccuracies and distortions and generally gives a false picture of us both."

But only after the negative publicity started did Kurt and Courtney truly understand the full implications of the story.

"I wouldn't have thought that I could be dwarfed or squashed or raped or incredibly hurt by a story in that magazine," Courtney later said. "But the power of it was so intense. It was unbelievable.... I knew that my world was over. I was dead. That was it. Not only was I going to walk around with a big black mark but any happiness that I had known, I was going to have to fight for the rest of my life."

Kurt was equally devastated by the story. The birth of his daughter, which he saw as his crowning achievement, was only two weeks away. He was the biggest rock star in the world. He should have been happy. But all of a sudden people were coming down on him and Courtney as if they were demons. It was causing a lot of tension between them.

A few days after the article was published, Kurt returned with Dylan to the home he and Courtney were renting in the Fairfax district of L.A. The two were obviously high.

"I'm going to fucking kill you, you bastard," Courtney yelled at Kurt. "I don't even want you to see the baby when it's born. You're a fucking basket case."

Kurt was too strung out to yell back. He went upstairs and climbed into bed. The next morning he decided to check into a detox centre in another effort to clean himself up.

Courtney was growing more depressed. She told Eric that she wanted to commit suicide so that Kurt would lose both her and the baby.

"He's a shit," she complained. "I've gone through hell in the last year and all that the fucker could think about is getting his next fix."

At the urging of Danny Goldberg, who was worried about the effect the turmoil was having on her pregnancy, Courtney checked into an L.A. hospital two weeks before she was expected to give birth. Ironically, Kurt was checked into an adjoining room trying to kick his drug habit.

Kurt was bitter about everything that had happened. His first thought, he would tell Michael Azerad, was to quit the band and kill Hirschberg.

"As soon as I get out of this hospital," he remembered thinking, "I am going to kill this woman with my bare hands. I'm going to stab her to death. First I'm going to take her dog and slit its guts out in front of her and then shit all over her and stab her to death." He said he admitted he even considered hiring a hit man.

But there was little doubt in the minds of the Cobains' friends and record management that most of Hirschberg's article was accurate.

"The Geffen people freaked out after that article came out," recalls Courtney's father. "They tried to do everything possible to revamp her image so that fans would not be offended. But Kurt got depressed and went on a huge drug binge that annoyed Courtney. They started arguing constantly and Courtney was a total wreck."

The rest of Nirvana was growing increasingly ambivalent toward Courtney. "She's going to break us up," Krist Novoselic would say. "She totally controls Kurt and she's turning him against us."

As if the article weren't damning enough, Courtney had allowed the *Vanity Fair* photographer to shoot her in see-through lingerie, smoking a cigarette and looking very pregnant. The editor, Tina Brown, ordered the cigarette airbrushed from the photo, but Courtney was desperately afraid the negatives would make their way to the tabloids and prove that she showed a reckless disregard for the health of her unborn baby. Eventually, she paid the photographer a reported $50,000 to get the negatives back.

She later said that, during the photo shoot, she just took one puff of a cigarette and the photographer happened to catch it. But according to one of the techs present at that shoot, "That's an outright lie. She was practically chain-smoking the whole time she was there." Indeed, *Vanity Fair* had other photos of her smoking that day, and Hirschberg described her as smoking throughout their interview.

"I want you to sue their asses off" Courtney told her lawyer. "They've fucked up my whole life. Everything is going bad. And Kurt's freaking out." Courtney claimed she had been quoted out of context and that she had said she had only done heroin early in the pregnancy before she knew she was pregnant.

When Kurt heard that Courtney went into labour, he rushed down the hall in a hospital smock to be with his wife. But the combination of sedatives and lack of sleep made him totally incoherent when he approached Courtney.

"You fucker," Courtney screamed. "Now you decide to come to the rescue. Get the fuck outta here. It's me who's experienced all the pain."

Courtney's doctors tried to calm her down but to no avail. Kurt started to yell back at her but he collapsed. After a few minutes, he was revived and escorted out of the room.

Frances Bean Cobain was born at 7:48 a.m. on August 18, 1992. She weighed seven pounds, one ounce, and doctors said she was born healthy. Courtney says she was named after Frances McKee of the Scottish duo the Vaselines. However, others still believe that she was named after Seattle's Frances Farmer – the controversial Hollywood actress driven to an asylum and eventually lobotomized – whose life was something of an obsession for Kurt. Her middle name was given to her because Kurt thought she looked like a bean when he was shown the ultrasound before she was born.

Courtney later claimed that Kurt brought a gun to the hospital the next day and threatened to commit suicide. She also claimed that he tried to convince her to kill herself too.

"I just started talking him out of it," Courtney said in a 1994 *Rolling Stone* interview. "And he said 'Fuck you, you can't chicken out. I'm gonna do it.'"

She also said that this was not the first time he asked her to take her life. She says she talked Kurt into handing over the gun to Eric Erlandson, who was at the hospital checking on the newborn baby and tired mother.

Tabloids had a field day with the birth of Frances. Headlines like "Cobain Baby Born a Junkie" or "Baby Born Deficient" were read by millions of Nirvana fans, prompting Gold Mountain to issue a press release denying the rumours. Kurt tried to ignore all the negative publicity and concentrate on his new baby. Friends say he underwent a transformation when Frances was born.

"I believe the day I saw a change in Kurt was when he had these ultrasound pictures of the baby," Danny Goldberg of Gold Mountain told the *Los*

Angeles Times. "They were like little black-and-white Polaroid photos and you see the baby's hands and things in the womb. He put it up on his wall at home. I think that took him out of thinking about himself and made him start thinking about the next phase of his life, where no matter what happens, this person was going to be in his life. He came out of the 'Oh man, I was a punk rocker and now I'm a rock star and I never wanted to be a rock star' attitude. He was so thrilled about having a baby."

Frances got to see Kurt's side of the family on an almost daily basis. Kurt's mother, Wendy, was ecstatic over the birth of her new granddaughter. But Hank Harrison wasn't so lucky.

"The biggest regret that I have is that I felt Kurt wanted to meet me but Courtney wouldn't let it happen," says Harrison. "And the day Frances was born I left a message for Courtney. She had called me a few times since but she was adamant on never letting me see my grandchild.

"My mother's been really sick in the last year and I called Courtney and begged her to let Frances see her great-grandmother. I even promised not to be present. But Courtney refused, saying, 'What have those people ever done for me?' I don't know how she could deprive her daughter of a family life."

Five days after Courtney gave birth, an article appeared in the *Los Angeles Times*, which had received a fax of her medical records from somebody in the hospital. The paper reported that a pregnant woman had checked into the hospital under an assumed name, listing Kurt Cobain as her husband. The records revealed that the woman had received "daily doses of methadone, a heroin substitute used to treat narcotics addiction." It quoted the director of a nearby drug rehabilitation centre saying that an addict should not detox while pregnant.

"The standard practice is to continue the use of

methadone through the pregnancy and deal with the chemical dependency when the pregnancy is over," he said. "And when the baby is born, then the baby is chemically dependent and it will go through methadone detox. Babies go through that well."

Kurt and Courtney later sued the hospital for leaking her records and insisted that the records only reflected her drug use in the first month of pregnancy (before she knew she was pregnant).

The article sparked further outrage. Courtney's lawyer called and told her that the Los Angeles child welfare authorities were threatening to take custody of Frances because of the allegations that Courtney had used heroin during her pregnancy. Courtney was livid.

"You tell those fuckers that if they touch Frances they'll have to kill me first," she fumed.

An emergency meeting was called, with Kurt, Courtney, their lawyer Rosemary Carroll, and Danny Goldberg present. Frances was only a few days old and already the Cobains were about to lose her. The four devised a plan to create as much positive publicity as possible, with Kurt and Courtney posing with Frances and looking like loving parents. Interviews and photos suddenly appeared in a string of magazines including *Spin*, *Rolling Stone*, and even *Time*. The Cobains were convinced they would beat the charges and keep their baby.

In September, Kurt told Robert Hilburn of the *Los Angeles Times* that he was entirely clean of drugs since the birth of his baby. "Holding my baby is the best drug in the world," he said.

But the child welfare authorities persisted. Their investigation confirmed Kurt and Courtney's drug abuse, and custody was temporarily revoked from the parents. Kurt and Courtney were ordered to give Frances to one of Courtney's sisters until they cleaned up their act. They also had to submit to regular urine tests and meet with a social worker weekly. Worst of all, they weren't allowed to be alone with their daughter for an entire month.

The new parents were devastated and urged their lawyers to fight back. Kurt later called the whole episode a conspiracy, claiming, "It was all a total scam. It was an attempt to use us as an example because we stand for everything that goes against the grain of conformist American entertainment."

In March 1993 they finally won their court battle and regained full custody of their daughter.

"That was the toughest moment of Kurt's life," said Dylan Carlson. "Kurt realized that he had to change his life dramatically or else he would probably lose Frances. So, contrary to what the press said, he calmed down his heroin habit and became a loving father. Frances was what he lived for."

It's late autumn and Kurt is strolling through the La Brea Tarpits, one of his favorite places to visit when he wants to escape the turmoil at home. He seems like a man caught between two cultures, Seattle and L.A. But Hollywood has disappointed him. There's no place for punk ideals amongst the phony glamour.

"Seattle's more down-to-earth, there's some soul over there," he would tell his friends. "L.A.'s for pretenders caught up in all the hype."

Kurt and Courtney have just had another falling out after Courtney brought up the unpopular subject of buying a home in Beverley Hills. Kurt insisted that Frances Bean be raised in Seattle because it's safer and offers a more stable environment.

"I'm not going to let our daughter grow up in a place where she could get her head shot off at any time," he told Courtney, who considered Hollywood her mecca.

Walking through the tarpits, Kurt notices a couple of kids wearing Nirvana T-shirts. He approaches them.

"Nice shirts," he says casually. "By the way, I'm Kurt."

One of the youths, who is carrying a skateboard,

looks at him and says, "Take off your sunglasses. Prove it."

Kurt lifts his blue-rimmed shades over his head. "Recognize me now?" he asks. The kids look at him in disbelief. Kurt autographs their T-shirts and then walks off after they have thanked him.

"He used to go to parks whenever things got tough at home with Courtney," says Dylan Carlson. "And he was so good with kids. Whenever someone recognized him, he would never refuse an autograph. He kind of liked the adulation after all the abuse he took at home."

Gold Mountain was acutely aware that the Vanity Fair controversy had been a public relations disaster which threatened to derail Nirvana's success. They concocted a PR plan which would have the new parents give as many interviews as possible with friendly music media along with photographs of Kurt, Courtney, and the new baby to gain sympathy. The new strategy seemed to be working and the negative publicity died down considerably, although some accused Kurt of exploiting Frances.

Kurt had already been approached by two British writers, Britt Collins and Victoria Clarke, who were interested in doing a biography of Nirvana. Although Kurt wasn't overly enthusiastic, he gave them an interview and put them onto a few leads. A few months later, Courtney heard the two writers had been in contact with *Vanity Fair's* Lynn Hirschberg, who claimed to have tapes of Courtney's infamous interview. She went ballistic.

Courtney immediately called Clarke and left a message on the answering machine telling her they better back off. When Kurt heard the news, he blew up, revealing his increasingly ugly side in a shocking manner. Clarke later released a tape to Britain's Select magazine with nine messages Kurt left on her answering machine the next day.

"If anything comes out in this book which hurts my wife, I'll fucking hurt you," he threatens on one message. Another has him saying, "I love to be fucked, I love to be blackmailed, I'll give you anything you want, I'm begging you. I'm on my knees and my mouth is wide open. You have absolutely no idea what you are doing." He then threatens to cut "out your fucking eyes, you sluts...whores...parasitic little cunts!" Courtney is heard in the background egging her husband on. "I don't give a flying fuck if I have this recorded that I'm threatening you," he continues. "I suppose I could throw out a few hundred thousand dollars to have you snuffed out, but maybe I'll try it the legal way first."

Clarke and Collins also have several tapes of Courtney calling with similar threats, including a vow to "spend every cent we have to make sure your book never comes out."

Gold Mountain's Danny Goldberg told the *New York Times* that Kurt denied making the calls and said he thought it was a prank to publicize their book.

Kurt, however, later admitted to Michael Azerad that he had made the threats and that he wanted to kill the two writers. "Obviously I have a lot to lose right now so I won't be able to do it," he said, "but I have all the rest of my life. If I ever find myself destitute and I've lost my family, I won't hesitate to get revenge on people who have fucked with me. I've always been capable of that. I've tried killing people before in a fit of rage....when people unnecessarily fuck with me, I just can't help but want to beat them to death."

Gold Mountain contacted everybody connected to Kurt and asked them not to cooperate in the women's unauthorized biography, which was scheduled to be released by Hyperion Books, a division of Disney. Conflicting stories have surfaced as to why the book was never released. The writers have told friends they were paid a large sum of money to abandon the project.

BBC filmmaker Nick Broomfield investigated the suppression of the book for a forthcoming documentary about Courtney Love. He says a source told him that David Geffen called his friend Jeffrey Katzenberg – at the time president of Disney, currently Geffen's partner at Dream-works SKG – to shelve the book, reputedly offering to buy the contract. Melissa Rossi reports that the Cobain lawyers faxed to Hyperion fifty-six pages of sections in the book they intended to legally pursue, which begs the question of how they obtained an advance copy of the manuscript. Ironically, the same thing would happen after Rossi released her book, *Courtney Love: Queen of Noise*. Simon & Schuster received a huge list of supposed errors from Courtney's lawyers.

Hyperion failed to return several calls asking for their version of why the book was never released.

In November, Courtney spotted Clarke at a Seattle bar and hit her with a glass, prompting the writer to file a civil suit which Courtney later settled out of court. Later, Collins had her apartment broken into and suspected Kurt and Courtney's camp was responsible, an accusation promptly denied.

Meanwhile, Kurt and Courtney were anxious to give their side of the story to head off the damage they expected from Collins and Clarke.

Kurt approached Michael Azerad, a respected *Rolling Stone* journalist who had been covering Nirvana for some time, and asked him to write a biography of Nirvana. Azerad insists the book was unauthorized although, in the acknowledgements, he thanks Kurt and Courtney for their "assistance and encouragement".

The couple gave Azerad complete access to friends, family, and band members, which resulted in the release of a very thorough but incomplete biography of Kurt in late 1993, a few months before Kurt's death.

Kurt and Courtney saw Azerad's book as a way of rewriting history in their favour, especially when it came to Kurt's drug use and the *Vanity Fair* episode. Although Azerad truly believed the information he was given, it became apparent only later that he had been used to clean up the Cobains' tarnished image. (Although the book is still a must-read for anybody interested in Nirvana along with his many excellent behind-the-scenes accounts in *Rolling Stone*.)

Azerad detailed a number of factual inaccuracies in the Vanity Fair article in an attempt to discredit Hirschberg and implied that the writing misunderstood Courtney's sense of humour. He seemed to believe Courtney had not used heroin while pregnant.

Indeed, after Hirschberg's article, Courtney herself had told Everett True of *Melody Maker* magazine that "I didn't do heroin during my pregnancy." She added, "And even if I shot coke every night and took acid every day, its my own motherfucking business."

In 1995, Courtney finally admitted to *Request magazine* that she had indeed done heroin during her pregnancy "or else I would've sued her [Hirschberg's] ass off."

6

The Road to Rome

The last year of Kurt's life was a year of contradictions. After the Vanity Fair controversy, Kurt made a genuine attempt to give up heroin, substituting methadone. But the stomach pain was getting worse, and smack was the only thing he knew that would take away the pain.

In the media, however, he regularly portrayed himself as someone who had experimented with drugs but then rejected them, calling them "a total waste of time."

"I knew that when I had a child," he told Robert Hilburn of the *Los Angeles Times*, "I'd be overwhelmed, and it's true... I can't tell you how much my attitude has changed since we've got Frances. Holding my baby is the best drug in the world."

He went on to say he had only "dabbled" in heroin for years, defining dabbling as using once or twice a year. He then admitted that around the time of the

Saturday Night Live appearance he had formed a "little habit" which had lasted about three weeks.

His public affection for Frances, however, was more than just a publicity ploy. By all accounts, he doted on his new baby. Soon after he won his battle with Children's Services, freeing the couple from social worker visits, Kurt paid $400,000 for a weekend estate in Carnation, Washington, where he could spend time alone with Courtney and Frances. He also rented a four-bedroom house overlooking the water on Lakeside Avenue. He talked frequently about how Seattle, which has been named America's "most livable city," was a good place to raise a family.

Royalty money kept pouring in from *Nevermind,* enabling Kurt to live the kind of life he had only dreamed about, although he kept insisting he didn't have as much money as everybody thought.

Kurt revealed that in 1992, the couple had spent about $1 million — $80,000 for personal expenses, $380,000 in taxes, $300,000 for a house in Los Angeles, and the rest in legal bills as the result of the Vanity Fair story and the custody battle.

Although *Nevermind* sales kept the cash flowing, Kurt again betrayed his punk ideals in a bitter dispute with the other band members and almost broke up the band before it could make another album. When the band had signed with Geffen in 1991, Kurt had agreed to a deal which would allow him, Krist, and Dave to split the songwriting royalties equally. At the time, he didn't realize the financial implications, but, when sales of *Nevermind* took off, he saw that the arrangement could cost him millions of dollars.

After the royalty checks started coming in, Courtney was shocked that Dave and Krist were getting the same amount as Kurt. She hounded Kurt to do something about it.

"Anybody can do what they do!" she screamed. "You're the one with all the talent." Finally, Kurt relented to her constant complaints and told the other band members he wanted a bigger share, not for the money but in acknowledgment of his greater contribution to their success.

"I write the songs, I come up with the basic idea, and then we work on it as a band," Kurt would later explain. "Most of the time that I'm asking Krist and Dave their opinion, it's just to make them feel a part of the band. I always have the ultimate decision."

It was true that Kurt was the principal songwriter, and Dave and Krist knew that they probably deserved a smaller share of the royalties. They were willing to discuss a change for the next album. The shit hit the fan, however, when he informed them he wanted the new arrangement to be retroactive to the release of *Nevermind*. He even threatened to quit the band unless they agreed.

Dave and Krist were shocked. Their old friend had completely abandoned his punk ideals and replaced them with greed. At one point they decided to call Kurt's bluff and break up. Only after heavy pressure from Geffen, friends, and family did they capitulate to Kurt's demands, aware they could never equal the success of Nirvana without Kurt. The dispute left them bitter – feelings they defused by blaming Courtney for manipulating their old friend.

Financial disputes weren't the only thing causing tension in the band. Dave and Krist were becoming increasingly alarmed at Kurt's heavy heroin use, calling him a "junkie asshole" behind his back.

They were scheduled to go back into the studio to record their next album with a new producer, Steve Albini, whose punk credentials impressed the whole band. Albini had produced PT Harvey, Superchunk, the Jesus Lizard, and other bands Kurt admired. Best of all, he had heard through the rock grapevine that Albini hated *Nevermind* and had labelled it a complete sellout.

In late 1992, Geffen had released a compilation of outtakes, rare live footage, and unreleased tracks from some BBC Nirvana sessions called *Incesticide*. This pseudo-album presaged Kurt's repudiation of the popular *Nevermind*. The sound was much harsher. But it was the liner notes, rather than the music, that really signaled Kurt's new attitude. In the original version Kurt had submitted to Geffen, he launched a vitriolic attack on Lynn Hirschberg and aspiring groupie writers who "surround us now like celebrity-worshipping jackals moving in for the kill."

When the lawyers vetoed this section, he substituted a paragraph praising Courtney and Frances Bean and included "a big 'Fuck You' to those of you who have the audacity to claim that I'm so naive and stupid that I would allow myself to be taken advantage of and manipulated." In conclusion, he vented his outrage over the growing legions of Nirvana fans who clearly didn't share Kurt's punk ideals. He warned the homophobes, racists, and sexists in their audience to "leave us the fuck alone."

Kurt was acutely conscious of what people in indie circles thought of his mega-selling album and was anxious to redeem himself through his next project which he told people was going to be "as raw as they come."

In February, the band headed to Pachyderm studios in Minnesota, booking themselves in as "the Simon Ritchie project." Simon Ritchie was the real name of Sid Vicious, and around this time Kurt was anxious to invite comparisons between himself and Courtney and the legendary punk couple Sid and Nancy. This was a conscious effort to avoid a more common comparison to John and Yoko, which, despite Kurt's efforts, was being made with increasing frequency. It didn't help that Kurt repeatedly expressed his admiration for John Lennon, whom he once called his "musical god." The comparison between him and

John, therefore, was almost flattering, but that's not what irked him. In every interview he gave, he went to great lengths to praise Courtney and dismiss the growing chorus of criticism leveled against her and their marriage.

"Courtney's had misconceptions about herself all her life," he told the *Advocate*. "I talk to people who knew Courtney five years ago, and she was more of a volatile fucked-up person than she is now. She was insane at times. People would see her at parties just begging for attention. I never could have predicted a successful marriage with this person a few years ago. It just couldn't have happened."

Meanwhile, Courtney was enjoying the increased attention which came from being Mrs. Kurt Cobain. Almost daily, she received requests for interviews and photo shoots. One of the more bizarre interviews she gave during this period was to a magazine called *Roller Derby*, in which she held forth on a number of topics not normally associated with Courtney Love, including diet tips. When the interviewer mentions weight loss at one point, Courtney jumps in:

"I have a tip! I lost 40 pounds, and I have a real tip. I was fat from 14 to 24. When you're fat like I was – which is five feet eight inches and 150 to 170 pounds – you do not get to fuck the boys you want to fuck. Right?... Right?"

"What's your tip?" asks the interviewer.

"The thing you gotta do is A) Stop counting calories! Okay? B) Do not get on a scale! 'Cause lean muscle weighs more than fat. All right? I cut out FAT! That's all you gotta do. FAT! No cheese. That's it, Lisa. Period. NO CHEESE. I told this to KROQ, I told this to my nanny. People I tell this to lose 10, 30 pounds. STOP CHEESE. You know why the Orientals are not fat? 'Cause they look on cheese as this gross Western habit – it's like sour, mild, LARD. They don't want anything to fucking do with cheese. If you're gonna eat cheese, take it out on a picnic, cut it up carefully, and really taste it – with wine or something. Don't melt it on shit. And I lost FORTY POUNDS by not eating cheese. And I even ate a little mayonnaise. All right? Skip the butter and skip the cheese and you will lose weight. I swear to God, Lisa. I was a fat girl my whole life. No one would fuck me, and when they did they'd do things like fart in front of me. I told my friend that this guy farted in front of me, and you know what he said? He said, 'Well, look at her; wouldn't you fart in front of her?'"

A week into the recording session for Nirvana's new album – which up to that time was going smoothly – Courtney showed up. That's when the problems started. Nobody minded her hanging around the studio. Other people had brought their wives or girlfriends along. The sparks started to fly when Courtney began to interfere. She would constantly take Kurt aside to give him advice and occasionally publicly contradicted the suggestions of Albini, who wasn't amused. He thought he had scored a coup by avoiding interference from Geffen, and all of a sudden here was a woman with, in his opinion, no talent telling them what to do. This sparked a number of screaming matches between Albini and Courtney, with Kurt usually taking Courtney's side. Twice Albini threatened to quit.

Albini refused to publicly comment on the feud, which had already been leaked to the media. "I don't feel like embarrassing Kurt by talking about what a psycho hosebeast his wife is," he would tell reporters, "especially because he knows it already." Reports also came out of a vicious fight between Courtney and Dave Grohl, who nearly came to blows at one point.

Part of the problem was the perception that Kurt was being completely controlled by Courtney. Krist told people his old friend was "completely pussywhipped." Indeed, Kurt seemed to have become emotionally dependent on his wife.

"It was like she was his drill sergeant," said one

person close to the recording. "She would give him an order and he'd snap to attention and carry it out. At times, he was a simpering puppy dog. It was kind of pathetic."

At the session, Kurt recorded a song with only three words, "I'm married. Buried." In another song, "Heart Shaped Box," which was about Courtney, he wrote, "Throw down your umbilical noose so I can climb right back."

A senior Geffen executive described to biographer Christopher Sandford evidence of Kurt's dependence he had witnessed a month earlier when Nirvana toured Brazil:

"It was obvious Courtney was never just 'Mrs. Kurt Cobain,"' he said, "and that if anything she saw herself as the big star and him as the groupie. He worshipped her."

He described Kurt clinging to Courtney's hand "like a man under arrest" for all but the two hours a day he was actually onstage, and, said that she took responsibility for literally everything that was not vital for him to do herself (After Kurt's death, Courtney would claim that "Kurt couldn't catch a fucking taxi by himself.")

When the recording sessions wrapped up, the band settled on the name *In Utero*. Kurt originally wanted to call the album *I Hate Myself and I Want to Die*. This was Kurt's favourite expression when anybody asked him how he was doing. It was obvious to anybody who heard it that he was being sarcastic.

He said he meant the title as a joke, telling *Rolling Stone*, "I'm tired of taking this band so seriously and everyone else taking it so seriously and trying to read things. Basically that's what all our songs are about – confusion and I hate myself and I want to live, so I thought it was really appropriate. I'm thought of as this pissy, complaining freaked-out schizo-phrenic who wants to kill himself all the time." The media would seize upon these references after Kurt's death to conclude his suicide was inevitable.

After strong objections by Krist and Geffen, the title that was finally settled upon was taken from a poem Courtney had written. On *In Utero* Kurt had deliberately avoided the catchy pop punk which had characterized *Nevermind*, preferring a darker, rawer sound which would regain his credibility in punk circles.

Albini had banished Geffen representatives from the sessions, and the company was getting nervous over rumours about the band's new direction. They had good reason to worry. *Nevermind* had been one of their most successful albums ever, grossing more than $50 million. The company was salivating at the prospect of even bigger numbers for Nirvana's next effort.

When the master was finally shipped to Geffen president Ed Rosenblatt and the music people had a chance to listen to the results, panic gripped the company. As Kurt described it, "The grown-ups don't like it."

Almost immediately, pressure was mounted on the band to go back into the studio and add some catchier material or, at the very least, to bring in another producer to remix what they had done.

Kurt wasn't sympathetic to these efforts. "I'm just putting out a record that I would listen to at home," he said. "I never listen to *Nevermind*. I haven't listened to it since we put it out. That says something. I can't stand that kind of production and I don't listen to bands that do have that kind of production, no matter how good their songs are. It just bothers me."

In fact, according to friends, Kurt had nothing against a commercial sound and still loved to listen to pop groups. His words, like *In Utero* itself, were meant to redeem him in indie punk circles, where accusations of him as a sellout still hurt him.

Everybody in Nirvana knew the new album wouldn't sell as much as *Nevermind*. They were resigned to the fact, with Kurt predicting *In Utero* would rack up only half the sales. In the end, the band relented slightly to the pressure, asking Albini to make changes. He refused, citing their agreement to give him creative control.

According to Dylan Carlson, it was Courtney who convinced Kurt to back down. "He was so determined to say 'fuck you' to the industry and reclaim his roots, but Courtney kept talking about the millions of dollars he was giving up and how he had no right to deprive Frances of her future."

In the meantime, Albini had given an interview to the *Chicago Tribune* predicting Geffen would reject the album, even though Nirvana's contract ruled this out. This set off a national wave of media speculation that Nirvana was through and that *Nevermind* had been a one-hit wonder.

Finally, Kurt went over Albini's head, agreeing to bring in R.E.M. producer Scott Litt to remix some tracks. A bitter Albini never talked to him again. When *In Utero* was finally released in September, it debuted at number one and received mixed reviews.

After the recording sessions were over, Kurt returned to life as a husband and father. Countless photos from this period show him holding Frances in one hand with a bottle or a stack of diapers in the other. But while he relished his role as daddy, the husband part was getting more difficult. He was becoming more aware of his dependence on Courtney and he didn't like it, especially when she hurled verbal abuse at him night and day.

"She would call him a dumb fuck all the time," remembers Peter Cleary, a Seattle drug buddy of Kurt's. "He would just stand there and take her abuse... he was like a baby. One day he was talking to me and another friend and I guess she thought she was being ignored so she started calling him a 'dickless jackoff' right in front of Frances Bean.

"A lot of women," Cleary continued, "are very

possessive about other women, but she was possessive about anybody. She didn't want him to have any friends except her. Don't get me wrong, she could be really nice too, but the way she treated him was sad."

As his frustration with Courtney became worse, so did his drug habit. On Sunday, May 2, 1993, at 9:10 p.m., the Seattle police department received a phone call to come to Kurt and Courtney's Lakeside Avenue home. Wendy and Kurt's sister, Kim, had come for supper, but Kurt had never come down to greet them.

Two hours earlier, Wendy told the police, Kurt, had injected thirty to forty dollars' worth of heroin at a friend's house. When Kurt had got home, he had gone to his room, where he started shaking, became flushed and delirious, and talked incoherently. Any experienced junkie knows what to do in this situation. Courtney took out a kit she kept for such occasions and injected Kurt with buprenorphine. She then gave him a Valium, three Benadryl tablets and some codeine. Usually this combination was enough to bring him out of it, but Kurt vomited, causing a worried Wendy to call 911. When the police arrived, they took him to Harborview Medical Centre, where he was treated and then released. Despite Courtney's admission to injecting Kurt with an illegal drug, no charges were filed against her or Kurt.

A little more than a month later, at 3:00 on the afternoon of June 4, police received another 911 call to come to the Lakeside home. When they arrived, a shaken Courtney – wearing a red bathrobe, a soaked t-shirt, and sweatpants – told the officers she had gotten into an argument with Kurt over guns in the house. She said that she had thrown a glass of juice into Kurt's face and that Kurt had then pushed her. When Courtney had pushed him back, she claimed, he had thrown her to the floor and begun choking her, leaving a scratch.

Kurt was arrested for assault and locked in the King County Jail for three hours before his lawyer arrived with the $950 bail. Police also confiscated three guns they found in the house, which were registered to Dylan Carlson.

Courtney had decided against pressing charges, and the Seattle police had little choice but to drop the case. According to an internal department memo, "The victim will testify that nothing happened, contrary to the police report. Additionally the [911] tape is probably not admissible because it neither describes an assault, nor do her hearsay statements fall under an exception to the hearsay rule.... Since we are unable to prove that an attack causing bodily injury occurred and that there was an absence of self-defense, the City declines to file."

Christopher Sandford quotes a friend of Kurt's who arrived at the couple's home around this period to find "Courtney throwing everything that was loose against the wall and screaming at Kurt for being useless. His fault, as she saw it, was not being able to come up with a song."

In the summer of 1993, Kurt experienced what he called "a miracle." After years of consulting specialists about his debilitating stomach pain, he found a doctor who finally diagnosed the problem – a pinched nerve relating to his scoliosis. Once the problem was diagnosed, it became treatable and Kurt finally rid himself of his daily agony.

From this point on, many people detected a change in Kurt's personality. "Kurt became a new person after that," says Dylan Carlson. "He stopped retreating into the dark side that everybody came to associate with him and actually seemed cheerful. Part of it was Frances, I think, but the stomach thing was the most important."

Kurt had been resisting pressure to tour because of his stomach pain, but with the pain out of the way, he agreed to do a forty-five-date tour. By this time, Nirvana had added a rhythm guitarist, Pat Smear, so that Kurt could concentrate more on his vocals.

That summer, he collaborated with one of his heroes, Beat writer William S. Burroughs, author of *Naked Lunch*. Kurt added guitar to a Burroughs spoken word piece and released it as "The Priest They Called Him."

As Nirvana embarked on their tour in October, Kurt was in an upbeat mood. He told *Rolling Stone* that month that he had never been happier in his life. He loved showing off pictures of Frances Bean to anybody he met, and when Courtney brought her on tour, he could dote on the real thing. In November, Kurt agreed to do *MTV Unplugged*, giving him a chance to show off his unique vocal talents through an acoustic set.

Although Kurt's stomach pains were gone and he had an excuse to stop taking heroin, it became evident that he was a full-scale addict. In interviews, he repeatedly claimed he was clean, terrified that Children's Services would take away his daughter again. But friends and band members noticed when Kurt would spend long periods in the bathroom only to emerge in a slight daze. In late 1993, it seemed just about everybody in Seattle had spotted Kurt buying drugs at some point.

After the tour ended, the problems with Courtney started anew, this time over money. The royalty checks kept pouring in and Courtney was anxious to spend them. Unlike Kurt, she liked the high life. "What's the use of having money if you don't use it?" she would repeatedly ask him.

Finally, in January 1994, Kurt agreed to buy a huge mansion on Lake Washington Boulevard in the wealthy Madrona district of Seattle. They paid $1,485,000 for the property, which included a beautiful view of Lake Washington. Kurt and Courtney's new neighbours included some of Seattle's most prominent citizens. The head of the Starbucks Coffee chain,

Howard Schultz, lived just up the hill, while the world's richest man, Bill Gates, resided on the other side of the lake. Kurt frequently told people he was embarrassed to live in such opulent surroundings.

The couple had barely moved into the new house when Kurt agreed to go on a European tour Gold Mountain had scheduled for the group. He had considering refusing to do so because he was still exhausted from the recently completed American dates.

His friend Peter Cleary describes Kurt's state: "He and Courtney hadn't been getting along. The only thing keeping them together was Frances, but Kurt had been talking of a divorce and trying to get custody."

Cleary continues, "The thing about touring is that Kurt said it's the only time he gets to call the shots. At home, he was like an emotional cripple around his wife, but on tour it was different. He was the centre of attention and he was the boss."

Cleary believes this is the reason Kurt agreed to the European tour. The whirlwind trip started in Lisbon on February 6. Kurt travelled on a separate bus from the other band members and reports were that he was constantly tired. Courtney, who was preparing to record her album *Live Through This*, later told *Rolling Stone* that Kurt called her constantly saying he hated the tour.

"He called me from Spain," she said. "He was in Madrid and he'd walked through the audience. The kids were smoking heroin off tinfoil and the kids were going, 'Kurt! Smack!' and giving him the thumbs up. He called me crying.... He did not want to become a junkie icon."

Most people on the tour describe Kurt as very tired. The sets didn't have the same energy as previous concerts, and Kurt seemed almost listless onstage. On March 1, Nirvana was performing at Terminal Einz in Munich when, a few songs into the set, Kurt lost his voice.

The next day, he went to see a throat specialist, who diagnosed severe bronchitis. He was given medication and told to rest for a couple of months. That day, Gold Mountain announced the remaining twenty-three dates would be rescheduled, although Kurt's doctor advised him to cancel the tour altogether. Later that evening, Kurt flew to Rome, where he checked into suite 541 of the Excelsior hotel right across the street from the American embassy.

The next day, Courtney arrived with eighteen-month-old Frances and a nanny to join Kurt at the Excelsior. They did some sightseeing and went out to dinner that evening with Pat Smear while Frances stayed at the hotel with the nanny. Almost all of what the world knows about what happened next comes from Courtney Love. The events of that evening would be a crucial piece to the puzzle of Kurt's death.

When they returned to their suite, Kurt called the front desk to send up a bellboy, whom he sent out to fill a prescription in Courtney's name for a drug called Rohypnol, which is a powerful tranquillizer. He also ordered two bottles of champagne.

Early the next morning, Courtney claims, she awoke to find Kurt unconscious. "I reached for him and he had blood coming out of his nose," she told Britain's *Select* magazine. "I have seen him get really fucked up before but I've never seen him almost eat it."

Courtney rang the front desk clerk, who called an ambulance that quickly whisked Kurt to Rome's Umberto 1 Polyclinic and then to the American Hospital. The press learned of the incident and they descended en masse on the hotel, where photographers captured Courtney hurling abuse at reporters.

News reports flashed all over the world, including one CNN bulletin that Kurt was dead. A little over twenty hours after Kurt had arrived in the hospital, he awoke and scrawled a note to Courtney: "Get these fucking tubes out of my nose." Next he asked for a strawberry milkshake.

A frighteningly prophetic pose from Kurt in Paris, just before his death. This was his last photoshoot.

Top: Courtney Love at fifteen, shortly after being released from an Oregon reform school into her fathers custody.

Bottom: Six-month-old Courtney Love on the lawn of her parents' San Francisco home.

Dear Hank
Thank you for the stay
I know it has been
Terribley difficult at times
due to me & the Company
I keep. I hope to see
you fully recovered
from my Regressed
Experimentation near
Xmas. Thanx Esp. for
School Support & letting me
walk on the ice w/ thickness
of my own choosing
Love
Courtney.

A note Courtney sent to Hank Harrison after she spent the summer with him in the early eighties.

The greatest rock-band – Nirvana. Taken from the Parisian shoot, Kurt changed and applied makeup before these pictures were taken.

Top: Courtney and Kurt with one-year-old Frances Bean at the MTV Music Video Awards, 1993.

Bottom: Kurt performing in Paris during his final tour, two months before his death.

View of the greenhouse at Kurt and Courtney's Seattle estate where Kurt Cobain was found dead of a gunshot wound in 1994.

Top: The Cobain country house in Carnation, Washington, where police say Kurt spent at least one night with an unidentified woman while he was missing shortly before his death.

Bottom: Courtney's father Hank Harrison, signs autographs for teenage fans during a cross-Canada lecture tour to promote his book *Kurt Cobain: Beyond Nirvana.*

Courtney unveils her new image, arriving at a post-Oscar party in a Versace dress, March 1997.

The following day, Gold Mountain issued a statement that the Rome incident was an accident. "It was definitely not a suicide attempt," it said. "He wanted to celebrate seeing Courtney after so long." Courtney continued to tell the same story and no one ever heard her say Rome was a suicide attempt until after Kurt's death, when she would offer a completely different version of events.

The doctor who attended to Kurt in Rome also says it was an accident, a story he maintains to this day. "We can usually tell a suicide attempt," says Dr. Osvaldo Galletta. "This didn't look like one to me. He mixed tranquilizers and alcohol and when you do that, you're playing with fire." More importantly, Dr. Galletta denies later claims by Courtney that fifty pills were pumped out of Kurt's stomach – a story which, if true, might confirm a suicide attempt.

Five days after Kurt awoke, he was given a clean bill of health and released to return to Seattle. Before he had left for the European tour, Nirvana had been scheduled to headline Lollapalooza, the mega alternative tour for which they would make millions. After Kurt returned from Rome, he told Courtney he had changed his mind.

"She went ballistic," says Dylan Carlson. "She kept on screaming at him about how much money he was giving up and said if he didn't want to do it, she'd be glad to take his place."

There are several conflicting reports about whether Kurt was sleeping with other women during this period. His biographer Christopher Sandford writes that he sent a young art student several love notes, a hand-drawn valentine, and an invitation for the woman to join him in a Seattle hotel. When she declined, he phoned a dozen times a day and sent her a message stating, "I'm not obsessed with you. I just wanted to talk to you about conceptual art." Melissa Rossi spoke to several of his friends who told her he wanted a divorce from Courtney.

On March 18, Seattle police received another 911 call from Courtney. When they arrived, Courtney informed them that Kurt had locked himself in a room with a gun and threatened to kill himself. When police knocked on the door, Kurt let them in and said he wasn't suicidal but that he was actually hiding from Courtney.

When the officers took Courtney aside for questioning, she admitted that he hadn't threatened suicide and that she hadn't really seen him with a gun. When asked why she had lied to police, she said he wouldn't open the door and, knowing that he had guns in the room, she called 911 for his well-being.

The officers warned her against making false statements to police and then confiscated two guns they found in the house. They also confiscated some stomach medication they found in Kurt's pocket.

Four days later, on March 22, Kurt and Courtney took a cab to the American Dream used-car lot in downtown Seattle, which specialized in vintage cars. In early January, Courtney had purchased a Lexus even though she didn't drive. Kurt refused to be seen in a luxury car and made her return it.

The cab driver, Leon Hassan, reported that the two "quarrelled viciously" in the back seat en route to the lot. When they arrived at American Dream, a classic '65 Dodge Dart caught Kurt's eye and, over Courtney's objection, he decided to buy it.

Joe Kenney, the salesman who sold them the car, recalls that they "weren't wearing six dollars worth of clothes between them." He says they talked about the Lexus a little bit, with Kurt trying to convince Courtney that the Dodge would do everything the Lexus did.

He recalls Courtney had to use the bathroom and on the way in she dropped a handful of pills and had to pick them up. He remembers remarking to another salesperson that he thought he should get Kurt to autograph his CDs soon because it didn't look like either of them would be around much longer, they were so strung out on drugs.

"She was really tossing down the drugs," says the other salesperson. "They were certainly uptight."

After Rome, officials at Geffen Records were terrified about Kurt's close call. He was worth millions to the label and they couldn't afford to lose him. "If that sounds cynical," says one Geffen source, "you don't know the music business. They couldn't have cared less about his well-being, except as it affected their bottom line."

Geffen contacted Gold Mountain and ordered them to do something about Kurt's drug use. Danny Goldberg in turn contacted a drug intervention counsellor named Steven Chartoff in Port Hueneme, California.

"They called me to see what could be done," Chartoff told Christopher Sandford. "He was using, up in Seattle. He was in full denial. It was very chaotic. And they were in fear for his life. It was a crisis."

Kurt refused to go through Chartoff's program, prompting Gold Mountain to contact Courtney to set up an ad hoc intervention of their own.

On March 25, Love, Novoselic, the nanny Michael Dewitt, Pat Smear, Danny Goldberg, Nirvana manager John Silva, Janet Billig of Gold Mountain, and Dylan Carlson brought Kurt into a room for more than four hours and confronted him about his drug use, telling him he had to stop.

According to the Geffen source, the entire episode was a charade. "How could anybody expect him to take something like that seriously? For god's sake, three of the people ranting at him in that session were junkies themselves (Carlson, Courtney, and Dewitt)."

He goes on to speculate that Courtney was compelled to participate because the company had threatened to drop him from the label if he didn't get clean, and "Kurt was her meal ticket."

After Courtney threatened to prevent Kurt from

seeing Frances Bean unless he went through detox, Kurt finally agreed to check into the Exodus Recovery center in Los Angeles, where he had detoxed once before. Courtney had to go to Los Angeles to check on the upcoming release of Hole's new album, *Live Through This*, and she left with Frances and a different nanny on March 28. When she arrived, she checked into a $500-a-day suite at the Peninsula Hotel in Beverly Hills. She later claimed that she was there to undergo outpatient treatment of her own drug problem with her psychiatrist Dr. Steve Scappa so she could keep Frances with her and be supportive of Kurt's own treatment.

The day Courtney left for L.A., Kurt spoke to his grandmother on the phone. He made a date to go fishing with his grandfather the next week.

"When he talked to me he seemed to be happy," recalled Iris Cobain, Don's mother.

On Friday afternoon, March 30, Kurt went with Dylan Carlson to a Seattle gun shop, Stan Baker Sports, on Lake City Way. Dylan paid $308.37 cash for a Remington 20-gauge shotgun.

"He [Kurt] wanted me to buy it because the cops had recently confiscated all his guns and he was afraid they would take it away again if it was in his name," says Carlson, claiming Kurt was afraid of stalkers. This seems to be confirmed by a 1993 interview Kurt gave where he told a journalist, "Guns are protection. I don't have bodyguards. We know people who have been stalked or murdered. I'm not a very physical person. I wouldn't be able to stop an intruder without a gun."

Dylan pauses, clearly shaken up by the memory. "At the time, Kurt definitely wasn't suicidal or I would never have bought the gun," he continues. "He was my best friend. I would have known if Rome was a suicide. No way. A year earlier, I would have believed it because of the pain, but he wasn't talking like that anymore. He was making all kinds of plans for when he got back from rehab."

Kurt's state of mind at this time would, of course, become a contentious issue after his death. Was Kurt suicidal? Like his best friend Dylan, many other people who knew Kurt at this time maintained he was very happy. Anna Woolverston, a Seattle music journalist who covered Cobain for years and now works as a receptionist for Sub Pop Records, said she didn't believe Kurt was suicidal at the time of his death.

"I find it very strange that he would take his own life, because he loved his daughter so much," she told us in 1995. (Soon after, she says, she received "major flak" from her Sub Pop employers and others for daring to question the suicide.)

But some people on the Seattle scene find such statements absurd and say there is no doubt that Kurt was a prime candidate for suicide. "He was always a depressed individual," says Alice Wheeler, a well-known Seattle music photographer who knew Kurt and is good friends with Kurt's ex--girlfriend Tracy Marander. "Anybody who doubts he was suicidal didn't know Kurt very well." Wheeler, however, acknowledges that she had no real contact with Kurt in the last few months of his life.

"The thing you have to remember about all the talk of Kurt being suicidal," said Kurt's Seattle friend Peter Cleary, "is that all the talk only started when Courtney came out after the death and said Rome was a suicide attempt and the media picked up on all her examples of Kurt being suicidal. That's when all these people started saying, 'of course he was suicidal, just listen to his music.' But that's a bunch of crap. Sure he was a moody guy and got depressed quite often. That applies to a hell of a lot of people, including me. But nobody ever talked about Kurt being suicidal before he died, nobody. Why do you think everybody who knew him was so surprised when Courtney said that Rome was a suicide attempt? I've read all this ignorant bullshit in the media pointing to the fact that Kurt wanted to call *In Utero* '*I Hate*

Myself and I Want to Die.' It was a *joke,* for chrissake. That was his warped sense of humour. He was the most sarcastic guy you'll ever meet. I have no idea if he was murdered but I can tell you one thing. He was *not* suicidal, at least not when I knew him, and I knew him for the last year of his life."

The same night Dylan bought the gun, Kurt flew to Los Angeles. As he arrived at the airport, he realized he still had a box of cartridges he had bought with the gun and didn't think he could take them on the plane, so he gave them to the limousine driver, Harvey Ottinger.

He was picked up at Los Angeles Airport by Pat Smear and a Gold Mountain employee and driven to the Exodus facility in nearby Marina Del Rey, where he checked in. The last time Kurt detoxed at Exodus, which had always been a favourite of rock stars, he hated it.

"It was disgusting," he said. "Right away these forty-year-old hippie long-term-junkie-type counsellors would come in and try to talk to me on a rock-'n'-roll level, like, 'I know where you're at, man. Drugs are real prevalent in rock-'n'-roll and I've seen it all in the seventies. Would you mind if David Crosby came in and said hello? Or Steven Tyler?' Rattling off these rock stars' names. I was like, 'Fuck that. I don't have any respect for these people at all."' That time, Kurt left prematurely before his treatment was finished.

Two days after he checked in, on Good Friday, April 1, one of Frances's nannies, Jackie Ferry, arrived for a visit. Kurt played with his nearly two-year-old daughter for about an hour and then the two visitors left.

Courtney's phone records from the Peninsula show that she made thirteen calls to Kurt at Exodus over these two days.

One of Kurt's visitors later told *Rolling Stone,* "I was ready to see him look like shit and depressed but he looked so fucking great.

On Friday night, after visits from Gibby Haynes of the Butthole Surfers and an unidentified woman, Kurt stepped outside to smoke a cigarette at about seven p.m. He then climbed over a six-foot fence in the yard and took a taxi to the airport, where he booked a first-class seat to Seattle on Delta Flight 788 that night. He paid the $478 fare by credit card. He then called ahead to his car service, Seattle Limousine, to tell them he was arriving at Seattle [Tacoma Airport] at 12:47 a.m. While he waited at the airport, he was recognized by a number of people and graciously signed autographs.

According to Peninsula Hotel records, at 8:47 p.m. Kurt called Courtney and left a message which may be the key to the entire mystery. The message on the hotel log reads: "Elizabeth's phone number is (213) __________." Private investigator Tom Grant has the phone number, which has a Los Angeles area code, and the identity of Elizabeth. (He claims he will reveal their significance to the FBI if the case is reopened.)

When Kurt arrived in Seattle, Linda Walker from the limousine service was waiting for him and drove him to the Lake Washington house, dropping Kurt off at the driveway entrance at about 1:30 A.M.

The only occupant of the house while Kurt and Courtney were in L.A. was one of Frances's nannies, Michael Dewitt, who was known as "Cali." Dewitt was from California. Courtney had befriended him and hired him to look after the baby part of the time. He was the only nanny who lived in at the house.

Cali later told the police that he awoke at 6:00 a.m. to find Kurt sitting on his bed. They talked for a while before Kurt left to go into town.

At 8:54 that morning, Courtney recalled, Kurt tried to call the Peninsula Hotel to speak to her but couldn't get through.

According to the version she told Spin magazine about that incident:

"There was a block on the phone for everyone but

him. I did not sleep. I called the operator every couple of hours to make sure, in case they changed shifts. They all knew that if Mr. Cobain called, put the fucking call through to me. At 8:54 a.m. I was not asleep. He called, and for six minutes he tried to get through, and could not. For him to argue for six minutes on the phone is crazed. I cannot imagine him arguing for six minutes. He did, though. And what that told him is that I was on their side, that I had a block on the phone for him. And I did not. Kurt's whole plan was to try to wear everyone down, but he could never wear me down. I think, though, that at that very moment he thought I had given up on him."

The only problem with this story is that, according to a 1995 article in Spin, the Peninsula Hotel denies it ever took place. It seems strange that Courtney made this up.

Over the next two days, there were a number of Kurt sightings around Seattle, including one by Nirvana's manager, John Silva.

According to Christopher Sandford, Kurt – dressed in a heavy military jacket under his black overcoat – met a woman named Sara Hoehn on Broadway. She said he was in a foul mood over a report that forty-thousand fans had lined up that morning in L.A. to buy Eagles tickets. "We might as well not have happened," she quoted him as saying.

Other reports saw him hanging around with an unidentified woman. This may have been a friend of his who was also a drug dealer known as Caitlin Moore. Kurt was rumored to be having an affair with her, and Courtney was intensely jealous of the amount of time they spent together. "You're fucking her, aren't you, you bastard?" a friend of Kurt's remembers her screaming a couple of weeks earlier, just after Rome.

On Easter Sunday, April 3, Beverly Hills private detective Tom Grant was in his office working on a case with his associate Ben Klugman when the phone rang.

On the other end of the line was Courtney Love looking for a detective. Most likely the Tom Grant Company wasn't her first choice. She probably went through the yellow pages under "Detectives" calling the numbers at random, but because it was Easter Sunday, everybody was closed except for Grant, who was working overtime to finish up another case.

She said she needed to find out who was attempting to use her husband's credit card, adding, "We're kind of famous." Grant and Klugman arranged to meet her later that afternoon at the Peninsula.

"The first thing she said when we walked in," Grant recalls, "is that she had lied to me on the phone. It wasn't somebody else attempting to use her husband's credit card. It was her husband attempting to use his credit card and that he had just fled a rehab and she was trying to locate him. Initially our job was to contact the credit card company and find out where the activities were occurring and where the attempts were being made. She said she had already canceled his only credit card and without it he couldn't get any money or do anything. That was our first assignment, which turned out to be difficult because it's harder to trace a card after it's been canceled."

Courtney said she thought Kurt might have returned to Seattle but she wasn't sure and that he might be going back east to stay with Michael Stipe of R.E.M. Kurt had told a number of people in recent weeks that Nirvana had "become a Nazi state" and talked of doing some solo stuff with Stipe. Grant says she failed to mention that Cali had seen Kurt at the Lake Washington home the day before. Courtney's Peninsula phone records confirm she had talked to Cali since this sighting.

Meanwhile, back in Seattle on Monday, April 4, a Michigan investment counsellor named Brad Barnett claims he ran into Kurt in a park near the Lake Washington house.

"He was holding a pack of cigarettes in his hand,"

recalls Barnett, who had driven from Kalamazoo that week in his van. "I asked him if he had seen the father and son fishing out on the lake. He smiled and said wistfully that he had and how much he wished that his father had taken the time to do those types of activities with him."

Barnett said the two had a brief conversation and then Kurt invited him back to the house and brought him up to the room above the garage where Kurt would be found dead four days later.

"There were three books on the table," Barnett says. "I picked one up and was astonished to see that Cobain was reading F Scott Fitzgerald's *The Beautiful and Damned*. "I asked him if he was aware that Fitzgerald was only twenty-eight when he wrote *The Great Gatsby*, which critics believe was his best novel.

"The irony was not lost on Cobain and he quickly responded, 'Did Fitzgerald think it was his best work? I think many of his short stories are as good or better, and they were written throughout his twenties. Fitzgerald's art peaked after *Gatsby*, as he became lost in alcohol and personal despair.'"

Barnett says he wanted to follow this up with a question about Kurt's own much-publicized drug problems but thought better of it.

"Kurt lit another cigarette and I asked him whether he felt that Fitzgerald was considered the interpreter of youth and the spokesman for his generation, and if he too felt a responsibility to his generation. Kurt responded, 'I don't really think so, at least not entirely. The artist surely speaks to those he moves, but I think it's the critics that want to label Fitzgerald as the spokesman for the Jazz Age. I don't speak for my generation. I think I reflect the times I live in, but the artist only speaks from the heart and reaches some people but not a whole generation.'"

For the next two hours, Barnett claims, the two talked about art and literature. At one point, he asked,

"What do you think genius is?" to which Kurt replied, "John Lennon said he didn't know but if there was such a thing he was one. I don't think genius has anything to do with education and knowledge. It has absolutely nothing to do with intelligence. It's a kind of incommunicable power of creative thought that has nothing to do with traditional learning because it can't be taught."

Although it doesn't come across in his typical interviews, Kurt was extremely well read and loved to talk about literature, according to his friends, so this conversation isn't entirely far-fetched.

At one point, says Barnett, Kurt ran out of cigarettes and he drove Kurt to the store to get some more while he bought a six-pack of Miller Lite. They drove into the Capitol Hill neighborhood and Barnett said that as they drove through, Kurt turned to him and asked if he had ever been threatened. Barnett replied affirmatively, at which point Kurt told him he "feared for his life" – a comment which Barnett says has haunted him since Kurt's body was found four days later, although he says he still believes the death was "probably a suicide." (Although Barnett's story helps bolster Tom Grant's subsequent theory that Kurt was murdered, Grant says he doubts that Barnett met Kurt that day. Barnett, however, has supplied receipts and other evidence confirming he was in Seattle that day but can provide no witnesses who saw him with Kurt.)

In Los Angeles that same Monday, Grant met again with Courtney, who told him she had filed a Missing Persons Report with the Seattle Police Department claiming to be Wendy O'Connor, Kurt's mother.

The department has since said they didn't take the report too seriously, believing Kurt wasn't really missing but rather that he just didn't want to be found.

On Monday, Kurt seems to have spent the night at the Carnation, Washington getaway cottage with a woman (possibly Caitlin, his drug dealer friend). Police would later find an ashtray full of recently smoked cigarettes, some Kurt's brand – Winston Lights – and some Marlboro Lights (not Courtney's brand) with traces of lipstick. On the table was a black ink drawing of the sun above the words "cheer up."

Grant was in the process of making plans to go to Seattle to search for Kurt, but first he contracted a Seattle private detective named Ernie Barth to set up surveillance in a number of locations Courtney believed Kurt might have been.

According to Grant, Courtney demanded they keep a watch on the Capitol Hill apartment of Caitlin Moore (Kurt's heroin dealer). The Missing Persons Report actually mentioned the apartment, which it calls "a location for narcotics," as a possible location where Kurt may be staying. It also says he bought a shotgun and might be suicidal.

"That's one of the things that just didn't add up about this case," says Grant. "Courtney knew from Cali that Kurt had been to the Lake Washington house, but she never asked us to set up surveillance there. Instead, she mostly wanted us to watch Caitlin's place. She seemed to be obsessed with Caitlin."

On Wednesday, March 6, Grant flew to Seattle to take over the search. He claims Courtney's last words to him before leaving were, "Save the American icon, Tom." Courtney had arranged for him to meet up with Dylan Carlson to inspect the Lake Washington house. By this time she had finally told Grant about Cali's conversation with Kurt on Saturday.

"It was Dylan's job to show me around and look in all the nooks and crannies," Grant recalls. "We arrived at the house that night. It was pouring rain. Before we entered the house, I turned on a little pocket tape recorder I had with me to make sure I documented whatever was going to happen. I didn't know what we were getting ourselves into."

Grant plays the tape he made that evening as they are searching the house. In retrospect, it is quite eerie.

The sound of the door opening appears followed by two disembodied voices shouting, "Hello, Kurt," "Kurt, are you here? Where are you, Kurt?" After the two fail to find who they're looking for, they undergo a complete inspection of the entire house, searching elusively for clues. The two left, satisfied Kurt was nowhere to be found.

The next day, Courtney asked Dylan to go back to the house with Grant to look for the shotgun. She said it could be in a hidden compartment in her closet. "I wondered why she didn't ask Cali to look there before now", Grant says.

When they returned to the house that night, the gun wasn't in the closet, but they found a note from Cali placed on the main stairway and addressed to Kurt – a note that hadn't been there the night before. It read, "I can't believe you managed to be in the house without me noticing. You're a fucking asshole for not calling Courtney." It advises Kurt to "take care of business" and accuses him of mistreating his family.

"I had a feeling the note was there for me to find, not Kurt," says Grant, adding that Cali later told him he was rarely at the house from Monday on. "If that was true, why did he find it so hard to believe Kurt had been at the house? It is Kurt's house, after all, and he knew Kurt had already been there once."

According to Grant, Cali explained he wasn't staying at the house because Courtney kept calling and saying she knew Kurt was there. "If so, why wasn't she having us watch the house during our surveillance?" asks Grant.

That day, Cali flew to Los Angeles to meet with Courtney. He later claimed he went to persuade her that he hadn't been hiding Kurt. He left without ever talking to Grant, who got the impression the nanny was deliberately avoiding him.

"There were so many things that just didn't add up about this time, so many inconsistencies which didn't make sense. It really smelled," Grant says.

Courtney later claimed to be frantic about Kurt's disappearance during this period and said that she waited by the phone the whole time for his call. Interestingly, her hotel phone records show that she called the request line of the local rock station KROQ twice during this period. She was calling to request her own album, a not uncommon tactic employed by musicians to increase their radio airplay.

"I guess she wasn't so frantic that she didn't have time to think of her career," says Grant.

Back in Seattle, Kurt's friend Dylan took Grant to all Kurt's traditional hangouts, but nobody had seen him.

The same day, an emergency phone call was placed from Courtney's suite to 911 about a "possible overdose victim" at the Peninsula Hotel. The police, fire department, and an ambulance all arrived at the scene to find Courtney with Hole guitarist Eric Erlandson. Frances Bean was with Jackie (the nanny) in the room next door. Courtney was taken by police to Century City Hospital, where she was released into police custody two and a half hours later. She was immediately placed under arrest for "possession of a controlled substance, possession of drug paraphernalia, possession of a hypodermic syringe, and possession/ receiving stolen property." The stolen property was a prescription pad which Courtney's lawyer Barry Tarlow claimed was mistakenly left in the room by her doctor when he had visited earlier. Tarlow said that, contrary to published reports, Courtney wasn't "under the influence of heroin" and "didn't overdose" but that she had an allergic reaction to the tranquilizer Xanax. He explained that the controlled substance wasn't narcotics but rather "Hindu good luck ashes." He failed to explain the syringe. Courtney was released that afternoon after posting $10,000 bail and immediately checked into the Exodus Recovery Centre, from where Kurt had escaped six days earlier.

Rumours were already circulating around Seattle that Kurt had backed out of Lollapalooza. The influential music weekly the *Rocket* published a report that Nirvana was splitting up. The *L.A. Times* printed a similar report on April 7, the day before Kurt's body was found.

7
The End of the Road

On the morning of April 8, Grant and Dylan were scheduled to head up to the Carnation estate to look for clues to Kurt's whereabouts, even though Ernie Barth had previously set up a surveillance on the property.

At 8:40 that morning, Gary Smith from Veca Electric arrived at the Lake Washington house to install an alarm system. As he was standing on the balcony outside the garage, he looked through the glass doors and saw what he thought at first was a mannequin. "I noticed it had blood in its right ear," Smith would say. "Then I saw a shotgun lying across his chest pointing up at his chin."

Smith immediately phoned his boss, who, instead of calling the police, placed a call to radio station KXRX-FM and told DJ Marty Reimer the news. At first the station thought the call was a hoax, but they decided to phone the police just in case. Within a half hour, the news that a body had been found at the Cobain residence was flashed around the world.

As Grant and Dylan approached the Carnation property that morning, the two stopped for gas and Dylan got out to make a phone call. When he returned to the car, he said the friend he had called had told him about the body. They turned on the radio, and within minutes, the body was confirmed to be Kurt's. On the way back, the report said he was found in the greenhouse.

"What's the greenhouse?" Grant asked.

Dylan said it was a room above the garage, prompting Grant to ask why they hadn't looked there.

Dylan replied, "It's just a dirty little room. I think they keep some lumber in there or something." Later, Dylan would tell reporters he didn't know the greenhouse existed.

When Grant called his office, his associate Ben Klugman told him someone had tried to use Kurt's Seafirst Bank credit card to charge $43.29 worth of flowers just hours before the body was found. He didn't think this was significant until the coroner's report revealed that the body had been dead for at least two days. The card was not found with Kurt's body. Who was trying to use the card? Because Courtney had cancelled the card, the credit card company's computer could trace attempted transactions but not who made them or where.

Seattle Police Department spokesperson Sean O'Donnell, attempting to explain the transactions apparently made after Kurt died, claims that the times listed on the credit card statements only represent when the transactions were logged in on the bank's mainframe computer, not when the transactions were actually attempted. But according to Seafirst Bank, this discrepancy would only account for a few minutes difference in the times, not two days.

The first people to arrive at the scene at 10:15 a.m. were three Seattle Police Department officers, Joe Fewel, Van Levandowski, and Jeff Getchman, who arrived to find the greenhouse room locked. They could tell from looking that the body that lay sprawled on the floor inside was dead. Minutes later, the fire department arrived and broke the window, spreading glass fragments all over the room, some of which fell on the body.

On one of the walls of the nineteen-by-twenty-three-foot room was a planting tray containing a pile of dirt with bulbs in it. On top of the dirt pile was a note written in red ink and stuck into the dirt pile with a red pen. Officer Levandowski immediately concluded it was a suicide note and wrote in a report that the note "is directed to Courtney."

Kurt was lying on his back with his head to the west and his feet to the east. Just left of his head was a large drying puddle of blood. A Remington 20-gauge shotgun rested between his legs with its barrel pointed toward his head, his left hand wrapped around the barrel. A spent shell casing could be found on top of a brown corduroy jacket which in turn lay on top of a beige nylon shotgun case. On the floor was a wallet.

The officer took the State of Washington driver's license, identifying Kurt Cobain, out of the wallet and propped it up beside the body. Countless published reports later falsely stated that Kurt had taken the driver's license out of the wallet to help identify the corpse. They reported that his face had been blown off and the license was the only means of identifying the body. In fact, both officers said they instantly recognized Kurt's well-known face, which remained completely intact.

On the floor was $120 in cash and a cigar box filled with drug paraphernalia (syringes, burnt spoons, cotton, and small pieces of what looked like black tar). There was a brown paper bag containing a box with twenty-two live 20-gauge shotgun shells. The box had originally come with twenty-five shells. (Grant and others have questioned why Kurt loaded three shells if he intended to kill himself rather than for self-protection, as he told Carlson.)

To the right of the body on the floor lay a hat, two towels, the cash, the wallet, a pack of cigarettes, a lighter, and a pair of sunglasses. Inside the jacket pocket, officers found the receipt for the shotgun made out to Dylan Carlson.

At 11:05 a.m. three coroners arrived from the King County medical examiner's office. Three homicide detectives led by Sergeant Donald Cameron had already arrived on the scene. Dr. Nikolas Hartshorne took Polaroids of the scene and quickly concluded Cobain had died from a self-inflicted gunshot wound. After he told the detectives, the information was leaked to the media, and the world learned that Kurt Cobain had "committed suicide."

Tom Grant says that when he arrived, Sergeant Cameron told him that one of the doors to the greenhouse was unlocked but had a stool wedged against it, which proved that Kurt must have locked himself in before he pulled the trigger because nobody could have left the room. This incorrect fact becomes significant later on.

It was raining steadily outside as the media began to descend on the house, along with fans already forming a vigil. Courtney had been informed of the death and arranged to fly back to Seattle.

Kurt's mother arrived on the scene wearing a T-shirt which ironically read, "Grunge is dead." She told a reporter from the Associated Press, "Now he's gone and joined that stupid club. I told him not to join that stupid club." The club she was referring to was composed of rock stars who died young, their talent snuffed out before their time. The list includes Seattle's own Jimi Hendrix as well as Janis Joplin and Jim Morrison. By an eerie coincidence, they all died at the age of twenty-seven, the same age as Kurt.

The media circus continued unabated as various officials from Geffen and Gold Mountain arrived to deal with the situation. Only one reporter, Everett True of *Melody Maker,* was allowed inside the house, displaying the power commanded by the man whose articles had launched Kurt to superstardom.

Already on the scene were *A Current Affair, Entertainment Tonight, Entertainment Weekly, Rolling Stone, Details, Spin,* and the *Village Voice.* MTV's Tabitha Soren, who just happened to be in town, began two days of nearly nonstop coverage reminiscent of the Kennedy assassination. CNN provided live coverage. Satellite uplink trucks were everywhere.

A Current Affair wanted the inside scoop and quickly offered Gary Smith – the electrician who found the body – $1,500 to tell his story. He turned it down, as he has every financial offer since.

Nobody from Kurt's camp would talk to the press, which led to the curious spectacle of the media interviewing each other about the impact of Kurt's life and death.

Within hours, suicide prevention hotlines around the country reported a huge increase in calls from distraught teenagers.

Kurt's body was taken away to be autopsied, although the police continued to tell the media the gunshot was self-inflicted.

That night, Pearl Jam – Nirvana's rivals for alternative music superstardom – played a concert in Fairfax, Virginia. When Eddie Vedder, whom Kurt despised, took to the stage, he said, "I don't think any of us would be in this room tonight if it weren't for Kurt."

The next morning, the *Seattle Times* ran a poignant shot, taken by one of their photographers through the balcony windows, of Cobain's body surrounded by police, with only the body's jean-clad legs and running shoes revealed.

Record stores all over the world were already reporting Nirvana's albums flying off the shelves.

Meanwhile, Courtney revealed for the first time that the overdose in Rome was actually a suicide attempt, a PR move that backfired when virtually everybody close to Kurt demanded to know why she hadn't told them earlier. If they had known, they would have done more to protect him, complained everyone from his friends to his record company.

Blame for Kurt's death was already being meted out from all circles, who accused his camp of emotional negligence.

A memorial service with 175 invited guests was scheduled by Courtney for April 10, two days after the death, even though the body was still in the custody of the coroner and wouldn't be released in time for the service, which was scheduled to take place at Seattle's Unity Church of Truth with Minister Stephen Towles presiding.

Towles spoke first to the assembled crowd, describing suicide as "no different than having your finger in a vice. The pain becomes so great that you can't bear it." Krist Novoselic and Dylan Carlson delivered short eulogies. "We remember Kurt for what he was: caring, generous, and sweet," Krist read. He was followed by Dylan, who read Buddhist verses. After the service, Courtney invited guests back to a wake at her Lake Washington home. Most of Kurt's friends, however, chose to return to the home of Krist and Shelli, who were having their own wake. For many, this underscored the increasing acrimony between Courtney and the rest of Nirvana.

While the closed service was being held across town, a more public memorial had been organized by Seattle's alternative radio station, KNDD ("the End"). Thousands of people, mostly teenagers and TV crews, gathered at a park next to the Space Needle while Nirvana songs blared out of a loudspeaker. At one point, a group of kids publicly burned their flannel shirts, which *Spin* magazine would call "a truly awesome moment of pagan catharsis."

Finally, an announcement came over the loudspeaker that Courtney Love would address the crowd. But instead of the real thing, the onlookers were treated to a tape she had recorded earlier that day.

Courtney's unmistakable voice began:

"I don't know what to say. I feel the same way you guys do. If you guys don't think... I used to sit in this room, and then he'd play the guitar and sing... I'd feel so honored to be near him... you're crazy. Anyways, he left a note. It's more like a letter to the fuckin' editor. I don't know what happened. I knew it was gonna happen, but it could have happened when he was 40. He always said he was going to outlive everybody, and be 120. I'm not gonna read you all the note 'cause it's none of the rest of your fuckin' business, but some of it is to you. I don't really think it takes away his dignity to read this considering that it's addressed to most of you. He's such an asshole. I want you all to say 'asshole' really loud."

There's a pause for the crowd to comply, then she begins reading the note:

This note should be pretty easy to understand. All the warnings from the Punk Rock 101 courses over the years since my first introduction to the, shall we say, ethics involved with independence and the embracement of your community has proven to be very true. I haven't felt the excitement of listening to, as well as creating music, along with really writing it, for too many years now. I feel guilty beyond words about these things. For example, when were back-stage and the lights go out and the manic roar of the crowd begins, it doesn't affect me the way in which it did for Freddie Mercury, who seemed to love and relish in the adoration from the crowd...

Courtney interjects at this point: "Well, Kurt, so fucking what! Then don't be a rock star, you asshole!" She then continues reading:

... which is something I totally admire and envy. The fact is, I can't fool you, any one of you. It simply isn't fair to you or me. The worst crime I can think of would be to put people off by faking it or pretending as if I'm having 100 percent fun.... .

Courtney interjects again: "No, Kurt, the worst crime I can think of is for you to just continue being a rock star when you fuckin' hated it. Just fuckin' stop!" She goes on:

Sometimes I feel as if I should have a punch-in time clock before I walk out onstage. I've tried everything within my power to appreciate it, and I do. God, believe me I do but it's not enough. I appreciate the fact that I – and we – have affected and entertained a lot of people. I must be one of those narcissists who only appreciate things when they're alone. I'm too sensitive. Oh, I need to be slightly numb in order to regain the enthusiasm I once had as a child. On our last three tours, I've had a much better appreciation for all the people I've known personally and as fans of our music. But I still can't get out the frustration, the guilt and the empathy I have for everybody. There's good in all of us and I think I simply love people too much...

Courtney jumps in again: "So why didn't you just fuckin' stay?"

... so much that it makes me feel too fucking sad. Too sad, a little sensitive, unappreciative, Pisces Jesus man....

Courtney again: "Oh, shut up, bastard. Why didn't you just enjoy it... I don't know. And he goes on to say personal things to me that are none of your damn business. Personal things to Frances that are none of your damn business."

... I had it good, very good [authors' note: in fact, Kurt wrote, "I have it good," which some people believe is significant]. And I'm grateful. But since the age of seven, I've become hateful towards all humans in general, only because it seems so easy for people to get along and have empathy. Only because I love and feel for people too much I guess. Thank you all from the pit of my burning, nauseous stomach for your letters and concern during the last years. I'm too much of an erratic, moody person that I don't have the passion anymore. So remember...

Courtney: "And don't remember this, 'cause it's a fuckin' lie!"

... It's better to burn out than to fade away....

Courtney: "God, you asshole!"

... peace, love, Empathy, Kurt Cobain.

Courtney: "And then there's some more personal things that are none of your damn business. And just remember, this is all bullshit. But I want you to know one thing. That eighties tough-love bullshit. It doesn't work. It's not real. It doesn't work. I should've let him, we all should've let him, have his numbness. We should have let him have the things that made him feel better, that made his stomach feel better. We should have let him have it, instead of trying to strip away his skin. You go home and tell your parents, don't you ever try that tough-love bullshit on me, 'cause it doesn't fuckin' work. That's what I think. And I'm laying in our bed and I'm really sorry. And I feel the same way you do. I'm really sorry, you guys. I don't know what I could've done. I wish I'd have been there. And I wish I had listened to other people, but I didn't. Every night, I've been sleeping with his mother, and I wake up in the morning, I think it's him, 'cause their bodies are sort of the same. I have to go now. Just tell him he's a fucker, okay. Just say, 'Fucker. You're a fucker.' And that you love him."

Among the people at the memorial that evening was a twenty-eight-year-old named Daniel Kaspar. Hours later, Kaspar returned to his home in Maple Valley, Washington and shot himself dead. Neighbours said he was despondent over Kurt's death.

Kaspar was only the first in a string of copycat suicides reported over the next few days, which included two teenagers – one in Australia, the other in Turkey.

Meanwhile, Courtney was continuing to obsess in private about Kurt's female dealer friend, who she remained convinced was sleeping with Kurt before his death. She repeatedly called the Seattle Police Department asking them to bust her for dealing, which Courtney revealed in an interview with Gene Stout of the *Seattle Post-Intelligencer* without referring to her by name. In the interview, she contradicted her claim at the vigil that "we should have let him have the things that made him feel better, that made his stomach feel better" (obviously referring to heroin).

She told Stout she was disgusted that they couldn't shut down Cobain's drug sources.

"It's like apples in an orchard," she says about heroin. "It's falling off the trees. The Seattle police won't do anything about it. I asked them, 'Don't you get embarrassed when you hear that Seattle is famous for grunge, cappuccino, and heroin?'"

Many people in Seattle found this quote ironic. "At the time she said this," says a Seattle dealer named Walter, "she was shooting up a couple of hundred dollars' worth of junk every day. I know because I sold it to her."

From all the media accounts, the Seattle Police Department had closed the book on the case. The coroner, Dr. Hartshorne, officially declared a verdict of suicide after the autopsy, revealing the body had been dead at least two days before it was found. The case seemed to be closed. Once Courtney revealed that the Rome incident had been a suicide attempt, the media picked up on the theme of Kurt's suicidal tendencies and nobody seemed surprised he would take his own life. Most accounts treated it as almost inevitable.

But on May 11, a month after Kurt's body was found, a report came out in the *Seattle Times* by the paper's chief investigative reporter, Duff Wilson.

It began: "Kurt Cobain's death a month ago wasn't the open-and-shut suicide case Seattle police originally indicated."

Wilson revealed that homicide detectives had spent nearly two-hundred hours interviewing Kurt's family and friends, his heroin dealer, and others. They even hired a handwriting expert to review the note found by Cobain's body to make sure it was authentic before finally concluding that the death was indeed a suicide.

Why were the police so suspicious after publicly portraying the death as a definite suicide? When Duff Wilson was interviewed for this book, he talked about his own lengthy investigation, which failed to answer a number of mysteries involved in the case, including who was using the credit card after the death. As late as two hours before the body was found (which is at least forty-eight hours after Kurt died), somebody attempted to buy flowers for $43.29. Who was using the card?

Wilson says he still believes that the death was "probably a suicide" but he doesn't rule out the possibility of murder, "especially because of a number of strange things surrounding the Rome incident."

Wilson wasn't the only person with doubts.

8

Tom Grant, P.I.

Tom Grant sits in his unassuming Beverly Hills office surrounded by photos of his seven grandchildren. His graying hair and stocky build frame features that make him a dead ringer for Hollywood actor Brian Dennehy.

For seven years, Grant was a rising star in the Los Angeles County Sheriff's Department. In 1969, at the age of twenty-two, he joined the force, where his above-average investigative skills soon attracted attention. After only a year on patrol, he was selected to be a member of the elite Specialized Crime Activity Team (S.C.A.T.), which worked undercover to bust felony crime rings. In 1972, after being transferred to the Malibu Sheriff's Station, Grant was responsible for a major arson arrest and was promoted to detective, one of the youngest ever in the county. In 1975, Grant was feeling burned out by the dangerous job and decided to take a leave of absence to open up a retail music shop in Malibu. He had one year to decide whether to return to duty or continue his business.

"I was enjoying the relative peace of the music business better than the stress of police work. It was more fun selling equipment to the Beach Boys than dealing with murderers and thugs." Two years later the business went under, and Grant decided to set up a shingle first as a security expert, then as a private investigator.

There are no skeletons in his closet, it seems. His former colleagues and superiors at the sheriff's department say he was highly respected and have only good things to say about him.

Capt. Jack Sculley was Grant's sergeant at the West Hollywood Sheriff's Station and remembered Grant as a "very good patrol deputy."

As a private investigator, he has commanded similar respect, and his clients have included such well-known figures as Sammy Davis Jr. and Clint Eastwood's ex-wife Sondra Locke.

As Grant sits in his office talking about the case, he receives a number of calls. To one caller, he says, "You don't need a private investigator for that. You can do it yourself." He proceeds to tell her how. After he hangs up, he says, "I've been told I'm not much of a businessman. To another caller who wants him to bug her husband's office, he says, "That's illegal. I don't work like that. A lot of P.I.s will do it, but not me.

Grant doesn't look like his record collection contains many albums by Nirvana or Hole. Courtney Love must wish she had called another P.I. that Easter morning.

"I've never been much for conspiracy theories," says Grant. "I never even saw *JFK:* When I hear somebody else talking about a conspiracy, I usually scoff. That's why this whole case seems so unlikely to me."

Grant proceeds to explain the events which took place after the body was found on April 8.

"Courtney didn't seem to be mad that we had failed to find the body, even though we might have saved him, which kind of surprised me," he says, explaining that on the nights he and Dylan visited the house, there was a driving rain and a floodlight shone from the garage, making it impossible to see there was a greenhouse room above it. (For the purposes of this book, we visited the house in similar weather and confirmed Grant's explanation. Still, many have cited his failure to find the body as proof of incompetency.)

After Grant flew back to Los Angeles, he says he arranged a meeting on April 13 with Courtney's entertainment attorney, Rosemary Carroll.
Carroll was a good friend of both Kurt and Courtney and the wife of Gold Mountain's Danny Goldberg.

"At this meeting, Rosemary indicated her suspicions to me for the first time about Kurt's death," says Grant. "Among other things, she told me Courtney didn't show her the alleged suicide note. That's when I decided to return to Seattle for further investigation."

On Thursday, April 14, Grant returned to the Lake Washington house, where he found Courtney sitting at the dining room table.

"She said to me, 'I guess I really found the right P.I. this time.' The flattery was nice, but it didn't make much sense. Most would have thought I bungled the investigation."

They went to Courtney's bedroom to talk away from Kurt's mother, who was also in the dining room. Grant was intent on seeing for himself the suicide note, so he thought of a way he could trick Courtney into showing it to him.

"I heard you read the note on TV the other day," he told her. "I was confused about something. It sounded like the note said, "I'm lying here on the bed..." If Kurt was lying on the bed when he wrote the note, why was the bed so neat when I came in here the other night? It didn't look like anyone had been on this bed."

Courtney responded, "No, Tom. I was lying on the bed. I was lying on the bed recording the message to Kurt's fans."

Grant replied, "Are you sure that's what you said?" I got the impression that Kurt was saying *he* was lying on the bed."

"No, here, I'll show you," said Courtney as she reached over to retrieve a folded paper from under her pillow. She explained it was only a copy and that the police had the original.

Grant studied the note intently and then said, "I can't read this without my glasses. Can I go downstairs and make a copy on your fax machine? I'll look at it later."

"Yeah, sure," came the reply.

Grant takes his copy of the note from his files and illustrates one of the most compelling pieces in the puzzle.

After Kurt signs the note with the words "peace, love, Empathy, Kurt Cobain" there is a gap after which he writes, in slightly bigger handwriting, "Frances and Courtney, I'll be at your altar." Then, in a completely different size and style of handwriting, comes the words:

> Please keep going Courtney
> for Frances.
> For her life which will be so much happier without me.
> I love you, I love you

What's the significance of these words?

"If you look at the entire rest of the note [see appendix], there is absolutely nothing that indicates suicide," Grant says. 'It reads more like an explanation to his fans about why he is quitting the music business, which makes sense considering all the reports after his death that he had told people he was leaving Nirvana, which is why he canceled Lollapalooza.

"However," he continues, "anybody reading those last four lines would automatically assume that it was a suicide note. The question is, did Kurt really write them or were they added later?"

The Seattle Police Department obviously asked itself the same question when they saw the note. Internal department documents reveal they passed the note on to the State of Washington forensic laboratory for handwriting analysis. The analysis confirmed the note was written by Kurt Cobain, a fact that even Tom Grant acknowledges, with the exception of the first line and the last four lines, which he says is the only part of the note which points to suicide.

"The police forensic laboratory was never asked to analyse whether there were two different sets of handwriting," says Grant. "They were just asked whether Kurt had written the note. Of course, they refuse to say whether their lab found any inconsistencies at the end of the note."

In March, 1998, Dave Grohl confirmed for the first time in an interview with radio talk show host Howard Stern that Nirvana was indeed in the process of breaking up at the time of kurt's death. This lends strong credibility to Grant's argument that the note was actually a retirement letter from Kurt to his fans.

In February 1997, the American television show *Unsolved Mysteries* which is highly respected for solving mysterious deaths, hired two of the world's leading handwriting analysts to independently analyse the so-called suicide note. They provided samples of handwritten lyrics by Kurt Cobain in order to compare the handwriting.

Marcel Matley, an American expert, concludes, "The last four lines of the suicide letter, which include the words 'I love you, I love you,' were written by a different person. There are differences in the two." Matley achieved national recognition in 1995 when he sat on a national commission which determined the authenticity of the suicide note written by President Clinton's former White House counsel, Vince Foster.

The second expert, Reginald Alton of Oxford University, says, "There are more than a dozen discrepancies in the handwriting, definitely in the first line (where the word "Boddah" seemed to be added later) and in the last four lines." Alton cautions that he can't be 100 percent sure because he was not working from the original document but rather from a copy.

Both experts agreed that the body of the letter – the portion that doesn't mention suicide and which sounds more like a retirement letter from the music industry-was written by Cobain. Their analysis, arrived at independently, backs up Grant's theory completely.

Meanwhile, the *Seattle Post-Intelligencer* obtained a confidential copy of the autopsy report – a report that under Washington State law was never officially made public – and published its findings on April 14 under the headline "Cobain Lay Dead for Three Days." The autopsy revealed that Kurt had died three days before the body was found, probably the evening of April 5. More significantly, it revealed that Kurt's blood contained two to three times the fatal dose of heroin. Nevertheless, it concluded he died of a gunshot wound to the head, not a heroin overdose.

Grant points to the autopsy report as one of the most significant pieces of evidence refuting the suicide theory. He asserts that a heroin addict with this much heroin in his blood would not have been able to pick up a shotgun and shoot himself. Rather, he would have been unconscious before he could have raised and pointed the gun.

But Donald Reay of the Seattle medical examiner's office challenges Grant's theory. "That would be true with a normal person," he says, "but you have to remember Cobain was a heavy addict and could probably withstand a much higher dose than most people because he had built up a tolerance."

Medical literature does not support Reay's explanation. Although there is a tolerance factor, it is much less relevant for heroin addicts than other drug users, according to experts in the field.

Unsolved Mysteries asked one of the country's leading forensic pathologists, Dr. Cyril H. Wecht, to give his opinion on whether a heroin addict such as Kurt Cobain could have shot himself after injecting as much heroin as was found in his blood.

"With a level of 1.52 millilitres per litre of morphine as found in Kurt's blood level," said Wecht, "for the great percentage of people, including addicts, it would induce a state of unconsciousness quite quickly, in seconds, not even in minutes. It would be virtually impossible for him to have shot himself with that high a level of morphine. It raises a question if he shot that shotgun, a big question."

The authors of this book spoke to eleven different heroin addicts, who each categorically stated that it would be impossible for them to pick up a gun and manoeuvre it after shooting that much heroin, no matter what their level of tolerance.

Said one eight-year addict, "Anybody who says you can do that has never shot smack."

Grant theorizes that Kurt may have shot up with somebody he knew, somebody who supplied heroin pure enough to cause an overdose. Then, when Kurt slipped into unconsciousness, the person shot him and placed the gun to look like a suicide.

Some prominent law enforcement officials confirm this possibility. According to Police Detective Patterson of the New York City Police Department – which investigates more murders every year than any other force in the world – there are many examples of murders covered up to look like an accident or suicide.

"We've got several known cases where they intentionally OD someone with heroin to make it look like an accidental overdose," he says. "They'll give him a bad bag [a higher dose of purity than the user is used to] and he'll die, and it'll look like an accident. We also get people who are pushed off buildings to look like they jumped and sometimes there's a murder and the perpetrator sets a fire to make it look like he was killed by an accidental fire."

This possibility occurred to a Canadian chemist named Roger Lewis when he read media accounts of Cobain's death, especially after it was reported that his blood contained such high levels of heroin. Something about the death didn't add up to suicide, Lewis concluded, and he proceeded to embark on his own year-long study into similar deaths, hoping he could shed some light on the suicide verdict. Citing ninety-eight different criminology, pathology, and forensic texts, Lewis released his report in 1996, entitled "Dead Men Don't Pull Triggers." The results are interesting.

Lewis was curious as to how often murders were staged to look like suicides. Many criminology texts, in fact, discuss this very topic. According to the well-respected book *Fundamentals of Criminal Investigation* by C. E. O'Hara (1975), when someone who is drugged supposedly commits suicide, "the fair supposition is murder." He writes extensively on the common phenomenon of simulated suicides. "These are usually planned by persons wishing to defraud insurance companies or to arrange for a change of spouse." Interestingly, O'Hara discusses the rarity of suicides among missing persons. He describes how the myth of a suicidal missing person perpetuates homicides staged to look like suicides.

"To the layman," he writes, "the suicide theory is one of the first to suggest itself in a disappearance case. Statistically, however, it can be shown that the odds are greatly against the suicide solution.... A voluntary disappearance is motivated by a desire to escape from some personal, domestic, or business conflict. In the disappearance of approximately 100,000 people annually in this country, it is to be expected that personal violence should play a significant part in some of the cases. Murder, the unspoken fear of the relatives and police, must always lie in the back of the investigator's mind as a possible explanation. The suspicions of a shrewd investigator have not infrequently uncovered an unsuspected homicide."

Lewis cites the landmark 1986 criminology study *The Murderer and His Murder*, by D. Lester, which discusses at length the correlation between drugs, suicide, and homicide. "Narcotics were more likely to be present in the homicides," Lester writes. He also cites a Philadelphia study which concluded that "wives killing husbands constituted 41 percent of female murderers."

What about the autopsy which also came to the conclusion of suicide? Lewis cites two of America's foremost criminal forensic experts R. B. Hill and R. B. Andersen whose 1988 book *The Autopsy: Medical Practice and Public Policy* is considered one of the definitive texts. In their chapter "Missed Diagnosis" they write, "significant underdiagnosis occurs more often than overdiagnosis by a factor of 2:1." 5. B. Burgess agrees in his 1992 book *Understanding the Autopsy*. He writes, "There are many jurisdictions in this country where you would not have to be half-smart to get away with murder, quite literally... the fact remains that, in all too many places, the investigation of possible murder is undertaken only after pressure is brought by relatives or other interested parties, and when such investigation is instituted, it is done so incompetently that murder after murder goes unsolved and unpunished."

In his study, "Accident, Suicide, or Murder?" British criminologist Sir Sydney Smyth comes to a similar conclusion. "The question of whether a fatal injury was homicidal, suicidal, or accidental is as common in real life as it is in detective fiction... It is natural for a murderer to try to escape detection by making his crime look like a suicide or accident, and such attempts have been doubtless going on for a long time. One cannot say how long, for one never hears about them when they succeed. However, records of failures take us quite far back."

Lewis, a scientist himself reserves his most convincing arguments for the scientific possibility or impossibility that Cobain could have shot himself up with a triple lethal dose of heroin and then rolled down his sleeve, put away his heroin kit neatly and then lifted a shotgun and pulled the trigger, as the autopsy concluded. He cites more than sixty books and studies from forensic and medical journals, each proving that a man with 1.52 ml of morphine per litre (heroin is instantly transformed into morphine when it enters the blood) could not have remained conscious, no matter what his tolerance to the drug. This is significant because the Seattle Medical Examiner Dr. Donald Reay has justified his department's suicide verdict by saying that a severe heroin addict has a higher tolerance than nonusers.

In each of these studies, the only question for someone who injected as much heroin as Cobain did is whether he would have died immediately (often referred to as "a golden shot") or whether he would first have lapsed into a coma. In J.J. Platt's 1986 book *Heroin Addiction: Theory, Research, and Treatment*, he studied only severe heroin addicts. Platt concluded that the maximum lethal dose for *a 150* pound male (Cobain was 115 lbs. in 1993, which would have made the maximum dose even smaller), about 75 mg-80 mg, will result in a blood morphine level of .5 ml per litre of blood. Cobain's was three times that amount, 1.5 ml. In response to Reay's assertion that the tolerance level for an addict is higher than that of a nonuser, he is correct.

Platt's study concluded that, for a nonuser, Cobain's morphine blood level would be 75 times the lethal dose.

The *New England Journal of Medicine* published a study in 1973 by J. C. Garriott and W. Q. Sturner, entitled "Morphine Concentrations and Survival Periods in Acute Heroin Fatalities." In all the heroin fatalities they had ever studied to that point, the two had never encountered any blood morphine level over .93 ml per litre. In other words, Cobain's blood level was over 50 percent higher than the highest level they had ever encountered. They and others write of overdose victims lapsing into a coma immediately following a fix with the syringe still affixed into the arm or on the floor underneath the body. Yet, Cobain was supposedly able to put away his drug kit and then shoot himself according to the police report.

Lewis cites countless other similar studies, each reaching the same conclusion. Each study also proves that the dose Cobain took would immediately have rendered him unconscious or killed him, which backs up the view of the forensic expert quoted on *Unsolved Mysteries*. They completely contradict the findings of the Seattle Homicide Division and the Medical Examiner's Office.

On the basis of this study, Lewis concludes that somebody he knew must have given Kurt an overly pure dose of heroin, then – when he lapsed into a coma – took the gun and shot him, making it look like a suicide. But who?

Grant was interested in Michael Dewitt (Cali), the male nanny who was living at the house and who talked to Kurt on April 2. Cali later told police he had been friends with Courtney for years before she met Kurt.

When Grant told Courtney at the house that he wanted to speak to Cali together with Dylan Carlson, he says she told him, "Cali went to rehab in El Paso, or Georgia.... No, he's in L.A. with friends." He says she shouted to Eric Erlandson, "Call Cali and tell him to get back up here on the next plane." Grant then left the house and asked Eric to call him at the hotel when Cali arrived. A few hours later, Grant phoned the house and spoke to Eric, who told him that after Grant left, Courtney had him call Cali and tell him he didn't have to come to Seattle. Grant says Eric told him, "I don't know what's going on here." (After Kurt's death, Courtney awarded Cali's father, who owns a construction company in Washington State, a very lucrative contract to renovate her Lake Washington estate.)

Shortly after this meeting, Grant says he met with the lead homicide detective, Sergeant Cameron, and relayed his suspicions. He says Cameron was not impressed and dismissed his suspicions with the words, "Nothing you've said convinces me this is anything but suicide."

Grant continued his own investigation, determined to get to the bottom of what happened. On May 8, 1994, he wrote a letter to Courtney indicating his suspicions:

Dear Courtney,

I'm sure you know by now that my investigation has been somewhat more active than you might have been aware of. The purpose of this letter is to clarify my position regarding our working relationship.

You may recall our trip to Carnation on Thursday, April 14. I mentioned during the drive that I was beginning to turn over some "rocks" that I wasn't sure you'd want turned over. I asked you if you wanted me to continue digging. Kat [Bjelland, Courtney's friend], who was in the back seat said "Oh yeah, she wants to know everything." You responded, "Yeah, Tom, do whatever it takes. I want to know everything that happened." Your instructions were clear, so in the days and weeks that followed, I proceeded to do whatever it takes.

As the investigation continued, my attempts to get at the truth often seemed to be deliberately hindered. While reading some of the articles being written in newspapers and magazines, I discovered the information being released to the press was inaccurate and often cleverly misleading.

I consider the circumstances surrounding your husband's death to be highly suspicious. My investigation has exposed a number of inconsistencies in the facts of this case as well as many contradictions in sound logic and common sense. I'm required to report findings such as these to the police, so on Friday April 15, I spoke with Sgt. Cameron about some of what I've learned so far.

As I've experienced in past cases, police detectives don't often welcome the work of outside investigators. I've learned it's somewhat idealistic and naive to think the truth might be more important than professional pride.

I've decided to continue working on this case until I see it to its conclusion, without additional charges. Attached you will find an invoice which accounts for the charges billed for our services, including time and expenses. As you can see, prior to my return to Seattle on April 13, these charges exceeded the retainer amount. However, please consider your bill paid in full. There will be no further charges.

As I pursue the truth regarding the events surrounding your husband's death, your co-operation and assistance will be appreciated, but not required.

Sincerely,

Tom Grant
The Grant Company

"I thought Courtney would hit the roof when she received this letter," Grant says. "Instead she hired me to do some more work for her, things that had nothing to do with Kurt's death. I think she wanted to shut me up and she thought she could buy me off with this money.

Why did Grant accept the commission?

"I thought of refusing the work but then I figured that as long as I was working for her, I could more easily keep tabs on her."

He says that, during this seven-month period, Courtney would repeatedly attempt to sabotage the investigation. "Whenever I started to talk to people close to her about Kurt's death, she'd hire me to do another job. She didn't have a lot of options at this point, because cutting me off would keep her in the dark about what I was doing."

Grant continued to meet with Courtney's lawyer Rosemary Carroll, who he says was also growing more suspicious. It was at one of these meetings, Grant claims, that Carroll supplied him with information that may indicate a motive for Kurt's death.

Grant says, "Rosemary told me that, shortly before Kurt died, he asked her to draw up a will excluding Courtney because he said they were getting a divorce. At around the same time, she said Courtney called her up and told her to find 'the meanest, most vicious divorce lawyer' she could find and asked whether it was possible to void the prenuptial agreement. This would obviously be a pretty good motive for murder. If the divorce had gone through, Courtney wouldn't have received a dime because of the prenuptial agreement they had, or at least she would have only got a small settlement. Instead, she inherits an estate worth tens of millions of dollars in future earnings."

In fact, after Kurt's death, it was revealed that there was a will but that Kurt had not yet signed it. Therefore it was invalid. This would seem to confirm Grant's claim that Carroll revealed he had a will drawn up just before his death. Police have refused to reveal the contents of the unsigned will or whether Courtney was indeed excluded.

Grant claims that, at a meeting with Carroll at her Hollywood office on April 13, she said, "Kurt wasn't suicidal, Tom. He wasn't suicidal." He says she was also disturbed and somewhat suspicious that Courtney wouldn't let her see the alleged suicide note.

"Rosemary was very instrumental in initiating this investigation and encouraging me to dig into this further," Grant claims. "She knew something was wrong, she suspected there was foul play from the beginning and she played a major role in initiating this investigation."

Carroll, who was good friends with both Kurt and Courtney besides being their lawyer, is not allowed to comment on Grant's allegations because of her lawyer-client privilege. (Interestingly, Carroll is married to Danny Goldberg, former head of Nirvana's management company, Gold Mountain. Goldberg has repeatedly publicly praised Courtney since Kurt's death. She is also the ex-wife of the famous junkie Jim Carroll, author of *The Basketball Diaries*.) In a November 1996 public debate with investigative attorney Jack Palladino who was hired by Rosemary Carroll to determine what information we had on this case – the authors of this book stated that they would disavow all Tom Grant's claims if Carroll would simply deny she expressed these suspicions to Grant. She has so far declined to do so.

Grant produces a number of documents Carroll gave him and opens up his safe to reveal more than a hundred cassette tapes, saying, "I tape every conversation I participate in to cover myself. That's why you haven't seen anybody deny the conversations I quote. They know I have the proof."

To illustrate this point, he proceeds to play a number of conversations between him and Courtney – tapes which confirm key portions of his story but nothing directly linking her to any crime. He says he is saving crucial tapes for when the case goes to court.

In the fall of 1997, we told Grant that the only way he could establish his credibility in this case beyond a shadow of a doubt would be to play us the tapes proving Rosemary Carroll expressed her own doubts about Kurt's suicide. He did so and demonstrated once and for all that he did not concoct the murder theory for his own financial gain as his detractors charge.

On the tapes, Carroll talks about her belief that Kurt was murdered and tells Grant that she believes the so-called suicide note was forged by tracing over a "pastiche" of other things Kurt had written in the past. She does not say who she thinks forged the note.

On December 15, 1994, Courtney Love gave an interview to *Rolling Stone* about Kurt's death. For the first time, she revealed that Kurt left her another note besides the suicide note. In this note, she claims, Kurt wrote, "You know I love you, I love Frances, I'm so sorry. Please don't follow me. I'll be there. I'll protect you. I don't know where I'm going, I just can't be here anymore."

The most bizarre thing about this note, says Grant, is that it seems to confirm that Kurt wasn't planning to commit suicide at all but that he was just planning to leave Seattle and he wanted to be left alone.

After the Seattle police homicide team completed their investigation and concluded the death was a suicide, Grant succeeded in obtaining a copy of the police report. The report contains a number of interesting facts which he says lend more credence to his case.

First, the fingerprint analysis of the shotgun shows four latent prints were lifted from the gun. But, according to the department's senior ID technician, T. Geranimo, none of the prints were legible.

How is it possible that Kurt handled the gun without gloves and didn't leave one set of legible fingerprints? If somebody else had handled the gun, however, they could have made an attempt to wipe the prints off, accounting for the illegibility of the prints. As Courtney's father, Hank Harrison, puts it, "Dead men don't wipe the fingerprints off their own guns." (Law enforcement experts have told us that it is rare but not impossible for this to happen and that there are a number of similar cases with no legible prints, so this by itself proves nothing.) However, even more puzzling than the absence of legible prints on the shotgun is the unexplained fact that there were also no legible prints found on the box of shotgun cartridges or the pen used to write the note.

Just as interesting is a line in the original incident report by Officer Levandowski, the first officer on the scene when the body was found. Levandowski wrote, "There are stairs in the west side leading to the french door entry and another set of french doors on the east side which lead to a balcony. These doors are unlocked and closed but there is a stool with a box of gardening supplies on it in front of the door."

This would seem to contradict Detective Cameron's previous claim that the stool was wedged against the doors, proving nobody could have left the room. This is actually of little relevance one way or the other, since these doors only led out to a balcony. The important door was on the other side of the room and it *was* locked, but it was the kind of lock which can be locked on the inside before leaving, so it does not rule out murder.

After acquiring Courtney's telephone records from the Peninsula Hotel, where she was staying when Kurt was missing, Grant says he learned the 911 call which resulted in her arrest originated from her own room. "She obviously needed an alibi," he says. "She got herself arrested so she would be in jail when Kurt died."

It was about this time, Grant says, that he became convinced that Cobain's death was the result of a conspiracy between Courtney Love and Michael "Cali" Dewitt. Grant, however, has not shown us any evidence that Dewitt was involved but he insists he will produce this crucial element of his case to an outside law enforcement agency or in court.

Sergeant Cameron dismisses Grant's allegations, saying, "He hasn't shown us a shred of proof that this was anything other than suicide."

Asked why his department took so long to investigate the possibility of homicide, he said they only wanted to cover all the bases because of the intense media scrutiny and the fact that the death involved a celebrity.

"If it hadn't been Kurt Cobain, the case would have been closed after the medical examiner's verdict. We never took the possibility of homicide very seriously," he said.

Indeed, we obtained an internal homicide unit investigation summary dated April 8, 1994 – the day the body was found – which seems to confirm the department never had any doubts about the cause of death. In the space marked "Subject," instead of marking "Death of Kurt Cobain" or "Death of white male," the homicide detectives simply typed "Suicide."

According to Cameron, Dr. Nikolas Hartshorne – the chief medical investigator – declared the death a "self-inflicted gunshot wound" soon after he arrived on the scene. Usually, he says, this is enough to close a case. Hartshorne has been quoted in a number of media accounts as saying, "I've never seen a more open-and-shut case of suicide."

In 1988, when Hartshorne was still in medical school, he and a group of friends had a side business promoting punk rock concerts. That year, long before Nirvana hit it big, he booked the group for a gig at Seattle's Central Tavern, Nirvana's third Seattle show. Ironically, the group was opening for the Los Angeles band Leaving Trains, whose lead singer was James Moreland, Courtney Love's first husband. According to many on the eighties punk rock scene, Moreland and Hartshorne were good friends and frequently socialized together with the then unknown Courtney Love in Los Angeles.

In a December 1995 interview conducted in his examining room at the King County medical examiner's office, Hartshorne – confronted with our findings – agreed he was friends with both Courtney and Moreland in the eighties when they lived in Los Angeles, long before she met Kurt. Asked whether he thinks his friendship with Courtney may have con-stituted a conflict of interest in the case, Hartshorne – who says he was a big punk rocker at the time responds "absolutely not."

Hartshorne confirms the case was never really investigated as a homicide. "They [the homicide unit] came to the scene because of the popularity of the individual. I mean Elvis is still walking around out there, and when you have somebody this prominent, you like to get the best people in there to make sure all your i's and t's are crossed. Look at all the people who think it's a conspiracy. If they hadn't done all this work, you would have many more people mucking about saying it's murder.

"The suicide was his [Cobain's] decision and you have to respect him for whatever his decision was. He had that right," says Hartshorne. He labeled the conspiracy theories as "ludicrous" and said he has seen no evidence indicating anything but suicide.

Asked whether a paraffin test or any other forensic exam had been done to indicate whether Kurt had shot a gun before his death, Hartshorne cited a State of Washington law forbidding him from revealing medical information about the autopsy but he did say "that test isn't always reliable."

Strangely, on the wall of Hartshorne's examining room is an old concert picture of Kurt Cobain.

Hartshorne's potential conflict of interest certainly does not suggest he was involved in a cover-up. It is probably nothing more than a coincidence. In fact, the authors of this book had given several media interviews specifically stating that we didn't believe

Hartshorne was hiding anything but rather that the "*appearance* of conflict of interest" is often the most important factor in determining public perception and that therefore the medical examiner's office should have sent somebody else to investigate Kurt's death. We were surprised, then, when Hartshorne gave a 1997 interview to *P.O.V.* magazine about our findings. He did not deny his previous friendship with Courtney. Instead, he accused us of getting the information by "secretly tape-recording" him.

In fact, the entire interview was conducted on videotape and it is obvious from watching the video that Hartshorne was perfectly aware he was being recorded. Why, then, did he not say this to the magazine reporter?

Shortly after we first revealed Hartshorne's potential conflict of interest, Hartshorne left the King County medical examiner's office and took a job as the medical examiner of a small town in Florida. Officials of his old Seattle department refused to confirm or deny if his departure was related to the Cobain case. Seattle's chief medical examiner, Dr. Donald Reay, however, insists that the suicide ruling was correct and that Hartshorne followed all the proper procedures.

According to a source in the Seattle Police Department familiar with the investigation, Hartshorne's potential conflict wasn't known at the time but others in the department had their own doubts about Cobain's death.

"The clincher for many of us was the note," the officer told us in 1996. "Anybody who saw it thought it was strange. The handwriting changes at a very suspicious place. But that wasn't all. Love gave us another note which she said Kurt had written in Rome. She said it was a suicide note, but it wasn't. It was a rambling letter which was very unflattering to her. There are some veiled references which you'd have to stretch to conclude referred to suicide."

The source maintains that Cameron, who he says

is an "excellent detective," made it clear that the so-called homicide investigation was just a show and that "we weren't supposed to take it seriously." To illustrate what he calls a shoddy investigation, he revealed that a number of rolls of film taken at the scene of Kurt's death by a police photographer weren't even developed. He says Cameron thought the Polaroids were sufficient.

"I don't necessarily think the death was a murder," he says, "but there are too many inconsistencies to just call it a suicide. The case should be investigated by an outside force such as the Washington State Police to clear up all the BS. Cameron will never admit he made a mistake; he is very concerned about his reputation."

At the beginning of 1995, Tom Grant finally decided to make his findings public by appearing on the nationally syndicated *Tom Leykis* radio show, the third highest rated radio show in the country, and indicating his suspicions that Courtney was somehow not revealing everything she knew about Kurt's death. For two hours, he outlined the case against Courtney in detail.

At four a.m. the morning after his interview, he received a call from Courtney, who had heard the show. He plays a tape of this call:

> Hi, Tom. This is Courtney.... I just heard the radio thing.... I haven't heard you tell an out, ya know, I listened to the thing and I didn't hear you tell, tell like outright lies.... I wish you were doing it for the money and the realization that you're doing it because you think that it's right hurts me a lot....

Soon after his talk-show appearance, Grant says, Courtney terminated his employment, and they haven't talked since. Several weeks later, he received a call from one of Courtney's lawyers, who said he could make it "worthwhile" for Grant to let his investigation rest. Grant plays a tape he made of this conversation.

"Basically, they were trying to tell me to shut up," says Grant.

Courtney has refused to talk publicly about the murder allegations, but in a February 1996 posting on the Internet, she stated her opinion of Grant:

He does not deserve my energy, he's already destroyed so much. The man doesn't like me.... WOW. He's also totally unsueable living in a garage and driving a used Datsun. No one in the legit media world will touch him – he's got nothing, the entire Seattle infrastructure would get homicidal, and he'd be sooo in trouble – he's not worth my time, he's horrible and gross and I have a bad anniversary coming up. no fun... okay bye... Courtney.

Friends of Courtney have accused Grant of trying to cash in on the story and say he is nothing more than a conspiracy theorist.

"He's obviously a crackpot," says Seattle DJ Marco Collins. "He doesn't have anything to back up his theories and he's just trying to make a buck." Kurt's friend Dylan Carlson also dismisses Grant and his murder theory.

In fact, Grant has refused countless financial offers to tell his story, including two by television tabloid shows.

"People keep offering me money to tell my story," he says, "and I have never accepted a dime. If I take any money or try to write a book or something, my credibility will be shot. Courtney will come out and say, 'You see, he was just after the money.' I'm never going to get in the kind of position where she can say that."

Why then has he dedicated himself to this case so doggedly? Some have even compared him to Inspector Javert pursuing Jean Valjean in *Les Miserables*.

"The thing that keeps me going," he says, "is when I read about all those copycat suicides of kids who kill themselves because they think Kurt Cobain did. If I can prevent another one, it's worth it."

(In 1997, three years after he began his investigation, Grant finally began to accept financial donations from supporters. A year earlier, he was involved in a very costly fight to keep his private investigator license after Courtney tried to have it revoked. He was successful but says it left him nearly broke, leading to his decision to finally accept donations. Six months later, he made available what he calls the "Kurt Cobain murder investigation manual" – basically a compilation of the information available on his Web site – for eighteen dollars. Doesn't this contradict his earlier claim that he would never compromise his credibility by accepting money? "I wrestled with that," he explains, "but if I go broke, I'll have to give up my pursuit and Courtney wins.")

So far, there have been at least sixty-eight suicides directly attributed to Cobain's death, and some experts say there are probably significantly more. One of the most striking of these incidents came in late 1994. Three Quebec teenagers, Michael Cote, Stephane Langlois, and Stephane Dallaire, travelled more than 3,000 miles across Canada by car. When they arrived in Vancouver, they entombed themselves in a storage locker and slowly inhaled the exhaust fumes from their car. As they took their last breaths, they listened to the strident melodies and bleak lyrics of Kurt Cobain on a Nirvana cassette. Their journals later revealed they were all depressed about Kurt's suicide months earlier. One entry read, "Kurt Cobain was a God! When he died, I died with him." Stephane Dallaire was also distraught about the suicide of his best friend, who had taken his life in May in a fit of depression over Kurt's death.

A week later, another Quebec youth committed suicide by jumping off Montreal's Jacques Cartier Bridge. Police found a Nirvana cassette in the Walkman he was listening to as he jumped off the bridge.

Only a month after Kurt died, an eleven-year-old

boy in South Los Angeles lifted a .38 caliber semiautomatic handgun from his father's closet and brought it to school in his backpack. While the other students were congregating before school began, he stood at the entrance of the school and shot himself in the head. Two Nirvana CDs were found in his backpack. These last two examples aren't even officially classified as Cobain copycat suicides.

Obviously, nobody takes their own life just because of a dead rock star. This is too simplistic. Ther are always other factors involved – emotional instability, personal crisis, etc. But the sister of copycat suicide victim Bobby Steele insists that Cobain had a special hold on his fans.

"I've read through Bobby's journals," says Sharon Steele, "I talked to him about Kurt quite often when he was alive, I knew him better than anyone in the world. I know that Bobby would never have committed suicide if he didn't believe Kurt had. Bobby had his problems, obviously, but Kurt and his music seemed to have a special power or something over him and a lot of teenagers. It's hard to explain, and it's kind of scary, but it's undeniable. Just ask the families of the other copycats, they'll tell you the same thing."

As late as April 1997, reports were still coming in from around the world about copycat suicides. In a small town in northern France, two schoolgirls – twelve and thirteen years old – committed a double suicide. They left a note saying they were in love with Kurt. "When I hear these kinds of stories," says Grant, "it kind of sickens me that they are all because of a suicide which never happened. As the father of three grown daughters, this waste of precious life is especially disturbing to me. To repeat what I've already said, kids are not killing themselves simply because Kurt died. In this case [the French schoolgirls], these kids were only nine and ten years old in 1994. They probably didn't even know who he was at that age.

Nirvana is still gaining new fans every day. Kids continue to kill themselves because they *think* that's what Kurt did."

Whether or not Grant's suspicions of murder are well founded, publicity of his findings, which have circulated on the Internet, seems to be having a positive effect on the thousands of teenagers who are still depressed over the death of their idol. He pulls two boxes from his closet full of hundreds of letters and e-mails he has received since he went public. Among them:

Dear Mr. Grant,

Before I read your summaries and updates, I was really depressed about Kurt and I got really angry at people who talked about you and how someone planned Kurt's death and other things because I was in denial. I was extremely suicidal and even tried killing myself once by taking five Contacs. Obviously I failed.... I was sad because I thought that Kurt killed himself, I was confused, and I couldn't imagine living life knowing he was gone. I don't want this letter to be long, so I just want to say I'm elated that someone is clearing up all this confusion....

Tom Grant,

Thank you so much for sending this information to me! I've been really depressed ever since Kurt Cobain's death. I've considered suicide a number of times because of it. But I just barely finished reading your updates and summaries and I'm convinced that Kurt did not kill himself. This makes me feel a lot better. It may seem far-fetched but you could say I owe you my life....

Dear Tom,

I'm a VERY big fan of Kurt Cobain... I have

to admit that I have come close to suicide myself... in a big part because of you know what.... Your work to find the truth is VERY APPRECIATED!...

Despite Grant's extensive findings, however, he has yet to provide genuine evidence proving the death was a murder and that Courtney knew anything about it. Detective Cameron of the Seattle Police Department has publicly stated he would be glad to reopen the case if he had some evidence. Grant says he doesn't have faith in Cameron.

"I have never said I can prove it was a murder by myself," says Grant. "My goal is to have the case reopened so that the police start asking the right questions and get to the bottom of all the still-unexplained questions. But it was obvious to me that Cameron doesn't want to look into the possibility of murder. It would make it look as if he bungled the investigation from the beginning. Come on, it's not so far-fetched that somebody could make a murder look like a suicide, especially when drugs are involved. It's actually not very difficult, although maybe I shouldn't say that in case people start copy-catting."

Grant says his goal now is to have the case taken over by the FBI, whose jurisdiction would apply if a conspiracy was involved.

Meanwhile, Tom Grant is not the only person pursuing the possibility that Kurt's death was a murder.

Only five days after the body was found, on April 13, 1994, a journalist named Richard Lee broadcast a segment on Seattle's public access TV channel 29, entitled "Was Kurt Cobain Murdered?" The answer, according to Lee, is yes. Every week since then, Lee has done an hour-long show doggedly pursuing his theory that Kurt's suicide was actually foul play and that the Seattle Police Department didn't follow up all the leads in the investigation.

In the strange cast of characters that dot this

case, perhaps none is more bizarre than Richard Lee. Lee is a rather odd character. He comes across as the stereotype of a wild-eyed conspiracy theorist but in fact has a somewhat impressive journalistic background as a longtime contributor to the respected *Chicago Reader* and other publications. He seems to be bitter that Tom Grant, whom he calls a "junior G-man," has received all the attention on the case while he has been virtually ignored, despite the fact he went public with his murder theory months before Grant. For his part, Grant says, "It's not a competition. We're both after the same goal."

Lee points to many of the same inconsistencies as Grant but differs in one respect. He believes the entire suicide note is a forgery and offers a rather detailed analysis of the handwriting to back up his theory. But since he is not a handwriting analyst, it is difficult to take this claim seriously.

Another of Lee's arguments centres on the lack of blood at the crime scene. If Cobain had shot himself in the mouth, he says, it would have resulted in a huge pool of blood, much more than the small amount visible in the only published photo. However, according to several pathologists we have talked to, it is not at all unusual for this kind of shotgun wound to yield a relatively small amount of blood. It would be different, they explain, if he had been shot in the head rather than through the mouth.

He also has some pretty far-fetched theories involving David Geffen, the City of Seattle, and Courtney Love, which tend to reinforce his reputation as a conspiracy theorist.

Several months after Lee started his weekly broadcast, he received a letter from Courtney Love accusing him of being "obsessed" with the case. She also enclosed an autographed backstage pass from a Hole show, which she told him "you can show to all your friends."

"I think she thought I would be happy to get her autograph and that would shut me up, that I was just doing it for attention," Lee says as he sits in his small rooming-house apartment, where he is literally surrounded from floor to ceiling by his files and videotapes on the case.

Much of Lee's case focuses on the sloppy police work in the investigation. Shortly after he received the letter from Courtney, he also received an anonymous letter which he believes is a death threat from a local Seattle Police precinct. It reads:

"We sit around every week at the tavern laffing [sic] at your hilarious show.... Who's going to investigate when you are murdered?" The return address on the envelope is for a Seattle police station.

Lee, like Grant, doesn't believe there was necessarily a police cover-up involved in the case but rather that the police immediately concluded it was a suicide and didn't seriously investigate the possibility of murder.

He says he spoke to a Seattle Police Department spokesperson, Vinette Tichi, on April 13 and that she was surprised that he would have any questions about whether or not Cobain had killed himself.

"Didn't you know that we had a suicide attempt on him last month?" he quotes Tichi asking. He says Tichi told him there was no real reason to investigate Kurt's death.

"We don't normally even investigate suicides," he says she told him. "You know, this was a king of high-profile person, so our homicide detectives did go out to the scene that day to do an investigation, but our case is closed. It was determined that it was a suicide, self-inflicted, and we aren't doing any further investigation regarding his death."

It may have been Lee's broadcast that day, only five days after the death, that prompted homicide detectives to go through the motions of an investigation.

Three years later, he is demanding a real investigation take place and has issued a sort of manifesto on the Internet along with a set of recommendations to serve as guidelines for a murder probe: just as any person does, Kurt Cobain deserves justice. In very many ways, Cobain exemplified Seattle and the Northwest in the hard- bitten, individualistic character of so many of its natives. His popularity here was not merely due to commercial success and popularity elsewhere, people really felt he was one of us. The way in which the handling of his death investigation was carried out casts shame across the character of the official bodies that govern our locality. In this case, the local agencies have shown themselves to be uncaring, incompetent, and possibly criminal in their actions. There is still time, I believe, to largely correct this situation and to bring those who murdered Kurt Cobain to justice. Failure to do so can only be considered a further compounding of the errors already made.

Recommendations

1. The City of Seattle and King County government should take any and all actions necessary to secure the greatest pool of extant evidence in this case, and to safeguard it from possible destruction from those who might prefer that it not exist.

2. The King County Executive has in his power the right to order an investigation and inquest into the causes and circumstances surrounding the death of any individual. The King County Medical Examiner's staff could not possibly be employed to investigate their own work to report gross misconduct. Therefore, experts from outside the local pool of those whose professional paths cross with those of the pathologists in question should be brought in for consultation and/or to conduct the investigation of this inquest.

3. Because this case involves mishandling of the

case by SPD, and quite possibly inappropriate actions, the City of Seattle should petition for the participation of the U.S. Justice Department in investigating this case. If the investigation is to get anywhere, it is probably advisable that diligence be made to request that investigators be brought in to investigate this matter from elsewhere, at least in a supervisory role.

Despite Lee's weekly pursuit of the murder theory, he was making no headway into reopening the case. Neither was Grant having much success in achieving this goal. He continued to track down leads and pursue the truth, but it didn't seem anybody was listening, at least in high places, and the case languished in his files until a significant development in early 1996.

At first glance, it's hard to take someone who calls himself El Duce seriously, especially not somebody who plays in a band who call themselves the "kings of porn-metal." El Duce, whose real name is Eldon Hoke, had been the leader of the Mentors since 1977 and had developed a notorious reputation around Los Angeles, where he lived. His stage persona included dressing up in the garb of a medieval executioner. The underground cult band, whose songs include "Heterosexuals Have the Right to Rock," made national headlines in 1985 when the lyrics of their song "Golden Showers" was quoted by Tipper Gore during her well-publicized crusade against obscenity in the music industry.

Why, then, would anybody believe his claim that in late December 1993 a limousine pulled up to the Rock Shop – a Hollywood record store where he worked part-time – and out of the car came Courtney Love.

He claimed she brought him outside on the sidewalk and said, "El, I need a favor. My old man's been a real asshole lately. I need you to blow his fucking head off."

"Are you serious?" Hoke asked.

"I'm as serious as a heart attack," she replied. "I'll give you fifty thousand dollars to do it. I'll fly you up to Seattle and tell you what to do."

"I told her I'd do it if she was serious," Hoke said. "She said she'd even give me a blow job if I did it. I said, 'Forget the blow job, just give me the money.' She asked me where she could reach me and I told her I take my messages at the Rock Shop. We went inside and I got her a business card and I said, 'You can reach me here.'"

Hoke said he was Courtney's friend in the late eighties when his band's guitarist was dating Hole's original drummer, Carolyn Rue. Several musicians on the Los Angeles music scene have confirmed this. Interestingly, Krist Novoselic once played bass in a Mentors cover band started by members of the Melvins. His stage name was "Phil Atio."

Anybody seeking notoriety can make this kind of claim, of course. It's hard to take it seriously, except for the fact that there was an eyewitness. Karush Sepedjian manages the Rock Shop and remembers Love's 1993 visit. "It was sometime during the holidays, just before New Year's Eve" says Sepedjian. "I remember Courtney pulls up in this limo. She starts talking to El in front of the store and my counter is right near the door so I could hear part of the conversation. She said to him, 'Look, can you handle doing this, can you get this done? What do you want for it?' They were talking about Kurt Cobain. Then they come into the store and El whispers to me that she just offered him fifty thousand dollars to get rid of her old man. He was pretty excited. Courtney tells me she'll be calling me soon, and then she left."

Sepedjian says he also knew Courtney when she lived in L.A. through Carolyn Rue's same boyfriend, who briefly played in Sepedjian's former band Godrod. He says that, after a couple of months went by and they heard nothing, he and El Duce thought it was just a joke and didn't take it very seriously. Then, in March, Sepedjian received a phone call.

"Courtney called looking for El. At the time, he was out on tour with his band. I told her I didn't know where to reach him. She was all frantic. She says, 'I need to talk to him. He's got a job to do.' I told her I had no idea and she starts screaming at me. I told her I've got a business to run and I hung up."

A couple of weeks later, when the two heard Kurt committed suicide, they thought it may not have been a joke after all. "I wondered if she found somebody else to do the job," Hoke says.

Asked why he thinks Courtney would have approached Hoke to kill her husband, Sepedjian says, "Everybody thinks he's crazy, which he probably is. He's also got a reputation that he'll do anything for a buck."

The fact that a witness to the incident exists still doesn't prove anything. Maybe Hoke and Sepedjian concocted the whole story together to cash in. That's what Tom Grant thought when he heard their story.

"I was pretty sceptical," says Grant. "Why didn't they come forward sooner? At first I thought maybe Courtney put them up to it to set me up. I would start talking about these guys as proof and then they would come out and say they made the whole story up. I would then be discredited and have no more credibility."

Grant's skepticism is understandable. But on March 6, 1996, Hoke underwent and passed a lie detector test administered by Dr. Edward Gelb, considered the top polygraph examiner in the United States. Gelb is the instructor for the FBI's advanced polygraph course and uses the most sophisticated and accurate polygraph equipment in existence. It was recently revealed that Gelb administered a polygraph to O. J. Simpson two days after the murder of his wife and that O. J. failed the test quite badly. According to Dr. Gelb, Hoke's story is completely truthful. To the question "Did Courtney Love ask you to kill Kurt Cobain?" Hoke's positive response showed a 99.91

percent certainty that he was telling the truth, says Gelb, which falls into the category "beyond possibility of deception." Hoke also received the same score the next time he was asked the same question. (When he was asked the question "Were you offered $50,000 by Courtney Love to kill Kurt Cobain?" Hoke scored a slightly less impressive 99.84 percent score.) An attorney named Jack Palladino, hired by Courtney to discredit the murder theory, admits that Gelb is "very highly respected."

What about the cliché that psychopaths and sociopaths can beat a polygraph? We asked Gelb in a recent interview. "That's a myth," he asserts. "In a recent British Columbia study of these type of mental patients, it was found that the polygraph is actually *more* accurate in testing these people." He explains that many of these misconceptions about beating a polygraph stemmed from the test's early days, when the technology was much less sophisticated. Now, he says, the polygraph is so accurate that it is being accepted in many court jurisdictions, although he admits it isn't 100 percent foolproof.

Following his polygraph test, Hoke contacted the Seattle Police Department Homicide Division and the Los Angeles Police Department. Both he and Sepedjian have offered to take a similar test for the police but both departments have declined to pursue an investigation. (In fact, Sepedjian, an admitted junkie, took a polygraph as well but, according to Gelb's office, he kept dozing offæa common symptom of heroin addiction – and the results were dismissed as "inconclusive.")

Love and her legal representatives have refused to confirm or deny whether she was in Los Angeles during this period, despite our repeated requests. We have told them that if they can provide concrete evidence she wasn't in L.A. at the time of Hoke's claim, we will dismiss his story as a fabrication. Her lawyers, however, have been anxious to discredit other elements of Hoke's account. According to her attorney Seth Lichtenstein, Hoke claimed in one interview that he was seated on a bench outside the Rock Shop when Courtney approached to make the offer. Lichtenstein correctly asserts that there is no bench outside the store and concludes that Hoke must be lying. However, both Hoke and Sepedjian claim that Hoke actually said he was sitting on a bench *inside* in *the front* of the store, not outside *in front* of the store, and that he may have been misquoted. Indeed, in an interview he gave to the authors of this book long before Lichtenstein's criticism, he made no mention of sitting on a bench outside the store.

Even if Courtney's offer took place, it is not proof that Kurt was murdered, but it might be enough to reopen the investigation.

Recently, the story of El Duce took a bizarre and unexpected twist. On April 19, 1997, Eldon Hoke was killed by a train in Riverside, California. Events surrounding the death are still cloudy. Only a week earlier, he had told his story about Courtney Love to BBC filmmaker Nick Broomfield, who was investigating Kurt Cobain's death for a forthcoming documentary.

At five o'clock in the afternoon on the day of his death, Hoke arrived at his ranch house with a man he said he had just met. The man, whom he introduced to his roommates, wore a baseball cap, jeans, and a T-shirt. After a short while, Hoke announced that he and his new friend were going to the liquor store and would be back in an hour. They never returned. At nine o'clock that evening, Hoke somehow was hit by a train going sixty miles per hour and killed instantly. There were no witnesses and the train driver did not see what happened.

Police were unable to locate the man Hoke left with and, after a short investigation, the death was officially ruled an "accident."

According to Hoke's longtime friend, music journalist Al Bowman, "There is something very, very strange about his death. Anybody who knew El knew that you could make friends with him by offering to buy him a drink. He had a problem with alcohol."

Bowman, who is a well-known fixture on the Los Angeles music scene as an organizer of the L.A. Music Awards, says Hoke was definitely not suicidal at the time of his death. "No way. He was all excited about his upcoming tour. He was in good spirits. He didn't kill himself. I'm convinced this has something to do with Kurt Cobain.

Another of Hoke's longtime friends, a Los Angeles musician named Drew Gallagher, claims that he talked to Hoke at the Mentors' last show, two days before the death. According to Gallagher, "Duce was acting very freaked out. He had heard that he might be in danger and he asked me if I knew where he could get a fake driver's license. I asked him why and he said, 'People get buried in cornfields, people get lost in swamps.' I asked him what he was talking about. He said he had recently been told who killed Kurt Cobain and he was super paranoid. I knew all about the thing where he said he was offered $50,000 but he said this was different."

Gallagher makes the dubious claim that Hoke told him the name of the killer and he plans to reveal it in a forthcoming book he is writing about the Los Angeles punk music scene. Isn't he afraid that he could share the same fate as Hoke? "The information is locked in a safety deposit box and will be made public if anything happens to me," he says.

For his part, Grant remains cautious about the El Duce revelations and is unwilling to speculate on the cause of Hoke's death, saying he doesn't have enough information.

Some of Grant's claims, however, reveal a decidedly less sensible approach. For example, he insists that during the drug overdose in which Courtney injected Kurt to revive him, the drug she used, buprenorphine, could have killed him, which may have been her intention. But experienced junkies have told us that the technique is common and that many heroin users often do the same thing for friends to save their lives. In a number of other instances as well, he seems to exaggerate to prove his point.

The most significant inconsistency in Grant's murder theory, however, centres on the Rome overdose. Grant is convinced that Rome represented Courtney's first attempt to murder her husband.

The drug Kurt overdosed on was Rohypnol, which is better known as the "date rape drug." Hundreds of reports have circulated of men mixing the drug in their girlfriends' drinks, inducing a confused or unconscious state, and then having sex with them. Grant believes Courtney may have mixed a large number of pills into Kurt's champagne so that when he took a drink, he was actually unknowingly ingesting large amounts of the drug, enough to kill him.

But if that's the case, why did she call the police when she found him unconscious on the floor? If she wanted Kurt dead, why didn't she just leave him on the floor until he died? Grant offers a number of questionable theories to answer this contradiction. Maybe she realized too late that he hadn't taken enough to kill him, he speculates, and she wanted to make herself look good by appearing to save his life. Maybe, but where's Grant's proof for this serious accusation? He offers none.

It is interesting to note, however, that the Rohypnol was Courtney's prescription, not Kurt's.

There is no doubt Grant is sincere in his crusade, but it is important to note that he has not produced any smoking-gun evidence linking Courtney to her husband's death (he claims he is saving it until the case is reopened by the FBI), and until he does, she is entitled to the presumption of innocence. This is a rather bizarre catch-22. Surely if Grant produces credible evidence, the FBI would agree to reopen the investigation?

"I would need official access to a number of documents first, such as the forensic report – which Courtney refuses to allow the police and the medical examiner's office to release – in order to piece all the evidence together," Grant explains.

This explanation is only partially convincing. There is no question that there is enough evidence to justify reopening the investigation and even making a strong case for murder. But no such compelling evidence has yet been produced to justify jumping to the conclusion that Courtney Love was involved in a conspiracy except the El Duce confession, which is still a somewhat shaky incident on which to base a murder case.

To sum up the most compelling evidence that Kurt's death wasn't a suicide or that at the least, the investigation should be reopened:

1. There were no legible fingerprints on the shotgun, the box of cartridges, or the pen used to write the so-called suicide note.

2. Three times the lethal dose of heroin was discovered in Kurt's body at the time of his death. According to pathology experts, Kurt would not have been able to shoot himself after injecting that level of heroin into his body. He would have been unconscious within seconds.

3. The so-called suicide note does not mention suicide at all but reads like a retirement letter from the music industry. Only *after* Kurt signed his name were an additional four lines added that do sound like they may indicate a suicide, but according to at least two internationally renowned handwriting experts, these four lines were written by somebody else – not Kurt Cobain.

4. Three weeks before the death, police were called to Kurt's house, where he told them he was hiding from Courtney. Three days before the death, Kurt told somebody he "feared for his life."

5. Kurt's credit card was used at least two times after the medical examiner says he was already dead but before the body was found. The card was missing from his personal effects when he was found. The police never determined who was using the card and why.

6. The death was declared an open-and-shut case of suicide by Seattle medical examiner Dr. Nikolas Hartshorne, whose ruling was accepted by the Seattle police before any investigation was conducted. But in fact Hartshorne had a clearly demonstrated potential conflict of interest as a good friend of Cobain's wife. In normal circumstances, the spouse is often the first potential suspect in a suspicious death but, because of the potential conflict of interest, the investigation may (or may not) have been compromised.

7. A man has claimed that he was offered $50,000 to kill Kurt Cobain three months before his death, and passed a polygraph test on this assertion "beyond possibility of deception."

9

The Prodigal Father

Just after eleven a.m. on April 8, 1994, Hank Harrison was at his Northern California horse ranch when he received a call from his godson Joe Hickman telling him Kurt had just been found dead.

"I felt as if my heart had been ripped out of my chest," Harrison recalls. "Here was a son-in-law I had never met but that I had this kind of mystical connection to and now I was never going to meet him. I just felt this indescribable sadness for my granddaughter."

At the time of Kurt's death, Harrison hadn't seen or spoken to his daughter for more than five months. The last time father and daughter had contact was in November 1993 at a San Francisco club, Slim's, where Hole was opening for Fugazi and the Lemonheads.

"We got along pretty well that day," he says. "Before the gig, we went out for coffee at Cafe Trieste and she was fascinated by my Macintosh Powerbook.

She made me show her how to use it and asked me all kinds of questions about logging on to the Internet. At the gig that night, she introduced me to Evan Dando of the Lemonheads, who said he was a big fan of my book about the Grateful Dead and wanted an autographed copy. That pissed her off. She grabbed me, dragged me into her dressing room, and told me to sit there and not move. (Courtney seemed to confirm this when she told the *San Francisco Chronicle*, "He didn't even stay to watch one song of his daughter's rock band.... He was only interested in talking to people who were more famous than me." Harrison claims he stayed for the entire Hole set but decided to watch it from the back of the audience instead of backstage because the music was so loud.)

Harrison continues his account of the last time he saw his daughter. "Later, I met [Hole bassist] Kristen Pfaff who really impressed me. She used the phrase 'fugue state amnesia' to describe Courtney's personality changes, which I thought was interesting."

According to Harrison, he asked Courtney several times when he was going to meet Kurt and the baby.

"She told me they might come visit me soon, but she had said that before and it never happened. For some reason, she didn't want me to meet Kurt. I was always telling her that I wanted to take him bungee jumping, which is a proven treatment for heroin addiction. I'm convinced that I could have got Kurt off drugs. She thought I was crazy".

Indeed, Harrison's offbeat ideas about drug addiction sound flaky, but his credentials in the area are impressive. In 1965, he designed America's first telephone LSD intervention program – the Institute for Contemporary Studies and LSD Rescue – in San Francisco to help bring people down from bad trips. His pioneering work in the field was written up in many publications, including the *New York Times*.

He brings out a scrapbook from those days

proving, if nothing else, that he has led a colorful life. Photos of Harrison with Jerry Garcia at the top of the Eiffel Tower; photos of him with his old friend and Jack Kerouac sidekick Neal Cassady; photos with Ken Kesey and the Magic Bus; a handwritten letter from Charles Manson (pre-arrest) to Harrison bad-mouthing the Dead and signed with a swastika.

Finished with the nostalgia, Harrison returns to Kurt's death. He says that, "like everyone else," he had no reason to believe Kurt's death was anything but a suicide.

"When I heard about Rome and all the other stuff suicide made sense," he explains. "It really had an impact on me, especially when I started hearing about all the copycat suicides. I wanted to do something."

What he decided to do was to design a special Kurt Cobain T-shirt with a stylized heart and donate the proceeds to suicide prevention. His efforts received considerable local publicity. By late April, he had donated almost one thousand dollars to a Northern California suicide prevention centre. He also went on the Internet and conducted more than two hundred online "interventions" with kids who expressed suicidal feelings about Kurt's death. These were similar to the telephone drug interventions he had pioneered in San Francisco almost thirty years before. In early May, Harrison was invited to appear on Geraldo Rivera's talk show to discuss his son-in-law and suicide prevention.

During the hour-long show, Harrison came across as articulate and spoke fondly of his daughter and granddaughter. But two days later, he received a call from Courtney. "She was furious at me. She accused me of exploiting Kurt's death and she warned me to back off. I asked her what she has against suicide prevention and she hung up on me."

Soon after, he told the tabloid TV show *Inside Edition* he was worried his daughter would share the same fate as Janis Joplin. "She's so intelligent," he said.

"All she has to do is snap out of it."

Around this time, President Clinton's White House counsel and longtime friend Vince Foster committed suicide. Harrison decided to send an e-mail to the president expressing his condolences and sharing his feelings about his son-in-law's suicide. Kurt was a big supporter of Clinton and urged his fans to vote for the president, who once revealed that his daughter Chelsea loved Nirvana's music. On May 13, Clinton sent Harrison a personal response on White House stationery:

Dear Hank,

I was inspired by the message you sent me via electronic mail.

If anything can be gained from Kurt Cobain's death, perhaps it is a greater understanding of the sadness and depression felt by so many people today. Those who consider suicide have a hard time seeing the goodness in life, the other options, and the people who are willing to help. It is my fervent hope that, with understanding and awareness, we can better guide others through their hours of darkness to find the encouragement they need. I admire your dedication to filling this need and send my best wishes to you, Courtney and Frances Bean during this difficult time.

Sincerely,

Bill Clinton

Not long after receiving Clinton's letter, Harrison began to contact members of Kurt's family to offer support. For the first time, he says, he heard doubts about the suicide.

"Most of them believed it was suicide, but a few told me things that nobody knew about Kurt and Courtney, and one family member in particular thought his death was very suspicious. I thought this was a bit far-fetched, maybe the family just didn't want to accept that he would kill himself, but I heard some horrendous stories, and for the first time, I heard that Kurt was planning to divorce Courtney. I knew they had been having problems, but I never knew about that. She certainly never said anything to me."

Among the members of the Cobain family Harrison contacted was Kurt's father, Don Cobain. A letter Don sent him does not mention any questions about Kurt's death, but parts are interesting: "I get real mad at Kurt. I guess I feel I was cheated out of really getting to know him and being a part of his life, when we were starting to talk to each other again. I also get real mad at the people who were around him all the time for not letting me know that he was having problems, maybe I could have helped? The truth is, Kurt got what he wanted and nobody could have helped him, but I wish I could have tried."

According to Harrison, Courtney bought each of Kurt's parents an expensive house and has asked them not to talk publicly about their son.

"I think she wanted to buy their silence," he says, "but Wendy [Kurt's mother] seems to genuinely like Courtney, who's been very good to her since Kurt's death."

By the end of 1994, Harrison was still convinced Kurt's death was a suicide, but he began to post tribute messages about Kurt on America Online under the screen name "Biodad." This prompted Courtney – who had discovered the Internet after her father taught her the basics a year earlier – to launch a series of vicious public online attacks against her father. In one, she accused him of giving her LSD as a child, in another she implies that he molested her. And she repeatedly claims that she hardly knows her father and that she has only seen him about ten times in her life. But Harrison produces hundreds of photos, letters, and docu-ments –

including her 1979 State of Oregon parole release form granting Harrison custody – proving otherwise.

"We have always had this love-hate relationship thing," Harrison says. "For years, she would publicly brag about her father who used to manage the Grateful Dead, and she sounded so proud; now she barely acknowledges I exist."

What about the accusation that he gave her LSD as a child? "That's plainly ridiculous," he responds. "I definitely used to experiment with acid, but I had a bad trip and stopped using, and then I started to get people off acid. Why would I give a child that stuff? I think that's something her mother told her to turn her against me."

In 1995, asked about the allegation, Courtney admitted to the *San Francisco Chronicle* that "I don't know if it actually happened." According to Love's biographer Melissa Rossi, Courtney has told several people that it wasn't actually Harrison who gave her the drug but rather a hippie girl in a commune where her father brought her while he attended a Dead concert.

In early 1995, Harrison came across Tom Grant's murder theory for the first time. He began to track down some of the leads Grant had given him on his own.

"Suddenly a lot of the pieces came together. I certainly wouldn't put it past her to have Kurt killed. Face it, she's a psychopath," says Harrison, who claims to have a psychology degree. "It runs in the family. She's entirely capable of doing something like this."

"I hope I don't get killed for saying this but I'm now convinced that Courtney had something to do with Kurt's death or at least knows who did it."

Why would a father say these things about his own daughter? At times, one senses he is almost jealous of her success, and even a bit starstruck about having a famous daughter, but when he lets his guard down, he betrays a deep sense of hurt about the way she has treated him over the years. Tears come to his eyes as he recalls an incident while Courtney was on the Lollapalooza tour that summer. He still hadn't expressed his doubts about the suicide publicly. "It was just after Jerry Garcia died," he explains. "Courtney said to the crowd, 'I'm sorry to hear Jerry died. I wish it had been my father instead."' (In fact, she said, "I'm really sorry about Jerry Garcia, that means maybe that my real father will die, and that makes me happy.")

Harrison is quick to add that he is not trying to put his daughter in jail and claims he loves her very much. He produces a pile of letters from Courtney proving that at one point they were very close. In one of these letters, written when she was sixteen, she writes, "you're the only person who ever understood me."

"I've been caught up in a bizarre web of events which has affected my life," explains the fifty-nine-year-old Harrison. "It would be very much like if your child came home with plans for a nuclear weapon in their briefcase and you wanted to know where the hell he got them. Well, my daughter came home with a dead husband and I damn well want to know what happened."

Still, the spectacle of a father publicly saying these things about his own daughter seems to many unseemly.

"Look at Theodore Kaczynski," Harrison responds, referring to the accused Unabomber. "Nobody criticized his brother for turning him in."

How credible is Harrison? Certainly he can provide considerable insight into various periods of Courtney's life, bolstered by the huge volume of letters and documents which he produces to back up his accounts. But it must be remembered that he never actually met Kurt Cobain and much of what he says about his former son-in-law and his death must be taken with a grain of salt. Some of his detractors besides Courtney claim that everything he says must be questioned.

According to another former manager of the Grateful Dead, Rocky Scully, Harrison can't be believed. "He [Harrison] lies. In his book, he described events that he never attended such as the [Dead's] trip to Egypt. He wasn't in Egypt. He's a nonauthority." In fact, Scully joined the Dead long after Harrison parted ways with the band, but other members of the Dead have also dissed Harrison since he revealed in The *Dead, Volume 2*, that some members of the band frequently smuggled and sold drugs to finance their tours. As for the allegation that he wasn't in Egypt, Harrison produces numerous photos and other memorabilia proving he was there.

"The reason he might think I wasn't there," Harrison explains, "is that I didn't fly on the chartered plane with the rest of the band. I was in Amsterdam and I flew from there to Cairo to meet up with them. I spent three and a half days in Egypt. Here's the proof (producing a photo of him and Jerry Garcia in Egypt). Let's face it, they don't like that I revealed how they were dealing drugs. That's why I parted ways with the Dead. I couldn't handle that scene anymore. Now, they diss me any chance they get. I have a clear conscience."

In late 1995, after Harrison announced he was planning to write a biography about Cobain, he received a letter from his daughter's lawyers threatening a lawsuit. This prompted him to write her the following letter:

Dearest Courtney:

Since you refuse to call or answer my letters, I must assume you are hiding something. What gives with the rumours about Kurt's death?

As you know, I began to write a book about Kurt two years ago, but now you insist I cease development on this project. Why? You give me no good reason and yet you slander and libel me every chance you get. I won't sue you, but I will answer all allegations in the book.

Furthermore, I can't help but wonder why you want me to stop writing a book about this wonderful man? I will donate all my royalties to suicide prevention.

If you insist, I will stop work immediately and get on with the *Stones of Ancient Ireland* and my novel, *The Beekeeper*, but I need to know the truth. What is going on? Why don't you just come out and volunteer to take a polygraph test to silence the critics once and for all?

Please meet me halfway. I have arranged a lie detector examina-tion for you at my expense. The results, no matter what the outcome, will never be made public. If you pass, I will cease writing the book or collaborate with you as you see fit. If I do not hear from you I will continue writing.

Taking the test and passing it will also help assuage your grandmother's fears. I would like her to see the baby, but barring that at least she will know you had nothing to do with Kurt's horrible death.

In the final analysis, we have a dead poet and a lot of suspicions which will never go away without a public hearing. If Kurt wasn't murdered what is being covered up? Why the big silence? Why not throw open the case and get to the bottom of it once and for all?

Love always,

Hank

Courtney has never responded to this letter, but in a 1995 interview with the San Francisco Chronicle, she discussed her current attitude toward her father. "He's a rugged old cockroach and he's not going to go away. I know someday I'll have to come to terms with him and make amends but I can't yet. I'm a Buddhist and for some reason this is my Karma."

Although Harrison cites many of the same inconsistencies as Tom Grant, he also uses some considerably more subjective arguments to back up his suspicions. For example, he is fond of saying, "Kurt was a Zen master and Zen masters do not commit suicide." This kind of talk has earned charges that Harrison is a flake and can't be taken seriously.

"Let's face it," he responds. "I'm from California and that's the way we talk. Besides, I am a bit of a flake. A lot of that stuff has been taken out of context. That's the kind of thing I say when I'm trying to analyse his personality and I talk about his Buddhist beliefs, but obviously my suspicions rest more on the evidence."

Understandably, Courtney is not pleased with her estranged father's accusations. She has repeatedly claimed that Harrison is trying to cash in on his association with her. Indeed, Harrison has been known to use his daughter for financial gain. Several years ago, he attempted to auction off a number of Courtney's poems, and most recently he sold childhood photos of Courtney to Melissa Rossi for her 1996 biography, *Courtney Love: Queen of Noise*.

On the other hand, Harrison owns several very valuable artworks, including two Picassos and a Chagall, which he acquired when he was with the Grateful Dead. He says he doesn't want to sell his art but wants to leave it to his granddaughter Frances Bean when he dies. He also owns an old Jaguar, a horse ranch, and a publishing company and still receives royalties from seven books, including two bestsellers about the Grateful Dead.

Recently, Harrison completed his biography of Cobain, *Kurt Cobain: Beyond Nirvana*, which he has made available for free on his publishing company's Web site.

Currently, Harrison is preparing a lawsuit to force the State of Washington to reopen the investigation into the death of his son-in-law.

For his part, Tom Grant has completely distanced himself from Harrison and his public statements, fearing he will damage the credibility of the case.

10

New Deaths, New Suspicions

When Kristen Pfaff was found dead in the bathtub of her apartment on June 16, 1994, she was still striving to understand the death of her friend Kurt Cobain only a few weeks earlier. Both Kristen and Kurt had struggled to realize the American dream only to have death leave them at the peak of their success.

After weeks of arguing and turmoil among band members, Kristen was surprised that Hole even managed to finish the *Live Through This* album. Courtney had driven just about everyone in the studio, from the producers to the band members, up the wall. After another protracted day at Triclops Studio, Kristen headed to Mick's on Peachtree Street in downtown Atlanta to meet a friend. She looked tired and tense. She told her friend Roxanne that working with Eric and Courtney was the worst nightmare of her life.

"They think they're God's gift to music," she said. "But they really know shit about this business."

As she sipped a glass of freshly squeezed orange juice, Kristen assessed the situation and knew her escape routes were limited.

"Courtney's scary. If I take a hike, she'll make me look bad or do something to make my life miserable," she told her friend.

From the outset, Kristen's relationship with Courtney was plagued with problems. Kristen had first met Courtney when her Minneapolis band, Janitor Joe, was making the rounds of the California club circuit in 1993.

It was Eric who first spotted Kristen. The tall, skinny blond guitarist was not only impressed by her bass playing but also by her slim figure and swiveling hips. Eric and Courtney wined and dined Kristen in L.A. in an attempt to get her to join the band. At first, Kristen was reluctant. She was wary of Courtney's flamboyant reputation. But the idea of playing with a well-known band on a major label was enough to convince her.

"It didn't take long for her to regret her decision," says her father, Norm Pfaff a salesman in Denver. "She became almost instantly aware of the downside of being famous. She couldn't deal with all the attention surrounding Hole and the drug-infested Seattle music scene."

But Kristen lived life as if each day might be her last. That tenet lent an urgency and intensity to her life and became a guiding principle to those close to her.

"The day Kristen joined Hole is when we took off," Eric told Craig Marks, music editor of *Spin* magazine. "All of a sudden we became a real band."

Courtney was becoming increasingly jealous of Eric's fixation on Kristen. She would constantly show up at Kristen's Capitol Hill apartment unannounced so that she could keep tabs on the two, who quickly became more than just bandmates.

"Courtney was always hanging around the building," claims one of Kristen's neighbours. "Sometimes I would see her in the basement doing laundry. She always looked like something was bothering her and she'd be smoking like a chimney."

Kristen had replaced Jill Emery on bass. She was aware of Courtney's poor track record of labour relations with band members. In fact, when her romance with Eric became more stable, he constantly warned her about upsetting Courtney.

"Don't fuck with her," he would say. "Just bite your tongue when Courtney does something stupid or insults you. That's what I do. Courtney has the power to make us all a lot of cash."

While Kristen was a charismatic presence, no one considered her another Courtney Love. "No wonder she agreed to have me in the band," she would tell Eric. "Because I let the spotlight shine only on her. Courtney really doesn't care about the quality of musicianship or stage presence. As long as she has three puppets who agree that she is the star, there are no problems."

When Kristen told Courtney that she should try singing more in key during the recording of *Live Through This*, Courtney completely lost control of herself "Who do you think you are, bitch!" she screamed. "I give you the chance of your life and right away you try to change things. You fuck my guitar player, constantly make eyes at my husband and now you're telling me how to sing. Just don't fuck with me because you'll regret it forever."

Later that night, Courtney apologized to Kristen. She knocked on Kristen's hotel room and said she was sorry. She even brought her some pot and a flower. Kristen loved receiving flowers. But later that night Kristen discovered that it was Eric who had forced Courtney to apologize. "I'll accept it for now," she told Eric. "But after this recording, if we manage to get through it without murdering each other, I'm leaving. I've had enough of Seattle and all the shit that goes with it."

Kristen was not yet five when she first showed signs of musical talent. In the middle-class suburb of Amherst, New York – the same town O. J. Simpson had lived in while he played for the Buffalo Bills – Kristen studied classical piano. She told her parents that when she grew up, she would like to play music for a living.

A straight-A student, Kristen attended Buffalo Academy of the Sacred Heart, a Catholic girls' school, and then Boston College. After having an abortion, she decided that she needed a change of city to make a fresh start. She enrolled in the University of Minnesota and decided to settle in Minneapolis, where she created computer graphics for a bank. "I still don't think she should have taken that job," her father said. "Kristen wasn't that qualified for it but she still decided to take it. She really wanted it to give her a steady income."

That's when she became a bass player. After seeing a local punk band at the Rogue Bar on Fifth Street, she went backstage and asked the bass player if he would give her lessons. A few months later, she met two young Minneapolis musicians, Joachim Breuer and Matt Entsminger, and formed a trio called Janitor Joe. The band's hard-edge rock quickly gained them recognition on the local circuit. It was difficult for Kristen to accept Hole's offer because Janitor Joe was one of the few bands able to break out of the Minneapolis scene and gain some national airplay. College stations around the country were playing their newly released seven-inch vinyl and the band had started to tour regularly. But Courtney was persuasive.

It didn't take long for Kristen to regret her decision to join Hole. From the moment she stepped foot in Seattle, she could not avoid the drugs that permeated the city's well-known rock scene. She also quickly became wary of Courtney and the people who surrounded her.

"At first she's really hard to figure out," she told her mother, Janet, a trucking company executive. "Courtney's really nice to you to your face, but if you do something that she doesn't agree with, she'll do something behind your back to make you look really bad."

"Seattle was not a good place for her," Janet Pfaff said in a 1994 interview. "She hated it there."

Kristen was introduced to heroin at Kurt and Courtney's University district home shortly after arriving in Seattle in 1993. Eric and Courtney even teased her that she was a "Minneapolis square" because she had never done hard drugs before. Eric would spend endless hours with her at her N.E. Harrison Street apartment doing drugs and lounging in bed. That winter Kristen decided that if she didn't do something soon, she would destroy her life. So she checked into a drug rehabilitation centre and decided to split with Eric, who was shattered. He constantly showed up unannounced at her apartment. But Kristen was determined to kick her bad habits and to start hanging around with more positive people."

"I care a lot about you but you're such a lowlife," she once told Eric, shortly before slamming her front door in his face. "Your whole life is a fake. Everything. The people you hang with, the drug dealers, Courtney... even your guitar playing. You're so good at fooling the crowd. If I were you, I'd take a few guitar lessons, otherwise you'll always know the truth and any musician who plays with you will know the truth."

Kristen became totally clean and started to enjoy life again. Although she continued to live in the drug-infested Capitol Hill area just a block away from Broadway Avenue's morass of drug dealers, she kept to herself and spent lots of time alone in her apartment reading bestsellers and watching old videos.

When Kurt's body was found in April, Kristen was devastated. Kurt had always had a soft spot for Kristen. "She's a fucking talented musician" he used to tell Dylan

Carlson. "She's also a beautiful soul. I think she's so beautiful, but if I ever told her that and Courtney found out, it would be hell."

Kristen spent weeks dealing with Kurt's death. She was traumatized and made the decision to leave Seattle and start over in Minneapolis. But her life seemed to be haunted by Courtney's power.

"She was terrified that Courtney would do something to screw up her decision," said Laura, a close friend of Kristen's who also lives in Capitol Hill. "But she had enough of all the shit on the scene. Ever since Kurt died, she said it was over. She didn't even want to tour to support Hole's new album. She had lost all respect for Courtney and Eric and all the rest of them."

After Kurt's death, Kristen phoned Joachim Breuer, her Janitor Joe bandmate, and told him she needed to get away. He invited her to do a small east coast tour with her old band. Kristen did not hesitate to accept the offer. While on tour with Janitor Joe, Kristen realized that it was in her best interest to leave the drug-crazed Seattle scene.

"Those people are all crazy," she told her friend Matt Entsminger. "They're never happy with anything in their lives. No matter what, they always have to bitch and drive other people crazy. Courtney's going to have a fit when she finds out, but I'm leaving. Let them find another idiot to play bass. I'm history."

Kristen phoned Courtney and told her of her decision. She explained that she was finished with Hole and the whole Seattle scene. Courtney told her, "You'll fade into oblivion. Go join your old band. You don't even deserve the chance I'm giving you because you don't appreciate it."

But behind the scenes, Courtney's attitude was vastly different. "That bitch is going to ruin everything," she told her bandmates.

Courtney was irked that Kristen made her decision

so close to the release of *Live Through This*. She told Eric that Kristen had "planned this all along, to fuck us over just when we're so close to reaching the top."

Kristen returned to Seattle on June 14. Immediately, she went to a supermarket on Broadway and carted off about eight big cardboard boxes. When she returned to her apartment, she started packing up her belongings. She packed the dresses from her closet, the albums she had brought with her from Minneapolis, the lamp she had bought at a Minneapolis antique shop, and everything else that still had meaning to her. But everything she had accumulated since moving to Seattle she threw into a green garbage bag: the press clippings, her prized porcelain teacup she had bought at a thrift store on Elliot Street, and anything else that she thought might remind her of the city.

On June 15, she loaded up a U-Haul and planned to leave the next morning. Paul Erickson, a member of the group Hammerhead, helped her and offered to sleep next to the U-Haul that night, to guard her stuff. Erickson was a good friend of Kristen's. He respected her musicanship and creativity. And he thought she was a lot of fun to hang out with.

After packing all day, the two had a light dinner and a couple of beers. Eric had called and begged Kristen to see him because he wanted to say goodbye in person. Kristen agreed. Meanwhile, Paul decided to take a stroll on Broadway and check out the scene that night.

Eric arrived just before eight p.m. The rest of the evening's events remain cloudy. A neighbour says she saw Eric leave at about eight-forty p.m. Paul Erickson checked in on Kristen at about nine p.m. and could hear her snoring in the bathtub. Kristen loved taking long, hot baths to help her unwind. She would read in the bathtub and even occasionally eat dinner while relaxing in the tub. "It was common for her to fall asleep in the tub," says her father. Paul knew Kristen liked to spend lots of time in the bath, so he didn't think anything about it. He decided to go to sleep because he knew they had a long drive ahead of them the next day. He went down to the U-Haul and crashed.

Paul woke up at about nine the next morning. He went to Broadway to use a phone booth so that he could call a friend in Minneapolis and tell them that he and Kristen would arrive within the next couple of days. It was a sunny morning and summer was in the air. On his way back from Broadway, Paul noticed the birds in the park across from Kristen's apartment. It was the same park where many of the Capitol Hill drug dealers did their business at night.

Paul opened the front door of Kristen's apartment. "Hey, Kristen," he shouted, as he closed the door behind him. "Let's go. Today's the big day. We finally leave Seattle." But Paul did not get a response. He thought maybe she had gone out to get some breakfast. "Kristen, are you here?" he shouted again. After getting no response again, he thought maybe she was in the bathroom. After knocking and getting no response, Paul discovered the bathroom door was locked.

"Kristen, are you in there?" he yelled. "Open up, it's Paul. We gotta get out of here. We have a big day ahead."

After still getting complete silence, Paul kicked down the door. He saw Kristen curled up in the nearly empty tub, with syringes and other drug paraphernalia in a purse on the floor.

Paul approached her and started tugging on her cold body. "Kristen, Kristen, wake up, wake up." Paul broke down and cried. He knew she was dead. He went to a phone booth around the corner and called 911. It was just like Janice, Jimi, and Kurt. Another rock star was dead. A closer parallel was Jim Morrison, who was also found dead in a bathtub, in Paris. Like Janice, Jimi, Kurt, and Jim, Kristen was only twenty-seven years old.

News of Kristen's death quickly spread around

Seattle and the music world. Her ex-bandmate Joachim Breuer was completely shocked. He had spoken to Kristen the evening of her death. "She was as chipper and happy as she'd ever been," he said. "She said she couldn't wait to get back to Minneapolis."

Kristen's passing spawned tales of yet another mysterious and unexpected death in Seattle's drug-plagued music scene. It also triggered rumours of murder, drugs, and intrigue.

The King County Medical Examiner's Office reported no signs of injuries or violence when they found Kristen's body. Medical examiner spokesman Bill McClure said that Kristen had died of "acute opiate intoxication." He refused to say whether the drug involved was heroin. McClure, however, did not conduct the autopsy. Curiously, that task was performed by Nicholas Hartshorne, the previously discussed friend of Courtney, who declared Kurt's death a suicide.

Norm Pfaff said he believed something was wrong. The police indicated that Kristen's death was drug related, but Pfaff said he believed that at that time his daughter was not involved with drugs.

That feeling was echoed by Hole's drummer, Patty Schemel, a close friend of Kristen's. She said she believed Kristen had not used drugs since being in rehab the previous winter. "It was an accident," Patty said. "Kristen loved life and this shouldn't have happened. She was an amazing musician and a very beautiful person."

Ed Rosenblatt, president of Hole's label, Geffen Records, quickly released a statement to the media. "This is all the more tragic because she had gone through a drug rehabilitation program this past winter," Rosenblatt said in his statement. "She was in the process of moving back to Minneapolis to be with old friends until the Hole tour resumed."

Tom Grant was immediately suspicious of Kristen's death.

"To be frank, I'm almost sure Kristen was murdered,"

he said at his Beverley Hills office. "Nobody leaves Courtney and gets away with it. It was another perfect setup. But just think for a moment, why would Kristen OD or commit suicide the night she was planning on leaving? She had packed all her things, there's no way she would do something that stupid."

"Courtney's the type of person who is really nice to you when you do everything she says," Grant continued. "But when you defy her, she's a monster."

Grant speculates that perhaps Kristen knew something about Kurt's death she wasn't supposed to know. Again, however, he supplies no concrete or even circumstantial evidence to back up this claim. If anybody had an opportunity to murder Kristen, it is her old boyfriend Eric Erlandson, who was the last person to see her alive, but what motive could he have had in helping Courtney kill her? Grant doesn't say, and it seems unlikely he would be involved in such a plot.

On what, then, does Grant base his suspicion of murder? "A number of things made me suspicious. I talked to Courtney about Kristen's death and she told me conflicting stories about things that had been going on that night. But what really aroused my suspicion was a conversation I had with someone who was also there earlier that night. He was highly suspicious and he had some information which conflicted with the official reports." Grant says the truth about Pfaff's death will inevitably come out when the Cobain case is reopened.

Courtney issued a statement to the press that read, "I'm deeply anguished over Kristen's death. We are obviously very shaken by the tragedies affecting the band in the last months but have decided to continue on."

After Kristen's body was returned to her hometown for burial a few days later, Geffen Records contacted the Pfaff family and said the members of Hole would like to attend the funeral. Janet Pfaff rejected the request. She said her family would like to forget that part of her daughter's life.

"I don't know what's going on in that Seattle scene," she said. "But there's something wrong, terribly wrong."

Kristen's death suddenly forced a closer look at another Seattle death that had occurred less than two weeks earlier.

In the early morning hours of June 4, Detective Antonio Terry was driving home from work on Seattle's Interstate 5. Terry was dressed in plain clothes and had just come off duty. He was driving past the Swift-Albro off-ramp when he noticed four young men on the side of the road waving for him to stop. Two of the youths were Eric Smiley, twenty-five, and Quentin Ervin, seventeen. Their car had broken down. Terry stopped his unmarked car and offered to help the youths. The rest of the story is very sketchy, but to this day the youths claim that Terry got out of his car with a gun in his hand and demanded to know why they had waved down his car.

The two young men claim an argument and gun battle ensued. Ervin was wounded. Terry was shot but still managed to drive to the South Precinct, less than two miles away. Three hours later, he was pronounced dead at Harborview Medical Center – the first member of the Seattle police force to be gunned down in more than ten years.

That morning there was a huge buzz in Seattle over the slaying. Although there is still no evidence, many people who claimed a murder conspiracy in the deaths of Kurt Cobain and Kristen Pfaff tried to link Terry as the third victim.

Antonio Terry had built up a good reputation in the Seattle community. It was common for him to often stop and offer citizens help. One man came to his funeral to pay his respects because Terry had once given him a lift home after he had missed the last bus of the evening. Norm Stamper, chief of Seattle police, called Terry "a man who had dedicated his life to community service."

Terry's relationship with the Cobains was cordial. Many people say that he would stop by their home when he patrolled the area just to check that things were all right. Terry knew the Cobains were famous and therefore could be the target of intruders.

But Terry's connection to the case stems from four lines of the Missing Persons Report filed by Courtney Love after Kurt escaped from the Exodus rehab.

The bottom four lines of the report read:

"Mr. Cobain ran away from California facility and flew back to Seattle. He also bought a shotgun and may be suicidal. Mr. Cobain may be at a location for narcotics. Det. Terry SPD/Narcotics has further info."

Tom Grant remembers driving up to the Carnation estate after Kurt's death and Courtney making a phone call to Detective Terry on the car phone. He didn't think anything of this incident until he learned about Terry's death two months later.

It is still unknown why Terry's name was on the report. Sources claim his name was there at Courtney's insistence because they knew each other. Courtney was in California and thought that if a cop would have to answer to the press about Kurt's whereabouts, the only person she trusted was Terry.

Eric Smiley and Quentin Ervin were brought to trial for aggravated murder. The trial proved controversial because the defendants' lawyers claimed they were acting in self defence and that Terry's time sheet was altered after his death.

The defence attorneys claimed Terry's overtime records were changed to help the prosecutors' claim that the detective was on duty when he was shot. Killing an on duty police officer results in life imprisonment upon conviction in Washington State. The State Patrol Crime Lab analysed the time sheet and concluded it had indeed been altered in at least six places. Although this has no major bearing on the question of whether Terry was murdered, it illustrates the potential corruption of the Seattle Police Department and does little to help the department's credibility in the Cobain case.

When Terry drove to the precinct after being shot, a fellow officer claimed that the slain officer told him that one of the people in the shootings said, "He's a cop." Because Terry looked like a normal person in his off-duty clothes, it has never been determined how the suspect might have recognized him. However, if one of the suspects knew him, that could have been an indication that he was set up to be murdered.

Tom Grant is skeptical that Terry's death was a murder because of the unlikely chain of events. But he doesn't completely rule it out.

"I'm almost sure Kurt and Kristen were murdered," he says. "But the Terry case is a bit suspect. It most likely is a strange coincidence, but then again, what are the odds that the only police officer in Seattle to be murdered in years happens to be connected to the death of Kurt Cobain?"

11
"How Can I Go On?"

One day, a week after the near-fatal overdose in Rome, Kurt received a letter from a distraught ten-year-old boy. It read, "If you die, how can I go on?"

Kurt never liked being called the voice of his generation or the disciples which came with that role. "Why don't they get a life and stop worshipping me?" he would often ask.

Suddenly, after his death, there seemed to be a generation of youth expressing similar sentiments while parents, teachers, psychologists, and even suicide prevention professionals were at a complete loss to explain the phenomenon. Cobain's tragic ending inspired at least sixty-eight youngsters to take their own lives.

What was it about the death of this unkempt rock musician which could spark such an intense emotional reaction in so many kids? Something in Kurt's tortured, angst-ridden lyrics seemed to speak directly to the increasing disenchantment of the so-called Generation X, almost like a hidden code decipherable only to those whose troubled youth and cynical worldview paralleled Kurt's own. While he was alive, they devoured his music and his message, which, contrary to conventional wisdom, wasn't always one of despair. In 1992, he urged American youth to vote for Bill Clinton – saying he admired the politician's ideals – and they did, in record numbers.

Many teenagers said that, for them, Kurt and Nirvana's music represented hope for their generation.

"He was like my guru. I felt like he was leading me to something better;" said one fourteen-year-old boy, echoing the *Los Angeles Times* description of Kurt as "an awakening voice for a new generation." These teenagers had finally found a voice in a world dominated by baby boomers. And even though that voice reflected their angst, its very existence seemed to represent hope.

For millions of his followers, then, news of Kurt's suicide instantly shattered that hope. It was as if Kurt were telling them, "Why bother?" or, more appropriately, "Nevermind."

The tragic story of a Canadian teenager, Bobby Steele – poignantly profiled by David Staples in the *Edmonton Journal* – may serve as a barometer of the effect Kurt had on many of his fans.

Bobby's father was a major in the Canadian Air Force. The family – which also included Bobby's mother; Agnes, and his younger sister, Sharon – would follow him around the world from base to base. Every year or so a new assignment, new home, new school. It was hard to make and keep friends. When Bobby first heard Nirvana's *Nevermind*, he was sixteen. Something in the lyrics spoke to him. Kurt became his friend. He bought everything related to the group: posters, bootleg performances, rough tapes.

In July 1993 the Steeles were forced to move once

again – from Lahr, Germany, to a suburb of Edmonton. One more time, Bobby's life was uprooted. In September, when he turned eighteen, his parents bought him a computer. Now he had a new friend. At every spare moment, Bobby would use the modem to access newsgroups, bulletin boards, and chat rooms to talk about Nirvana with other enthusiasts who shared his passion. His passwords were "Cobain" or "NirvanaNirvana or "Bleach." Bobby would shut himself in his room, staying online into the early morning, Nirvana's anthems of alienation blaring from his headphones.

Sometimes he would ask his mother to listen to a Nirvana song, but they were too loud for her and she couldn't understand the lyrics, even when her son explained them.

Bobby said that he admired Cobain because the singer stood up for losers and nerds, for women who were raped, and for gays and lesbians. Bobby had dated girls for years, but now he started to explore his sexuality. In November, he started dating a twenty-five-year-old Native named Guy from a nearby reserve. In January, Guy left him for an old boyfriend.

On April 8, Bobby turned on the radio and learned that Kurt Cobain had just killed himself with a shotgun. He went down to the basement picked up a guitar, and wept as he thrashed away on the instrument for hours. The next day, he told several friends that Cobain was selfish, that he had thrown his talent away. "I would never do anything like that."

But he also had a friend named Connie who worked with him at an A&W restaurant. They would talk for hours on the phone every night during the week of Cobain's death. Bobby told her he wanted to kill himself, he just didn't know where or when. Connie tried to talk him out of it, to convince him that suicide was the coward's way out. She begged him to think of what it would do to everybody who cares about him.

Bobby started to enter his thoughts into a diary.

On April 13, five days after Kurt's body was discovered, he wrote a poem called "My Will":

Shoot the mouth and make it dumb
Shoot the brain and keep it numb
A kill me will
A kill me pill

The same day, Bobby wrote a short essay:

Often I think of trying my hardest to become famous and in my peak year of success (2003) die the same way Kurt Cobain died.
I feel I owe it to him, my life I mean, for being such an influence to my own. There is only so much I can do to let him know I really appreciated him. I can't wait to see him in heaven. Oh and if he's not there I'll be so pissed off....
I really hope that I get to meet him. Sure I have feelings for my family (who I think will go to heaven) but it seems I felt more love to a man I didn't even know than to my family....
I wish so much that I could put my words to music, but I lack the talent. Hopefully, I'll become better in practice, but for now I have very monotone music. And this is another thing. I need a band. I can't do a one man band for a career.

He applied to take computer courses at a nearby technical institute, but he was colour-blind and was told he wouldn't be able to distinguish the colours on computer chips. This prompted him to write a poem in his diary:

Rainbows are hard to find
When your eyes are colorless and blind
But please don't take my dreams away
from me.

A few weeks later, Bobby's father gathered the family together in the living room and told them about the suicide of a young man named Greg – a friend of the family – who had taken his life by locking himself in his car with the engine running, dying by carbon monoxide poisoning.

"Will you promise me you will never do anything like that?" their worried father asked his kids.

"No, Dad," Bobby replied. "I promise I would never do that." His father was relieved. He turned to sixteen-year-old Sharon.

"Sorry, Dad, I can't promise you because I've been depressed myself. I'm not going to make you a promise and then break it."

Major Steele exploded, "You make me sick with that comment. I hope you never do that."

That evening, Bobby talked to his sister about Greg's suicide. "Do you think he killed himself because of Kurt Cobain?" he asked.

"I don't know," she answered. "The chances are really high."

"Do you think he killed himself because he was gay or something?"

"Perhaps. Maybe that was a problem."

In the beginning of June, nineteen days before his high school graduation, Bobby suddenly quit school. When his mother found out, she forced him to return, driving him there every day.

On June 29, according to the *Edmonton Journal*, Bobby logged on to the Internet and entered his favourite chat room, where he discussed with another Nirvana fan the muffled lyrics to a song called "Endless Nameless." According to Bobby, Cobain always claimed he couldn't remember exactly what he was yelling in that song but it was probably "I can do" or "I think I can." Bobby, however, was convinced he was yelling something else. "It sounds like he is saying something like, 'Fire! Fire! Inside of me is Fire!

Imagining that... I am... deaf!' Something like that... but I REALLY don't know."

The next day, Bobby went for a job interview at a local Radio Shack. Because of his extensive computer knowledge, he beat out nine other candidates. He joined his friends Donovan and Wade at his favourite hangout, the Boystown Cafe, ecstatic about getting the job. His joy was tempered when Donovan started talking about a friend who was de-pressed because he didn't know what he wanted out of life.

When Donovan stopped talking about the friend, Bobby said, "I guess I'm going to go home now and blow my brains out." Wade and Donovan thought he was joking.

For the approaching Canada Day holiday weekend, the Steele family had made plans to visit Bobby's aunt in Fox Creek, Alberta. Bobby couldn't go because of his work.

On July 1, the family packed up the car and got ready to leave. Bobby was sleeping late, so his mother left him a note: "Please eat lots of food. Create yourself some fantastic meals. Love, Mom and Dad. P.S. Dishwasher can be unloaded. Love, Mom."

Before she left, Agnes wrapped a twenty-dollar bill around a second note and went into Bobby's room to put it in his wallet. "Enjoy the $20," the note read. "I thought I'd give you a pleasant surprise. Have fun. Don't forget to make yourself some meals. It will be like having your own apartment. Love, Mom."

When Bobby woke up, he got together with his old boyfriend Guy. The two ordered pizza, drank a six-pack of beer, and watched a video at Bobby's house. Guy left. At ten p.m., Bobby received a call from his friend Steve, who invited him over to watch a movie.

"No, I kind of feel like staying home," Bobby told him. He sounded bummed out, according to Steve, who asked him, "Are you okay?"

"Yeah, I'm fine. I just kind of feel like being at home."

Later that night, Bobby went downstairs to the basement, where his father kept four guns. Bobby picked up a 12-gauge shotgun and headed upstairs to his parents' room. In his father's dresser, he found three 12-gauge shells. He loaded the shotgun.

In the kitchen, he found the note his mother had left for him that morning. Over her message, he wrote, "Bye! I love you."

He took the gun to his room. He was wearing a black baseball cap, jeans, a Nirvana "Sliver" T-shirt, and a yellow and black plaid shirt.

On his stereo, he put on Nirvana's "Endless Nameless" – the song with the indecipherable lyrics – and hit the Repeat Play button.

Dave Staples of the *Journal* described the scene. "It was one of the group's most disturbing songs," he wrote. "Distorted guitar thrashed like a race car engine, then the guitars wailed like sirens at a death camp. Cobain's enraged, slurred words boiled out of the pit of his burning, nauseous stomach: 'Fire! Fire! Inside of me! Fire! Imagining that I am deaf!'"

Shortly after midnight, Bobby opened a file on his computer, but he seems to have abandoned it in favour of his little black diary, in which he started writing:

> July 94. I just can't live anymore. If you just think a lot, you just stop knowing that life has a purpose. I don't know what I want anymore. I just don't feel anymore. I fed the pets. I feel like total shit. I am not intoxicated or high... I just feel bad. It's been the most painful 84 days in my life [authors' note: it had been eighty-four days since Kurt's body was found]. I'm not happy... Never was. Never will be. I lack the strength. There is nothing left for me. Just nothing. I don't understand computers or music... I just wasn't meant to live here and now. I think... I don't think anymore. I'm dead... and nothing is left. There is really no explanation for what I did or even an excuse. I'm just morbid.... So I guess I just

> should be dead. Everything goes to whoever gets it first.... I DON'T care. I just need time by myself. Alone in the afterworld. I just can't live anymore... I'm dead. Say bye to everyone for me and also cremate me and prop me up on the fireplace by the propeller. This is my only last wish.

At the end, he added a reference from Cobain's purported suicide note, a quote from a Neil Young song. Cobain had written: "So remember, it's better to burn out than fade away." Instead, Bobby wrote: "It's better not to spark at all. Rob Steele."

After he signed the note, he used a Polaroid camera to take a self-portrait of the top half of his face with a Cobain poster in the background. Then he took another picture, reclining on his bed with Nirvana's *In Utero* CD above his head. He lined up the photos on his bed, perhaps because newspapers had mistakenly reported that Cobain had taken out his driver's license photo before he shot himself so that he could be identified.

He grabbed the shotgun, then positioned himself on the floor so that when he was found, it would look to anybody entering the room exactly like the famous photo of Cobain's death scene.

The same Nirvana song blared out from the stereo "Fire! Inside of me is fire!" Bobby positioned the gun in his mouth and felt the trigger. "Imagining that... I am... deaf!"

He squeezed the trigger.

Not every teenager affected by Kurt's death chose the route of Bobby Steele, although according to the volunteers staffing suicide hotlines, tens of thousands considered it. Some chose other, less extreme ways of venting their grief many in cyberspace.

Within days of Kurt's death, an online "e.zine" called "Kurt Is Dead" sprang up on the Internet's World Wide Web soliciting comments from Kurt's fans about his death. Hundreds responded. This outpouring contains some very eloquent answers to the questions music journalists and parents have grappled with unsuccessfully since Kurt died: Why was he so important to a generation? Why did they choose him as their voice? The results are as revealing about the generation as about Kurt himself.

Thomas Leavitt from Minneapolis was the first to post his thoughts, and his comments are representative of many others:

> Kurt Cobain's music reached right into the core of my consciousness and YANKED... it expressed the primal scream that echoes at the edge of my consciousness whenever I deal with the insanity of the world. The music always seemed to teeter on the abyss... there was a quality of suspension to it. Over the past few years, I've felt like I was running on empty.. like I was Wile E. Coyote, kept from falling only by my own inertia, held up only by my lack of recognition that I'd had the ground yanked out from underneath me ... much like the situation of my own generation. We're all wandering around, carrying big dreams, big hopes, while we scrounge for work, juggle two, three part-time jobs, and curse the obstacle course and barriers that seem to spring out of nowhere.
>
> Dammit. Kurt and his music were ANGRY, FUCKED UP CONFUSED, full of inchoate rage, bitterness, despair... driven by intense, slurred, blurred guitar riffs and bizarre, random lyrics. HE may not have spoken for my generation, but he spoke for me, and a lot of others I suspect... and his end, in a way, is quite fitting. Ultimately, he just couldn't deal with all the pain, the stress, the chaos and just totally freaked out and killed himself. Just as with River Phoenix, my initial reaction was: "That stupid fuck. Goddammit, why'd you have to go and do that, man?" (Kinda

> pleading bewilderment here.) Man... shit. (Anger at the absurdity of the world.)

A teenager named Peter wrote:

> What made him do it?
> He had a family and was a success blah, blah, blah. Well I can tell you that he probably got sick of this sick and festering disease of a world we live in. His death might not achieve too much, but it is an act that represents well our generation. It is not an avocation for suicide but more like a sign of our time. It's sad when we see an icon of our generation go like this. Its sadder to think that this was his last statement to the world: one of hopelessness. It's up to us to not let it go unnoticed.

Meanwhile, teenage fans weren't the only ones touched by Kurt's death. Fellow musicians from all spectrums of the music scene weighed in with their own thoughts.

Bruce Springsteen was one of the first. He told an interviewer: "I think he had a connection to his audience that was very, very deep. His music is powerful, very intense. That sort of power is rare. You hate to lose somebody like that, someone who keeps the music alive and moving ahead. Not many guys like him come along."

Rolling Stones guitarist Keith Richards, who had kicked his own heroin habit years before, seemed less sympathetic and blasted those around Kurt: "I figured he was in the wrong business. What's so tough about being lead singer in one of the biggest rock 'n' roll bands in the world? You just deal with it.... After the cat tried to off himself in Rome, I was surprised that the people who were supposed to be taking care of him let him buy a shotgun and mope around for days. They knew he barely escaped doing himself in already."

Singer-poet Leonard Cohen was always one of Kurt's idols. In the Nirvana song "Pennyroyal Tea," Kurt had written, "Give me Leonard Cohen afterworld / So I can sigh eternally." Cohen told the online magazine *Addicted to Noise* that he wished he had had the chance to speak with Cobain before his death; he would have tried to help the troubled star, perhaps by introducing him to the small Zen community on Mount Baldy, north of L.A., where Cohen now lived, working as cook and personal assistant to a Zen master.

"I'm sorry I couldn't have spoken to the young man," Cohen said, recognizing some of his own past excesses in Cobain's downfall. "I see a lot of people at the Zen Center who have gone through drugs and found a way out that is not just Sunday school. There are always alternatives, and I might have been able to lay something on him. Or maybe not."

Not everybody welcomed the universal eulogizing of a dead heroin addict. The Sunday after Kurt's death, TV commentator Andy Rooney angered many fans when he opined on *60 Minutes* that all the praise for Kurt was misplaced. "When the spokesman for his generation blows his head off" he said, "what is the generation supposed to think?... If Kurt Cobain applied the same thought process to his music that he applied to his drug-congested life, it's reasonable for a reasonable person to think that his music may not have made much sense either."

Right-wing radio-talk-show host Rush Limbaugh was less philosophical. "Kurt Cobain was, ladies and gentlemen, he was a worthless shred of human debris, who had been trying to kill himself for twelve years, and finally did it right, by using a shotgun, so he couldn't miss." His words were heard in millions of American homes, presumably by people who had never even heard of Kurt Cobain.

But even some in the music scene refused to join in the industry's rush to immortalize Kurt. "He died a coward," hissed one Seattle DJ, "and left a little girl without a father."

As the tributes and recriminations poured in, Kurt's death continued to cast a long shadow around the world. In November 1994, a nineteen-year-old British teenager named Jamie Petrolini murdered a London taxi driver. From his jail cell, he wrote a letter to the rock weekly *Melody Maker* explaining his actions:

"I was really lonely at school. This fact was really getting to me, so I failed my A-Levels. I went to college in Oxford to re-sit and I was really stressed and well, I suppose vulnerable.... I say I know how Kurt Cobain felt.... Please understand.... Please help. I don't want to end up like Kurt."

That same week, a sixteen-year-old schoolgirl in Dublin killed herself with a shotgun, leaving a note explaining she had "done it for Kurt."

A week later, a twenty-year-old California student named Gaston Senac was reenacting Kurt's death for some friends. He took a 12-gauge shotgun, propped it on the floor, knelt with his mouth over the barrel, and said, "Look, I'm just like Kurt Cobain." At that moment, the gun accidentally went off, killing him instantly.

In January an eleven-year-old boy from Quebec – which holds the unpleasant dual distinction of having the world's highest teen suicide rate and the highest rate of Kurt Cobain copycat suicides – was found hanged in the basement of his family home in Ile d'Orleans. At his feet, his father found a note reading, "I'm killing myself for Kurt." His mother, Hugnette, charged, "That singer stole him from us," and in the death notice she placed in the local paper, she pleaded for other children not to listen to the "negative music" of Nirvana.

Around this time, Kurt's mother, Wendy O'Connor, became alarmed at all the reports of copycat suicides and decided to give her first real interview since Kurt's death to *Entertainment Weekly* magazine, believing it would be cathartic to his fans:

> Kurt's problems were ongoing, and we struggled with them for years. I talked him through so many nights. He was probably a mis-or undiagnosed depressive, which runs in my family. My grandfather, I would say, died from that, 'cause he tried to commit suicide and eventually died from the injuries. Also, manic-depression is a progressive disease. Once you get past a certain stage it's almost unmanageable, even with antidepressants. I now know in hindsight that the sleeping he was doing in his teenage years was the very beginning of it. He was sleeping so much, but that was also masked by just being a teenager. But now I look back and go, "Ah-ha, that was the very beginning of it."...
>
> People have asked me, aren't you angry at Kurt for taking such a cheap way out, for leaving Frances and you, and I said no, not at all. People don't understand what depression is. The way I explain it is, have you ever been hit in the stomach and lost your breath? It's a horrible panicky situation. Can you imagine being in that state of mind, in that state of anxiety and fear for years? He was a wonderful person, but he just couldn't stand the pain anymore. That's why I'm not angry at Kurt.

Soon after, an Associated Press report hit the wires. It began with the headline "Parishioners Find Nirvana at the Church of Cobain." The AP story described the establishment in Portland, Oregon, of a fledgling church for disaffected youth which has chosen Kurt Cobain as its patron saint. It quoted the founder and pastor, Jim Dillon, as saying he got the idea from a church in San Francisco that incorporates the music of jazz legend John Coltrane into its services. Instead of playing "Amazing Grace" on an organ, the Church of Kurt Cobain would blast "Smells Like Teen Spirit." Dillon explained his sermons would be based on songs from

Nirvana. For example, he cited the song "Rape Me," which he explained is really about brotherly love.

Hundreds of newspapers around the world picked up the wire story about the Church of Kurt Cobain. When Charles Cross, editor of the Seattle music weekly the *Rocket* was asked about the church, he was outraged, saying Cobain would have been offended by the whole idea.

"This was someone who very clearly in his life was not someone who wanted to be held above his fans or worshiped," he wrote. "This may be a sign that our culture as we know it is coming to an end, or people can find spirituality in anything."

Two weeks later, it was revealed that the story was a hoax and that the church didn't actually exist.

Slightly more bizarre was a story which had been circulating around the Seattle music scene for some time after Kurt's death. In December 1994, a number of news organizations received a faxed press release by a group calling itself "Friends Understanding Kurt." In it, Steve Newman, the group's spokesperson, laid the blame for Kurt's suicide on a device called the "Dream Machine."

The group charged that in the last months of Cobain's life, he acquired the device from his old collaborator William S. Burroughs. The Dream Machine, wrote Newman, is "a dangerous trance-inducing contraption," and he claimed there had been a "string of suicides associated with the machine since the sixties."

Furthermore, he claimed, it was in fact, the catalyst in Kurt's unbelievably tragic, untimely death. To this day Courtney ponders whether the Dream Machine is really responsible for Kurt's death.... If Kurt had not come into contact with its manufacturer, he would be with us today."

The Dream Machine, according to *High Times* magazine, consists of:

a cardboard cylinder with holes in it attached to a

record-player turntable, in the middle of which sits a 100-watt light bulb. When the machine is turned on, the cylinder spins at 78 rpm. Subjects sit in front of the cylinder and close their eyes, and the light coming through the holes in the spinning cylinder reflects on the eyelids. The resulting flashes of light may, if the subjects are susceptible, create a mild sensation akin to the effect of the simplest light show. Aided by the inhalation of good pot and the sound of hot rock, the device might create at best a mild dreamlike sensation, or at worst (unless you're prone to epileptic seizures) an even milder headache. It's an adaptation of flicker technology, first seen with strobe lights and now packaged as brain machines.

In fact, Burroughs had been associated with popularizing the device during the eighties. He once said about the Dream Machine, "Subjects report dazzling lights and unearthly brilliance and color.... Elaborate geometric constructions of incredible intricacy build up from multidimensional mosaic into living fireballs like the mandalas of Eastern Mysticism or resolve momentarily into apparently individual images and powerfully dramatic scenes like brightly colored dreams."

The Friends Understanding Kurt press release goes on to state that a Dream Machine was found in the room with Kurt when he died and this is what drove him to his suicide. But the police report clearly contradicts this, as does the medical examiner, who said no such device was found.

In 1994, the San Francisco magazine *SOMA* located Steve Newman and, in a story headlined the "Dream Machine Hoax," he revealed that Friends Understanding Kurt consisted of himself, Courtney Love (who he said played more of a "low-key role" in the group), and Courtney's attorney Celeste Mitchell as well as other friends of Kurt. He insists that Kurt used the Dream Machine up to seventy-two hours at a time and it drove him to his suicide. The magazine dismissed the story and noted the acronym of the group (FUK).

Tom Grant seized on Courtney's role in the Dream Machine hoax to illustrate her desperation. "It all happened when the murder theory first started to circulate and she needed to get people believing it was a suicide," he said. "So she concocted this ridiculous story, made up a phony organization, and got this guy to front for her. The worst thing is that I've seen kids say, 'Of course he committed suicide. It was all because of that Dream Machine.'"

Soon after she helped spread the story of the Dream Machine to reinforce perception of Kurt's suicidal tendencies, Courtney was interviewed by David Fricke of *Rolling Stone* magazine in December, 1994. Since his death she had frequently stated that Kurt kept guns in the house because he was contemplating suicide. Fricke mentioned that Kurt had told him he actually kept guns for target practice, prompting Courtney to respond, "He totally fucking lied to you. He never went shooting in his life." But Dylan Carlson told us, "I don't know why she would say that. Me and Kurt went shooting all the time. He loved to shoot, not animals, just targets and cans and stuff. Courtney didn't like it but she knew about it." Indeed, Kurt talks about going shooting with Carlson in Michael Azzerad's book *Come as You Are*. Tom Grant believes Courtney's comments were another part of her ongoing effort to rewrite history in support of the suicide verdict.

Unfortunately, lost among all the psychological analysis, conspiracy theories, and recriminations over drug use, one supremely important fact has been overshadowed during the past four years. With Kurt's death, the world lost one of the great musical talents of his generation.

12
"Life After Kurt"

After a turbulent year, the deaths of Kurt and Kristen behind them, Hole is in the midst of another tour, storming from city to city on their lusty, groupie-dogged trail. Courtney seems to possess more energy, passion, and rebellion than ever. She is also undergoing a complete metamorphosis of her persona, orchestrated by New York's PMK agency, the renowned publicity firm her lawyers hired at $15,000 a month to revamp her image. But Courtney is more controversial than ever before.

The tour has moved to Vancouver. The last time Hole appeared in Vancouver – a town Courtney describes as having "really great-looking whores" – she stormed offstage after playing just a few songs. She was pissed off that the crowd seemed to be ignoring Hole's set. But on this night, the scene has changed dramatically. There are roadies, managers, and music industry VIPS catering to Courtney's every whim. The crowd is full of teenage girls who have come to see the woman they revere. And there is a new member on bass – Melissa Auf der Maur from Montreal, who was recommended by Billy Corgan after Kristen's death.

Courtney is in fine form for her fifth concert in six nights. Several hundred screaming fans have been turned away from the downtown club. Courtney says she prefers to play smaller venues, claiming, "I don't want the O. J. Simpson people attending my shows," although music insiders claim her fan base is limited and she could never fill the larger arenas and stadiums as Nirvana did. Midway through her set, she dives into the crowd and performs the traditional grunge show body-surfing exhibition.

As she is passed from fan to fan, men begin putting their hands under her dress. Her underwear is ripped, followed by her dress, before she returns nearly naked to the stage. (She later describes the experience as "rape.") Incidents like this are beginning to earn her headlines on her own terms, rather than as the tragic widow of a rock legend.

On and offstage, Courtney Love seems to have become a victim of her own success. Once she was a rocker who drew her lyrics and emotional power from the gritty traditions of punk rock. Now she appears to be trapped in creature comforts. Her lyrics of love, hate, suffering, and redemption seems to be premeditated by the pressure put on her by Geffen Records to succumb to a more commercial presentation. Her show, with its army of technicians, seems as fixed and rehearsed as the Ziegfeld Follies. The focus at a Hole show has clearly switched from the performance to raucous partying in the audience. It's obvious her managers and record company handlers have sanitized and repackaged the band's previously raw image, stripping them of their unruly free will – but not against the will of the band's leader.

Literally from the day Kurt died, Courtney immersed herself in promoting her music career. She became a slave to her audience, with its smug hedonism and short attention span and hunger for another outrageous Courtney Love incident.

Live Through This came out the Tuesday after Kurt's death and quickly sold out in some record stores. The day after Kurt's death, Courtney decided to grant an interview to MTV's Tabitha Soren. She used the opportunity to plug her forthcoming album "How's that for sick?" she asked. Instead of going into a deep depression or becoming more reclusive, she gave interviews to numerous representatives of the media within days of her husband's death. She seemed to jump at the chance to talk about Kurt even if the interviewer did not mention him first, prompting accusations that she was exploiting the tragedy to further her own career. Her friends, however, say the interviews were "cathartic." In these interviews, she spoke of Kurt's problems at length. "Kurt would have wanted me to talk about all the private details," she told one interviewer.

Courtney was becoming a money machine first and an artist second. She wasted no opportunity to give forth about Kurt's death, according to the growing legion of Courtney's critics.

"Her husband's dead less than a day and she decides to go on MTV to talk about it," says her father. "Courtney knew it was the opportunity of a lifetime. A new album coming out and her famous husband is found dead. There's not one media outlet in the world that did not want to get in a word with Courtney, and she knew it. She also did anything she could to make sure that they would all be granted their interview requests."

When the album was released, its quality surprised many people, and it received glowing reviews from most of the music press. The release was named top album of the year in a *Rolling Stone* readers' poll. Its catchy rhythms prompted some skeptics to charge that Kurt had probably written the musical bridges, a claim Courtney has never denied. Still, the album proved that Courtney had genuine talent and was not simply coasting on her husband's name. Nobody criticizes Elvis, Diana Ross, or Frank Sinatra because they didn't write their own music, but the Courtney-bashers seem to seize on any excuse.

Not long before, Courtney was determined to live the life of a struggling artist. She read poetry, studied Buddhism, did excessive amounts of drugs, and drew psychedelic visions in watercolors. But now she seemed more concerned with enhancing her fortune than her spiritual development as she drove around in a chauffeured limousine buying expensive clothes and dining with music industry executives.

"When Kurt died, Courtney immediately tried to get as much power as she could right away," says Harrison. "She inherited Kurt's percentage of Nirvana, which was worth millions of dollars, and she was determined to add to the fortune. You'd never know that she had just been widowed. There certainly wasn't any long mourning period."

Seattle DJ Marco Collins, Courtney's longtime friend, dismisses this kind of criticism. "She really needed to get busy," he says, "to forget the emotional abyss caused by Kurt's death."

One of the ways Courtney got busy was on the Internet. Ever since her father showed her his Powerbook and explained the basics of the Net in 1993, Courtney sensed the possibilities for expressing herself on this new medium. In the summer of 1994, she got herself an America Online account, chose the screen name BRRRKNSTOCK and plunged right into the fray. Her first posting was rather timid:

I am thinking heavily of trying Prozac.... I

> would appreciate info from intense, passionate, sexual (hetero, generally) and esp. CREATIVE females regarding this drug.... I'm NOT clinically depressed. I'm not even manic-depressive, just super neurotic and paranoid.

From then on, she took to her new toy with a passion she had heretofore reserved only for her music and her drugs. At first, her postings were anonymous, but eventually users caught on that it was Courtney and thousands waited anxiously for her trademark rambling posts, which could hold forth on subjects as mundane as the taxation of women's razors ("hmm... let's see, men's razors are not taxed – they are a necessity, women's razors are – they are a luxury. hmm, if I don't shave my legs i am a burning butch dyke outside of the main in patriarchal eyes...") and as personal as bashing her father ("remember BIODAD? well I happen to know his name as he is part of my conception and not even his NAME was true").

Sometimes she would log on late at night to publicly obsess about the woman she suspected was having an affair with Kurt when he died:

> She only sells speedballs and only to people in bands – she preys on the bipolar depressives AND the highly motivated, talented, pretty and genius alike. i would love the cops to pop her. i only call them hysterically every day (of course there's a needle hanging out of my butt 24-7 generally) but when I do find the time, I give them a jingle.

She seemed to take the greatest delight slagging her enemies like Trent Reznor of Nine Inch Nails over the Net ("well, Trent just wants to fuck us like an animal....) Occasionally, one of her posts would get her into trouble and she would have to claim it was a fraudulent message. The most infamous of these was the night she wrote about Dave Grohl, who had privately broken his silence and was venting to friends his feelings about Courtney. In the disputed post, she reveals that Grohl, who is referred to as "Dave Iscariot," had joined Pearl Jam (a group Kurt hated) but that Courtney didn't care because Kurt wasn't on speaking terms with the Nirvana drummer for over a year and that he didn't even call after the Rome overdose. "I'll be yer fuckin Yoko nightmare you fucking traitor," the Post declared.

As it turned out, Dave had been negotiating to join Pearl Jam around this time but in the end decided to form his own band. According to Dylan Carlson, Courtney did sometimes refer to Grohl as Dave Iscariot and constantly called him a traitor to Kurt after the dispute over *Nevermind* royalties. As well, it was Dave who began calling Courtney "Yoko." So many believe this is an authentic post, despite Courtney's denials.

Courtney, however, readily admits that she posted regularly to the Internet. "For a while, I was really addicted to it," she told *Spin*. "It was like my only friend. I just couldn't deal with humans. I was dealing with these cyberbeings, and having these inane conversations, banal conversations, crazy conversations, dealing-with-grief conversations with peo-ple from fucking God knows where who looked like God-knows-what." These online conversations are incredibly revealing about Courtney's psyche during this period.

For years, growing numbers of Seattle residents had recognized Courtney's unmistakable presence and trademark look wherever she went. But ever since Kurt's death, people no longer spotted her rummaging through flea markets and grunge stores in Seattle for plaids and prints to be worn together. Instead, she was frequently spotted shopping at the most expensive boutiques, something she had never done when Kurt was around. When Kurt was alive, the two were a fixture at the cheapest secondhand clothing stores, and Courtney took great delight in spending all night snipping and stitching, concocting skirts and jackets and imbuing all of them with a decidedly grunge flavor.

"She seemed to have forgotten all of Kurt's values," says Michael Hornburg, a former boyfriend of Courtney's when she lived in Portland, who in 1995 wrote a thinly disguised and unflattering novel called *Bongwater* about his time with her. "Maybe she was spending all that money to ease the pain of his death. But it's certain her lifestyle changed the day he died."

For a time, Courtney continued her riot grrrl image, at least in public. With the help of PMK, she became one of the world's most photographed entertainers. She would model cinched-waist dresses and incandescent red lipstick and heavy black boots. She also seemed to welcome the image of being deliberately dowdy to challenge the cultural expectation that women should be pretty.

Rumours about her love life started to circulate only days after Kurt died. Three weeks after his body was found, she checked into an Arizona health spa with her ex-flame Billy Corgan. The two spent several days at the Health Ranch and appeared to be, according to a Ranch employee, "on a honeymoon."

"I couldn't refuse Billy because he helped me get through everything," she told Tom Grant on the telephone from the spa – a tape he plays to confirm the story. "Billy's so nice; What am I supposed to do? It feels right."

She also got involved for a time with Trent Reznor of Nine Inch Nails. After he dumped her, she told the media his band should be renamed "Three Inch Nails" and constantly bad-mouthed Reznor on tour. This prompted him to complain to *New Musical Express*, "I didn't want to be her boyfriend and now she harasses me at any point she can. I haven't done or said anything else but she keeps blowing her fucking mouth at shows.... I guess I just have to wait for her to find something new to obsess upon."

Some tabloids also linked Courtney to film star Brad Pitt, and one even showed her in bed kissing the Lemonheads' Evan Dando, whom Kurt had constantly bad-mouthed during Nirvana's final tour.

In November, Courtney was seen running down L.A.'s Sunset Boulevard barefoot chasing indie folk singer Mary Lou Lord, who used to date Kurt in Olympia. Lord had showed up at an after-hours Hole party where Courtney was holding court for a number of celebrities including Lollapalooza founder Perry Farrell and actor Danny DeVito. When Courtney saw Lord, she went up to her and tried to push her, prompting Kurt's old girlfriend to run away, with Courtney chasing her, yelling, "I'm gonna kill you." Eventually, Lord flagged down a car and got away, although Courtney would later claim she found her hiding in a dumpster.

"There are five people in this world that if I ever run into I will fucking kill," Love said at the time, "and she is definitely one of them." Lord has declined to comment on either Cobain or Love.

Nobody knows what prompted the outburst, but a magazine called *The Nose* reported Courtney had started doing hard drugs again after she left a bent, burnt spoon – used for melting heroin – in the bathroom of a San Francisco eatery. In *Rolling Stone's* year-end issue, she admitted, "I take Valiums. Percodans... I have used heroin – after Kurt died."

Two years earlier, when Kurt was still alive, Lord had aroused Courtney's ire when the *Boston Phoenix* wrote a profile of Kurt and mentioned in passing that he had once dated Lord. The newspaper received two faxed letters signed by Kurt, but according to biographer Melissa Rossi, the bulk of each letter appeared to be in Courtney's handwriting, a fact confirmed by *Phoenix* writer Brett Milano, who wrote about the faxes. The first letter called Lord a "creepy girl," noting "I can't remember what happened, but it wasn't much" and added "now my life is plagued by this insane girl." The second letter had Kurt claiming he didn't even remember Mary Lou's name or face.

Rossi reported that Courtney later phoned Lord and threatened, "I'm gonna cut off your head and shove it up your ass – and Kurt's gonna throw you in the oven." In between the two incidents, Lord was inexplicably invited by Courtney to attend Kurt's memorial service.

Then, in January 1995, another incident fueled the media frenzy. Hole was on a tour of New Zealand and Australia when Courtney got involved in a midair mêlée. According to witnesses, she was in a drunken state in the first-class section of the Qantas airplane in Australia. A stewardess tried to convince her to behave herself but she only became more obnoxious.

"What the fuck do ya want?" she yelled at the stewardess. "I'm allowed to do whatever the fuck I want. Do you know who I am?"

Her bandmates Melissa, Patty, and Eric stared at Courtney in disbelief. But they didn't want to interfere because they knew from experience it would only make her more disruptive. Courtney placed her feet on the wall of the cabin and refused to move them. When the airline crew threatened to arrest her, Courtney quickly screamed, "Go the fuck ahead and arrest me." And they did. The story made headlines around the world. But Courtney was able to get sympathy and support from her fans thanks to the effective long-standing policy of her publicity firm, PMK: whatever Courtney gets herself into, we will come to the rescue and spin it in a positive light.

One incident that even PMK could not seem to cleanse was a March 1995 New York radio station event which fueled the probably unfair charge that Courtney is a racist. In front of a crowd of several thousand people, Courtney had led the crowd in a chant of "naughty words" which included "bitch," "cunt," and "nigger." At one point, she shouted, "Okay now kids, on three, you know you want to say nigger!" After a rambling discourse about the sexism of gansta rap and her refusal to play at Lollapalooza with Snoop Doggy Dog or Cypress Hill, two notoriously misogynistic rap groups. She then asked, "Does that make me a racist or a feminist?"

According to the *Village Voice*, her behaviour was met with "stunned silence" by the crowd. Courtney's spokesperson denied to the *Voice* that she was a racist, but the denial didn't seem to appease the writer who attended the event. "The fact is," he writes, "that she did use the N-word – and she did it at least twice."

Courtney later responded to the *Voice* criticism by explaining her purpose was to rile the crowd: "We got fucked on the bill. It was full of Bon Jovi fans. I'm a freak to them, might as well get on my broomstick." Asked what her thinking was behind the outburst, she said, "Yeah, well okay, maybe, but Christ I've got a stage, shouldn't I use it?"

Courtney continued to discuss her marriage to Kurt on America Online. She reported to her fans that after she had Kurt's body cremated, she had placed some of his ashes in an urn and some in a Buddhist shrine at their Lake Washington home. She also said she had buried some of the ashes at the base of a willow tree in the back garden. She talked about setting up a public memorial for Kurt and even publicly supported an Aberdeen artist's idea of erecting a statue in honour of Kurt. This incensed Nirvana's other members.

"If anybody puts up a statue of Kurt, I'll kick it down," said Krist Novoselic, a longtime Courtney adversary. "He would not have wanted it. That's not what Kurt was about."

Courtney's relationship with Krist and Dave Grohl has not been cordial. Publicly, both refuse to talk about her (fueling persistent rumours that they have signed a gag order in exchange for a greater share of Nirvana royalties), although Grohl told Rolling Stone in 1995 that seeing Courtney acting like a rock star is "the moment I've been dreading." Grohl has started the successful band Foo Fighters since Nirvana broke up. On the band's first album, he wrote a song which was clearly about Courtney, a fact he refuses to deny.

"How could it be / I'm the only one who sees your rehearsed insanity?" Grohl sings, and "I've been around all the pawns you've gagged and bound."

For her part, Courtney told *Rolling Stone* in December 1994, "There are issues between me, Krist, and Dave that need to be resolved. But I want the lines of communication to be open. For Frances's sake as much as mine."

Mark Connelly is a friend of Shelli Novoselic in Olympia, Washington, where Krist and Shelli still live. Connelly says Shelli told him that Krist and Dave have a pile of never-heard Nirvana material but they refuse to release it.

"She said Krist told her they won't release the music until the day after Courtney dies because they don't want her making a dime on it," says Connelly.

Grohl and Novoselic won't comment on Tom Grant's murder theory, but at a 1995 Foo Fighters concert, someone in the crowd shouted out, "Tom Grant is right!" and Grohl is reported to have given the thumbs-up sign.

In 1994, Courtney contacted two Seattle cemeteries about burying some of Kurt's ashes. One refused because of the possibility of huge pilgrimages by Nirvana fans. The other wanted to charge $100,000 a year for the extra security they would need.

Courtney frequently brags to her band and even the media that she carries Kurt's ashes wherever she goes. When she spent two weeks in Ithaca, New York, at the Buddhist Namgyal monastery in July 1994, she wore a teddy bear backpack which she claimed contained Kurt's ashes. The townspeople developed their own ideas of what Courtney was doing with the ashes. Some insist they were tossed in a lake. Others claim they were mixed with butter and used in a butter sculpture at the monastery. One even said that she smoked them in a huge joint – an example of the kind of bizarre rumors which follow her wherever she goes.

Courtney knew about the Namgyal through her longtime interest in Tibetan Buddhism. She had been referred to Losang Chogyen, known as "Pema," a founding member of the monastery who lived in New York City. When she met with Pema at the Four Seasons Hotel, he was slightly taken aback by his strange visitor.

"I didn't really know what I should be doing," he later recalled. "Kurt Cobain I had heard of because of Nirvana, the name of the band, but I had never heard the music. I didn't know about the existence of Courtney Love even. But I found out Courtney Love is a singer in her own right and has her own band. She was smoking constantly. She said she really tried to quit smoking, but she'd stop and start again. And so she was smoking and smoking, and the first thing I did right after we met was to light her cigarette."

Pema soon grew to like Courtney, who asked to chant with him. But before he would accede to her request, he asked her for a gesture of good faith.

"Stop smoking," he said, "at least while I'm here. Then we can chant." She told him she really wanted to go up to the monastery, but Pema was wary. "She was not in good shape. I think she was dozing off but she was trying to stay as clean as possible." When Pema informed the residents of the monastery about Courtney's request for a visit, they feared that she wasn't ready.

He went to see her again the next day at the hotel. "She talked about the ashes. She wanted to know the proper Buddhist ritual to honor them. She was so sweet. She was saying how much she cared for the teenagers. And she was saying most people think she's doing terrible things to the kids but she was saying 'I really want to help them.' She was really interested in what happens when people die." .

Finally, she was invited to the monastery. It was only a couple of months after Kurt's death. Courtney had all of Ithaca's attention. Some of the residents called the tabloids with wild Courtney stories. But most of the time, Courtney was seen in the company of video producer Frank Vidal, who had close ties to the monastery. He would arrive in the red Miata convertible he had borrowed from his father-in-law and drive Courtney down through the hills to the Namgyal monastery. By all accounts, he was very patient. He would even wait outside Ithaca stores while she spent hours shopping for new clothes and antiques. Once she forgot to use the changing room while she was trying on bras at the Isadora lingerie shop. The clerk said she noticed track marks and bruises on her arms. Courtney left the shop two thousand dollars poorer.

She would frequently stop to talk to total strangers while she was in Ithaca. She told them all about her life, including her frequent claim that she was more famous than Kurt when they first met.

One day, Pitt Doug, a salesman at the Ithaca Guitar Works, had to inform Courtney that her Visa card hadn't gone through. Courtney wanted to buy a vintage 1932 Martin C1 that she found in the store. She demanded to use the phone to call her bank in New York. She stretched the cord across the store's entrance so she could lie down on some speaker cabinets.

"She was dressed in a way that one of my schoolteachers described as 'just barely enough to cover the subject,"' Doug told Esquire magazine. When her card was refused, *Courtney* was livid. She started swearing at the staff before leaving in a rage. The store kept one of the many cigarette butts she left behind and placed it on a shelf next to a harmonica that Bob Dylan once threw away and a guitar pick from Buck Dharma of Blue Oyster Cult. Doug, however, was intent on fulfilling Courtney's wish and he contacted her management company in New York City. They made a deal to buy the guitar.

"Every time I see her waving it around on MTV I think about her screaming, 'I want my money to her banker,'" Doug says.

Wherever Courtney goes, publicity follows. The crazy shenanigans attracted the world's media corps to Ithaca. But it was an incident on her birthday that made the biggest headlines. Courtney was driven by limo to New York to celebrate her twenty-ninth birthday. That's when the candid shot of her in bed with Evan Dando was taken. It showed up in the tabloids immediately. Courtney's attempt to deny the affair almost became a full-time job. Another photo ran in the *New York Post* with Dando hugging the teddy bear with Kurt's ashes in it. He later explained his actions. "I had such respect for Kurt," he said. "And I was giving him a hug because I thought we could have gotten to be good friends."

When Courtney departed Ithaca in late July, she left behind about two handfuls of Kurt's ashes with the monks to complete the arduous task of consecrating them, mixing them with clay and molding them to make tsatsas – a Buddhist repository. A couple of weeks later, Courtney headed to Atlanta to undergo some facial surgery. She set up her altar at the hotel where she was convalescing. "Watch it," she instructed the cleaning staff "My husband's ashes are in there."

In September – after meeting with her advisers and hiring Melissa to replace Kristen – Courtney, Hole, and Kurt's ashes embarked on a tour to promote *Live Through This*.

Courtney sashayed onto the stage at her first appearance since Kurt's death. It was a benefit in Seattle and, although Hole wasn't the headliner, the attention of the crowd was definitely focused on her.

Courtney quickly got the crowd's attention by telling them Kurt was listening in from above. She also told them that he always liked her cover of "Where'd You Sleep Last Night?" better than his version. The concert was called "End It," a benefit to raise money for Artists for a Hate Free America. Joining Hole on the card were 311, Rancid, Weezer, Sky Cries Mary, and headliners Green Day.

The men in the crowd surged forward, extending their arms to receive the word from this new punk Madonna, with her flailing bleached hair and her seductive stage manner. But she slapped the men back. "Let the girls get up front," she yelled. "You men better let them up or I'll come after you all." Courtney set the tone for the set: Hole was delivering its wisdom to women, and the men had better behave themselves if they wanted to hang around.

"It was ironic because I went to interview Courtney after the set and she totally discarded me," says *Seattle Times* reporter Diedtra Henderson, who covered the event. "After giving that woman's speech, you would think she'd be more cooperative in giving another woman an interview."

Fans at the show also caught a glimpse of actress Drew Barrymore after Courtney challenged the Hollywood bad girl to come on stage. Then Courtney introduced two-and-a-half-year-old Frances Bean to the crowd. Frances's ears were covered with the kind of protective gear airport workers use.

"Say 'Hi,'" Courtney asked Frances a couple of times before Frances obliged. Courtney joked that she was "exploiting a child" in a sarcastic tone. Before receiving an encore, Courtney sang a hard-core version of "You Won't Remember Anything You Felt When He Cuts You All to Pieces With His Bible Belt." Then she left the stage, smashing a guitar and a couple of speakers and yelling obscenities at the crowd.

During Hole's tour, it came as no surprise to

anybody that Courtney didn't try to keep a lower profile. She told one magazine reporter that talking about "personal abuses and travails can make women stronger. She said she liked to address her crowd with firsthand experiences of "rape, incest, and insecurity." Her fans responded with more loyalty and support than ever.

"Courtney defined a more confident and less passive attitude about being a woman," said Lisa Anisman, sixteen, who was one of the lucky fans to get a ticket for Hole's sold-out Boston show. "I look up to Courtney because she's a woman who doesn't let society railroad her into the stereotypical image of a woman."

It is this attitude that has allowed many of Courtney's growing legions of fans to ignore all the nasty things written about her. She seems to fulfill the same role as a voice for disenfranchised young women as Kurt once did for his fans. But Courtney disavows the adulation. "I resent being a role model for marrying a rock star." she told Kurt Loder of MTV. "I wanna slap girls when they do that, I really do."

Soon after, negotiations started between Hole's managers and the organizers of Lollapalooza. Courtney was anxious to play the tour that Kurt refused to do the year before. She even leaked a report to the media that Nirvana was only offered about $150,000 to headline Lollapalooza in 1994. These remarks were immediately denounced as false by the two surviving members of Nirvana and also by Lollapalooza organizers, who maintain the true figure is in "the millions."

Meanwhile, Courtney's Beverly Hills lawyer Barry Tarlow had his hands full getting his client off one charge after the other. First, Tarlow successfully convinced a court that the material seized from Courtney during her arrest the day before Kurt's body was found consisted of a Buddhist good-luck charm containing harmless ashes, not drugs. Courtney was also charged and cleared of possession of stolen property. Tarlow argued that the stolen property was merely a prescription pad that Courtney's doctor had inadvertently left behind in her room. Her laywers have never explained the syringe police found in the same room.

Courtney's next legal wrangle was an accusation that she had assaulted two teenagers during a March 1995 concert in Orlando, Florida. Hole was playing at Edge in downtown Orlando and Courtney apparently jumped from the stage and punched eighteen-year-old Ryan O'Donnell five times in the chest after demanding that the men in the audience move back from the stage to let some women get closer to the band. The other alleged victim, Robert Lukas, a nineteen-year-old college student, claimed Love punched him three times in the chest. Courtney's entourage was incensed after the Orlando incident. They told her that she was going to get Hole erased from the Lollapalooza tour.

"Just when things are going great you have to pull another one of your crazy stunts," Eric told her. "Courtney, everything we've accomplished in the last year will get wiped out because of what you just pulled."

"They started it and I won't take any shit," Courtney replied. "Fuck Lollapalooza, it's a bullshit tour. Who gives a fuck? But they'll still keep us because everybody wants to see our fucking band."

Rob Lukas, a Canadian university student who was one of those allegedly assaulted by Courtney at the Florida concert, described the pretrial period as a personal hell.

"She had lawyers and private detectives harassing my family, my friends, my neighbors, trying to dig up dirt on me," he recalls. "I was threatened not to testify against her. It was a nightmare."

On November 6, 1995, an Orange County judge took the unusual precedent of dismissing the assault charges against Courtney just before the jury was to deliver its verdict, announcing that Courtney's behaviour was the type expected at a rock concert, especially in a mosh pit. The dismissal came after the prosecuting and defence attorneys had a sidebar with the judge. Afterward, jury members said that they had decided on a unanimous guilty verdict and Courtney would have been convicted if not for the judge's intervention. After the trial, Courtney told the press that she would have to rethink whether she would continue to dive into crowds at concerts. She also shed a tear in what clearly looked like an attempt to get some sympathy.

Not everyone believes Courtney's wild antics reflect her true personality. A 1995 profile in *Playboy* magazine describes a Hole concert at Detroit's St. Andrew's Hall where Courtney seemed too wasted to stand up.

"Backstage, after the show, she was as sober as Hillary Rodham Clinton," writes Neal Karlen.

Some of her friends echo this assessment. "You have to know the real Courtney," says Seattle DJ Marco Collins, who has been a friend for years. "She's a really good person. She's had a tough life. A lot of what you read about her or see onstage is just hype."

But *Playboy's* Karlen also discovered a darker side. He writes that she told him before her interview, "If you fuck me over, I'll hunt you down and kill you." Karlen writes that he believed her.

As Lollapalooza approached, Courtney continued to attract media attention. She adorned the covers of almost every major music and arts magazine, including a surprising cover story in the June 1995 Vanity Fair – the magazine that had nearly ruined her life three years before.

In the cover photo, Courtney was adorned with angel wings. It was clearly a payback by the magazine after Courtney shelved her threats of a lawsuit. This time, the article was almost entirely positive, describing Courtney as a "caring, if unconventional, mom."

"For Christ's sake, her and her friends were constantly

doing drugs in front of Frances and they're [Vanity Fair] making her into a saint," says Hank Harrison. "I'm sure Courtney's lawyers had something to do with this article."

Courtney was becoming more dependent on her high-priced legal team to control negative criticism. According to a member of her entourage, Courtney believes in using lawyers to intimidate her detractors. She never actually sues anybody because she doesn't have much of a reputation to defame and she is terrified that she will have to answer some dangerous questions about her own activities in a deposition or in a courtroom. But often a tough-worded lawyer's letter is enough to make somebody back off." Melissa Rossi reports that Courtney's boyfriend Rozz Rezabeck was considering writing a book about her around this time. When Courtney found out, she left him a message on his answering machine, "I am Jesus and my lawyers are my twelve disciples. Do not fuck with me."

Some of her detractors have figured out creative ways to express their feelings toward Courtney without worrying about legal consequences. Seattle's original grunge band, Mudhoney, recorded a song called "Into Yer Schtick" with the lyrics "Why don't you blow your brains out, too?" Asked by the press if the song was about Courtney, the band's leader Mark Arm said he didn't necessarily write it with one person in mind but added, "If the shoe fits, wear it."

Hole's Lollapalooza appearance let Courtney finally elbow her way onto the biggest world stage of alternative music. As the festival moved through North America, Courtney spent most of her time playing video games in the hospitality room backstage when she wasn't watching videos, usually *The Breakfast Club* (she claims she watched it twice a day for two weeks) with Frances Bean.

It didn't take long for Courtney to steal the limelight. On the tour's very first day, Courtney noticed Bikini Kill's Kathleen Hanna walk by with members of

Sonic Youth. Hole had just finished their set and Sonic Youth was getting ready to go on. While Courtney talked to Beck, Eric Erlandson came up to her and said, "Kathleen's behind you. You should give her some candy and freak her out." Courtney later claimed that when she turned around, Hanna was smirking at her. She also claims that Hanna said, "Where's the baby, in a closet with an IV?"

Courtney, who was holding some Tootsie Rolls and Skittles, went ballistic. She punched Hanna in the face before security guards broke things up.

Hanna was rumoured to have had an affair with Kurt a few years ago. Courtney claimed Hanna was "Kurt's worst enemy in the world" and that she was doing what Kurt would have wanted. But according to Slim Moon, Kurt's old neighbor in Olympia and head of Hanna's label, Kill Rock Stars Records, "Hanna and Kurt were good friends. He had nothing against her. I think Courtney was just jealous of their relationship."

After the incident, Hanna denied ever saying anything about Frances Bean. On September 26, 1995, Courtney pleaded guilty in a Washington State courtroom to assaulting Hanna. She was handed a one-year suspended sentence, forced to take anger management courses, fined $285, and ordered not to threaten anybody or to engage in any violent behaviour for two years or the sentence would be reinstated. Afterward, she told people, "The judge said I can't punch her in Grant County [where the Lollapalooza concert took place] but I can clock her again in Seattle."

The incident also triggered a bitter row between Courtney and Thurston Moore, whose band Sonic Youth was the tour's headlining band. He went online several times, posting scathing remarks about Courtney during the tour. He described Courtney's "puerile, useless rock-star shit." He also wrote in disgust after Courtney punched Hanna: "Everyone is disgusted and totally grossed out." Along with bandmate Kim Gordon, Moore threatened to quit Lollapalooza several times during the summer if Courtney was not removed from the tour. Courtney responded with a two-thousand-word online blurb attacking Hanna. Tour organizers calmed down Moore and Gordon, convincing them it was too late to dump Hole from the itinerary.

"One thing I can guarantee you, Thurston," said one high-ranking tour official. "Courtney Love will never be invited back. In fact, we won't even let her backstage next year. She's too much trouble."

Frances, however, was a hit backstage. Musicians loved to play with the three-year-old daughter of Kurt Cobain – who many said looked eerily like her father – before their set. Frances hung out with the children of the other musicians, including Thurston and Kim's daughter Coco. When Thurston remarked backstage that Frances seemed sad, Courtney told him, "Frances can kick Coco's butt any day of the week in terms of being a happy child."

Courtney's closest friend at the beginning of the tour was Sinead O'Connor, who was using Lollapalooza to launch her comeback. Sinead and Courtney liked to stay up all night in the tour bus watching depressing movies like *Ryan's Daughter*. Sinead was pregnant and she couldn't take the American Midwest summer heat. Before quitting the tour, she left Courtney a note saying, "They can sue me. I don't care. I'll find another line of work."

One night during the tour, Courtney spotted a teenage boy wearing a Nine Inch Nails hat. "Give me the hat and I'll give you my underwear," Courtney offered the youngster. When he agreed, Courtney took out a lighter and lit the hat and stamped out the fire in front of the kid. Then she took off her panties and gave them to the shocked youngster.

"Why did you burn the hat?" the boy asked.

"Trent's the biggest asshole I've met," she replied, referring to Nine Inch Nails singer Trent Reznor, with whom she is alleged to have had an ill-fated affair. "You should wear a hat like Smashing Pumpkins or Lemonheads."

Musicians on the tour started to notice that the heavy schedule was turning Courtney into a more refined musician. But a member of one band said sarcastically, "If Courtney could learn the basic chords and make music, anybody could."

Courtney soon became close pals with Hollywood bad girl Drew Barrymore, who became a sort of Lollapalooza groupie during the last half of the tour. Drew had just become involved with Eric Erlandson.

"Drew has the dirt on more celebs than anyone I've ever met, Courtney told anybody who would listen. "You know how you'll hear a rumor that so-and-so is gay, or that so-and-so does illicit narcotics, or that so-and-so likes girls' clothes. Well, Drew knows that stuff for real."

Courtney became drinking buddies with Drew and would often tease her about her breast reduction surgery. "Hey, everyone, don't you notice Drew's tits have shrunk?" Courtney said one night at the Lollapalooza backstage watering hole.

At the end of Lollapalooza, Courtney tried to make peace with Thurston and Kim. "She was afraid that they would blab about how fucked up she is to the press," says one Lollapalooza stage tech. "So Courtney gave them something valuable to make them shut up."

She handed Thurston and Kim the sole copy of a five-hour video she had of Kurt. "I know that Kurt would like to be remembered fondly and completely by Kim and Thurston," Courtney said. "Someday I'll figure out a way to do this for the world."

And despite the criticism that she exploits her daughter, most observers say it is obvious that Frances is one of the shining points of her life. Craig Marks of *Spin* magazine recounted a meeting he had with Courtney where Frances Bean was present.

"I'm not sure what sort of sociopathic mother-daughter relationship I had expected," he writes. "Mommie Dearest? Mildred Pierce? – But I was heartened, and admittedly relieved, to see Love gleefully singing the hits of Barney the Dinosaur with her child. 'I love you, you love me, we're a happy family,' cooed the pair, either oblivious or accustomed to the bustling surroundings."

The same night, Courtney told the crowd at her concert, "I don't care if people think I'm exploiting my child. She's the only successful thing I've done in my life."

Courtney maintains publicly that she has kicked her drug habit, but according to a Seattle heroin dealer named Walter, she continued to buy from him as late as January 1996.

"She doesn't buy as much as she and Kurt used to," he said, sitting in a basement drug den in Seattle's University district. "But every so often I get a call."

He also claimed Courtney pays the rent for his apartment and even bailed him out of jail on a drug charge in late 1995.

In the fall of 1995, Courtney and her bandmates rented a house in New Orleans across the street from one of Courtney's idols, author Anne Rice, to collaborate on Hole's follow-up to *Live Through This*. The music industry eagerly awaits this effort, anxious to discover whether Courtney can produce a solid album without Kurt's help.

In early December, Courtney called up Marco Collins's KNDD radio show in Seattle with what she called "amazing news." She had just landed the role in Milos Forman's film bio of porn king Larry Flynt. Courtney would play Flynt's heroin addicted, HIV-infected wife, Althea.

"Maybe I'll give up music and become a movie star," she announced.

Two weeks later, Courtney fulfilled a lifelong dream when she was interviewed by Barbara Walters on her year-end show "The 10 Most Influential People of 1995." Sitting in the Lake Washington home, Walters conducted an almost fawning interview during which Courtney cried several times when she talked about Kurt.

At one point, Courtney offered yet another explanation of where she got her band's name. "The name of my band came from a conversation I had with my mother. People always think it's obscene. And I guess it has that on top of it. As someone who always wanted to be a poet, there was no money in it. I've always been looking for the quadruple entendre, you know, the bard, you know, what Shakespeare could do. And my mother said to me 'Now, Courtney, you know you can't walk around with a hole in yourself just because you had a bad childhood.' And I remember thinking 'What a brilliant name, HOLE.'"

This account was later offered as proof by her critics that she is incapable of telling the truth, since she had previously claimed many times, and very publicly, that the name came from the Euripides play Medea. She also repeated the story that her father gave her LSD when she was a child, but this time she offered a new version.

"Apparently he wanted... he was a hygienics [eugenics] freak and I'm biologically part Jewish, part Irish. It's no wonder I'm neurotic. And he was anti-Semitic, his father was anti-Semitic, as was he, and he also made acid. Three people testified that he gave me acid. He wanted to make a superior race, and by giving children acid you could do that. Now he denies this and... who knows."

The most surprising revelation came when Walters asked her if she considered Kurt's death to be her fault after Courtney seemed to make that claim.

Walters asked, "Because you tried to get him off drugs and because he wasn't able to get off drugs, even though you were trying to do the right thing, it's your fault?"

"He thought he was a waste of space," Courtney responded. "Yes, yes... I told him he dropped the baby. And I was mean about it. I wasn't really mean, but I wasn't nice about it. [She sniffs.] You know, we were really polite to each other, generally. And I told him on the phone, I'm like, 'You know you dropped the baby... the other day [when he was in rehab], you dropped the baby.' He was like, 'What?!' I'm like, 'You dropped the baby, you dropped Frances on her head.' She was wearing a big hooded coat, He did not hurt her, and I did not need to tell him that."

Then came the tough questions.

"Have you ever done drugs in front of your child?" Walters asked.

Courtney seemed taken aback by the question. "My God. What a question," she protested in a high-pitched tone of surprise. "No!"

Meanwhile, Tom Grant's charges have shown no sign of fading away as his Internet Web site receives more than one million hits per year (it has been listed in the top 5 percent of Web sites worldwide) and the murder theory keeps gaining new proponents.

Long ago, Courtney's camp decided their best strategy was to ignore Grant and hope the mainstream media would follow suit. But it's a strategy that doesn't seem to be working as the story spreads throughout the world, for the first time receiving coverage in the mainstream media mostly negative and dismissive coverage, but attention nonetheless. One notable exception to the cynical tone of most mainstream reporting about the case came in a January 1997 article by Michael Saunders in the influential *Boston Globe*. The article focuses on the Web sites of Tom Grant and a Boston writer named Toby Amirault, another proponent of the murder theory. After summarizing their arguments, the article concludes: "If Grant and Amirault are right, then the Cobain case is either a classic travesty of justice or a supremely evil act gone unpunished."

In 1996, somebody finally decided to fight back on behalf of Love. An eighteen-year-old American university student named David Perle began to respond to Grant's murder charges on his own Web site which he called "Why Tom Grant Should Not Be Believed."

Perle explains what convinced him to start a Web site devoted to refuting Grant's claims. "When I read his files on the matter for the first time, June 26, 1995, I was so amazed at how ridiculous his written investigation read, saying outrageous things without backing any of it up; much of his investigation at that time (and even today) consisted of parts akin to: 'I heard this said, even though I have no evidence of it,' or, 'I saw this happen, and you'll just have to take my word for it.' And my favorite, 'This person gave me this really incriminating testimony, even though now she and her law firm deny it, and are threatening to sue me.... (Examples, not exact quotes.) I was amazed that that was what convinced so many people that Kurt Cobain was murdered."

Perle says a number of factors convinced him that Courtney couldn't have murdered her husband "It remains that first and foremost I am a Kurt Cobain fan," he writes, "and I still must hold certain respect for the fact that Courtney Love was one of the few people in Kurt Cobain's life whom he liked; trusted; loved. That must be remembered by all fans of Kurt Cobain, always."

Perle argues that Grant does not adequately prove his case and, during the first year of his Web site, he accused Grant of lying. But in early 1997, something seems to have changed his mind. While he is still reasonably convinced Courtney had nothing to do with Kurt's death, he now takes a very different tone about Grant's case and the possibility of murder.

"In a very slow process since the first time I read

his files, Tom Grant's claims have been a bit harder to disprove, and certain facts have arisen that may help show that Kurt Cobain may not have killed himself" Perle now writes. He even believes that the Seattle Police Department should reopen the case.

"If anything serious is to come of this matter," he writes, "pressure must be put on the Seattle Police Department (SPD) to re-investigate this case with or without the assistance of Tom Grant, so that all of the questions (whatever they may be) will finally be answered, and that everyone shall be satisfied that a serious and in-depth investigation has been completed, whether or not the case remains known as a suicide."

Before Perle changed his mind about Grant's case, he engaged in a lengthy correspondence with Courtney Love, who was grateful that somebody was defending her against Grant's charges. In July 1996, she e-mailed Perle after he informed her about his site:

> Go to the medical examiner, the chief of police, the chief and sgt in Homicide (because of the high profile of this death they were involved) – Grant had a PI firm for a few months he got real lucky. I couldn't find any lawyers so, hell, I used the yellow pages – he was/is a failed business man – also slow and ineptæthe people he consigned in seattle were slow – I sent someone over to the dealersæasked him had anyone been by? he said no... also lazy – Dylan says he barely looked at the house – also he never went up to the garage or greenhouse – wich i specifically asked as it was a "hiding" place for K. – theres nothing more to say because the actual authorities know all... BTW the 'Rome' note is xeroxed... and owned by the SPD – grant (who sells tidbits to the Star) wanted pictures, ballistics, forensics from me – I called Kimball, Cameron, all of them, they said he was a crank and ignore him. if he does go to the real

> media – who will not touch him as he has no facts other than he doesnt like me – gee! They get their fucking asses sued to hell – and they know that – thats all i have to say other than there is a date set to remove his license, and of course no one will publish his 'Novel' because its full of shit that the med examiner and cops will vehemently deny – they have all the evidence remember? If Tom grant had gotten a hold of a picture of Kurt – wed all have seen it – Frances too when she grows up – I could NOT take seeing such a thing, as far as our marriage PLEASE – divorce was NOT an option to either of us/we rarely fought and had a great marriage, PERIOD.

Two months later, Courtney e-mailed Perle about her father's accusations after he was quoted in a story about the murder theory in *High Times* magazine:

> High times smoked a few joints too many... get to the part about the "dream machine" hooboy! Also Hank OWNING something EG a House? HA! The guy is on WELFARE I've NEVER lived with him and have met him about ten times in my life. Yukky – its about my mother w/him also he thinks that through me he was some conduit that gave Kurt his Voice so ultimately this insane megalamaniac [sic] says that... KURT is really HANK-eg Voice Of A Generation rather than pathetic parasite/petty thief/child molester/All TRANSCRIPTS OF HIS CUSTODY BATTLE WITH MY MOTHER ARE PUBLIC RECORD EX GIRLFRIENDS/VARIOUS SCENESTERS TESTIFY THAT HE MOLESTED ME AS AN IN-FANT AND GAVE ME ACID PUBLICLY/ Not a pretty detail but anyone in the bay area can find them 1968 – Risi/vs harrison or State vs Harrison.... hes the lowest blowhole cretin, his mother took the stand

> accused him of some sick shit in that transcriptæhe was not allowed to EVER be near me my entire life by court order in the 60s! HARSH! Him and Tom Grant are peas in a pod unusable, and useless – Im not angry – its too typical, ba bing he hit the jackpot... just gross."

This last letter seems to be almost completely false. Transcripts of Harrison's divorce custody battle, in fact, say nothing about charges of molestation. We could find nothing about Courtney being given LSD, although it's possible that the allegations of LSD use, were made in supplementary documents which we could not access. The fact remains, however, that Courtney has admitted that her father did not give her LSD, according to her biographer Melissa Rossi. The decision did not bar Harrison from seeing Courtney for life (although an adoption proceeding years later removed his visitation rights) and there is incontrovertible evidence that Courtney not only saw her father more than ten times but that she frequently lived with him for long periods of time – evidence which includes an official State of Oregon parole document releasing Courtney from reform school into Harrison's custody as a fourteen-year-old. Perhaps it was these provable false accusations which convinced Perle to change his mind about the murder theory.

Courtney doesn't seem troubled by the turnaround of her most fervent supporter. She's made a career of springboarding off the heads of her critics up the ladder of success and she has no intention of falling down now.

13
Epilogue

We're still not quite entirely sure how it happened, but sometime between the time we started writing this book and its publication, we went from reporting the story to being the story.

In March 1996, after word got out that we were pursuing the controversy surrounding Cobain's death, we were approached by the largest rock radio station in Montreal, CHOM-FM, and commissioned to participate in a special series called "Who Killed Kurt Cobain?" Before this point, the only public airing of our findings was an article we did for *Canadian Disk* magazine in June 1995. In that article, we had been somewhat cynical about the case and had even speculated (this was before we met him) that Tom Grant was making his claims in order to make money off a book deal.

So, when CHOM hired us, we had no idea what was in store. Little did we know that the station was in the middle of its sweeps period and was determined to hype our project all the way to a ratings victory. For weeks, the station promoted the series with ominous voices and eerie music, promising explosive revelations. On the eve of the first broadcast, the station called a press conference to publicize the series and move the hype machine into overdrive. It worked. The press conference sparked a media feeding frenzy with a room packed full of media vultures eager for dirt.

Only afterward did we discover the source of their frenzy. It turns out that the station had sent out a highly sensationalized press release under the heading "Kurt Cobain Was Murdered" stating that we were calling Cobain's death a murder and implying that Courtney Love did it. It failed to mention that we were reporting on an allegation by her private investigator and that we were not making any accusations ourselves. And, although at the press conference itself this was made clear, the journalists had already jumped to their own conclusions based on the inaccurate press release and this was reflected in the subsequent reporting. It didn't help matters when one journalist inaccurately quoted Ian Halperin saying there would be an arrest in the case within a week (which a tape of the conference revealed he never said, although he did discuss a Los Angeles police officer's speculation on the possibility of an arrest if El Duce's claims could be proved) – a quote which was picked up over the wires.

When the series itself actually aired, we repeatedly emphasized that we were not accusing Courtney of anything, that we had never seen a "smoking gun" in the case, and that we weren't even 100 percent convinced the death was a murder. We just wanted to see the case reopened so that these questions could be answered once and for all. Of course, none of the media actually reported on the content of the series – just the press release and conference.

In a classic case of shooting the messenger, we

were written off by many as "conspiracy theorists" postulating ridiculous gossip. However, a handful of the more responsible reporters who knew we weren't making an accusation still rightfully questioned the ethics of our investigation – an issue we had ourselves agonized about. They questioned the propriety of reporting such a highly inflammatory charge by somebody else – that Courtney Love may have murdered her husband – and maintained this was just as bad as making the accusation ourselves.

Most of the critics, however, were not preoccupied with the ethics. Everybody knew that Kurt Cobain had committed suicide and, they implied, to suggest otherwise you would have to be a wacko.

Nevertheless, the story attracted attention. Within a week, we were inundated with hundreds of interview requests from as far away as Australia, Ireland, Germany and even Japan. And then, just as the media attention began to wane, we received an unexpected visitor.

About two weeks after the special aired on CHOM-FM, Ian Halperin returned home one afternoon and found a large bearded man waiting in his courtyard. The man introduced himself as Jack Palladino – an "investigative attorney" from San Francisco hired by Courtney Love. "I want to talk to you about your book," he said. "Let's go out to dinner, anywhere you want to go."

Curious, Halperin accepted. Over a four-hour dinner at a posh Italian restaurant, Palladino proceeded to charm and cajole the author, saying if he did not show him the manuscript, he could get in "big trouble." In between the subtle coercion, he told stories about his impressive roster of clients, which included Patty Hearst, Snoop Doggy Dogg, and John DeLorean.

On two occasions during the dinner, he seemed to hint that he could help get Halperin a recording contract if he cooperated. "You're a musician," he said, "and I have a lot of contacts in the music industry. I can help you out if you help me out."

Halfway through the dinner the investigator reached into his briefcase and pulled out a thick file containing a huge dossier on Halperin's life, including jobs he had held, names of old girlfriends, and much more.

Later, Palladino revealed that he had been hired by Courtney Love's entertainment attorney Rosemary Carroll, rather than by Courtney herself. And he seemed especially interested in determining whether we planned to publish the transcript of the alleged conversation between Carroll and Tom Grant where she purportedly expressed her suspicions about Kurt's death. (When we informed Grant of Palladino's interest in this tape, he said, "Give him my phone number. I'll be glad to play the tapes for him.")

Halperin told Palladino our price for a glimpse of the manuscript: An interview with Courtney Love to get her side of the story.

"That will never happen," he responded forcefully. After he flew back to San Francisco, Palladino called several times repeating his request to see the manuscript before he finally gave up.

While her lawyers engaged in damage control, Courtney showed no outward signs that the controversy was having any effect on her life. She was too busy changing gears on her image and career.

Long before she harboured ambitions to be a musician, Courtney wanted to be a movie star. In 1996, it looked like she was about to get her chance.

Oliver Stone had announced plans to produce a film about controversial porn king Larry Flynt, publisher of the hard-core *Hustler* magazine, and his notorious First Amendment fight with Moral Majority leader Jerry Falwell in the mid-seventies over a satirical ad in the magazine about the right-wing evangelist. The movie would be called *The People vs. Larry Flynt*. Stone had chosen as director the Czech-born Milos

Forman, who had won Oscars for *Amadeus* and *One Flew Over the Cuckoo's Nest*. Forman had already cast Woody Harrelson in the title role but he needed somebody to play Althea Leasure, Flynt's HIV-infected junkie/stripper wife.

Forman had been mulling the possibility of getting Patricia Arquette or Julia Roberts for the role. One day, however, the perfect choice was suggested to him while he was having lunch with Czech president Vá clav Havel, the writer-turned-politician whose close friendship with Frank Zappa and Mick Jagger gave him impressive pop culture credentials. Havel said there is only one person to play Althea, Courtney Love. Forman instantly agreed but was wary, given what he knew about Courtney's reputation as a troublemaker. He also knew the Hollywood insurance companies were getting much stricter about insuring known drug abusers, especially since the heroin-related death of actor River Phoenix the year before. But Forman vowed to fight for Courtney, convinced she was the ideal person to play Althea, and brought her to Hollywood for a screen test, where she dazzled Stone and Harrelson with her acting abilities.

The only remaining obstacle was a drug test insisted upon by the insurance company. Stone promised that if she passed, the part was hers. Courtney was told the date after which a urine test would detect illegal drugs in her system and warned that she better remain clean before the test. Reports conflict about whether she entered rehab, but on the day of the test, she passed and thought she had cleared the final hurdle. However, the insurer was still nervous. It took the unusual step of insisting on a hair sample to analyse for drugs. This procedure detects illegal drug use for a much longer period of time than a simple urine test. Courtney refused and the insurer wouldn't bond her.

Normally, this would have been the end of her chances. But by that time, Stone and Forman couldn't envision anybody but Courtney in the role of Althea. They finally found a company who would agree to insure her on two conditions. She would have to submit to weekly drug tests during the duration of filming and she would have to put up a $750,000 personal bond, to be forfeited if she failed any drug test. Courtney was furious, fuming about "Hollywood scum," but she desperately wanted the part she knew could be her breakthrough.

Meanwhile, she had won a minor role as a small-town waitress in another film, *Feeling Minnesota* with Keanu Reeves. Since her role wasn't considered major, she didn't have to face the same strict insurance guidelines. When the film was released in mid-1996, it was savaged by the critics and bombed at the box office, although some reviewers praised Courtney's competent performance.

Of course, Courtney was still known as a musician, not an actress, and people were beginning to wonder when Hole would release its long-awaited follow-up to *Live Through This*. The band had rented a house in New Orleans to write songs for the new album and Courtney often bragged that they had written the whole thing in less than two weeks. Where, then, were the results? asked the music press.

Reports were beginning to filter out of Los Angeles, where the new album was being recorded, that things were not going well. Courtney was desperate to prove that she could write music in her own right and put to rest the persistent speculation that Kurt had written the catchy musical bridges on the last album. But rumour had it that the new songs were awful. Courtney's old boyfriend Billy Corgan of Smashing Pumpkins was brought on as producer to rescue the album, but he frequently complained that he couldn't work miracles with mediocre material. Two years later, there is still no sign of the album.

To make matters worse, Courtney's old friend

Seattle DJ Marco Collins got hold of a studio quality recording from the *Live Through This* sessions proving for the first time that Kurt had played an active role in the recording – a fact rumoured for years. Collins played an alternate version of the hit song "Asking For It" on his KNDD radio show. On the recording, Kurt can be heard clearly singing behind Love's lead voice, on the second verse, the bridge and the fadeout of the song. "If you live through this with me, I swear that I will die for you," the two sing together. Kurt is also heard briefly by himself chanting, "Live through this... live with this." Later, his voice seems to have been removed from the version released on the album. An official from Courtney's management company, Q Prime, confirmed to the magazine *Addicted to Noise* that the voice did belong to Kurt, adding, "I'm not going to comment beyond that."

For many, this confirmed that Kurt had indeed been responsible for the quality of *Live Through This* and increased the pressure on Courtney to release a respectable follow-up. Montreal's *Hour* magazine reported that Jordon Zadorozny, who used to play with Melissa Auf der Maur's old band Tinker and now leads the respected alternative band Blinker the Star, had been recruited by Courtney to write new material for the album. Indeed, Zadorozny had flown to Los Angeles and spent time with Courtney, but he later denied he was writing songs for Hole. According to the report in *Hour*; however, Zadorozny's bandmates laughed at his denial and indicated that the rumours were true. (In the fall of 1997, with the album in chaos, Billy Corgan was removed as producer and asked to "collaborate" on some new material.)

About a month before the scheduled release of *The People vs. Larry Flynt*, we were inadvertently thrust back into the spotlight. We were approached by a Canadian promoter named Victor Schiffman with a unique opportunity. He proposed a Canadian lecture tour and multimedia presentation to discuss our findings and promote our upcoming book. It sounded promising. Then he threw in a twist, suggesting that we tour with Courtney's father, Hank Harrison, who would discuss his daughter and promote his own book about Kurt Cobain. We were understandably wary of this idea, lest we get lumped in with some of his own wild accusations. We knew, however, that Harrison's publicity value was incalculable, so we finally agreed to a compromise. The show would be split into two segments, with us, in effect, as the opening act for Harrison.

So in early November 1996, we hit the road with our odd tour, once again attracting a huge media buzz. The tour started out uneventfully enough with a sold-out appearance in Hamilton, Ontario, before a very receptive crowd of university students. We discussed our findings, showed slides and videotapes, and answered questions from the crowd. Then, Harrison came out and discussed his early days with his daughter, read some letters and poetry from Courtney, and mostly refrained from discussing the murder theory.

The next night, the fireworks began. We were scheduled to appear at Toronto's Opera House club, where, ironically, Nirvana had played several years earlier. While we were on the road, the club's house manager, Enzo Petrungaro, says he received some menacing phone calls pressuring him to cancel our appearance from MCA Canada, the Canadian distributor for Courtney's label, Geffen Records. "There was no direct threat of freezing the Opera House out of MCA acts," he told *Shift* magazine, "but I got the message that way."

Soon after the calls from MCA, Petrungaro received a call from our old friend Jack Palladino, Courtney's lawyer-investigator who had shown up in Ian Halperin's backyard months earlier. Palladino continued to apply pressure for the Opera House to cancel, threatening legal action against the club. But Petrungaro stood his ground. An hour later, he says he received a phone call from someone claiming to be Courtney Love, but he was out of the office at the time so he never spoke to her.

When we finally showed up that night, none other than Palladino himself was sitting in the front row with recording equipment and an entourage of three. During our presentation, he yelled out rebuttals of our facts a couple of times until we finally invited him to join us on the stage during the question-and-answer period to give Courtney's side of the story.

When he started to take potshots at us instead of addressing the facts, people in the crowd started yelling, "Get off the stage, fuckhead," and other such insults (although, granted, we were also heckled by two or three audience members). When we finally began a serious debate of the facts, Palladino acknowledged that we sounded "much more responsible" than we had been in March when we did our radio series. He was most anxious to discredit El Duce's story, repeating the allegation that the singer had falsely claimed he was sitting on a bench outside the Rock Shop when Courtney allegedly approached him to kill Kurt. After the show ended, Palladino vowed to journalists that he would follow us around on our tour.

The next day, one of the spectators told the *Toronto Sun* that he had entered the presentation "highly skeptical" about the murder theory but left believing it was very possible. He wasn't the only one who had his mind changed. While we were in Toronto, we were invited to appear on the network TV show *Jane Hawtin Live*, which is often described as Canada's equivalent to Larry King. The show is televised while being simulcast on a nationally syndicated radio network. We were brought on to debate the author of the *Encyclopedia of Alternative Music* about the murder theory and whether the case should be reopened. He argued that Kurt's entire history proved he was suicidal and the facts clearly indicated that he took his own life.

After the show, viewers and listeners are traditionally asked to call a 900 number and register their votes for and against whatever question is asked on a particular show. At the end of our hour-long debate, the question was posed: "Should the case of Kurt Cobain's death be reopened by police?" Thousands of people called to vote. The final result was 91 percent of the callers believed the case should indeed be reopened, with only 9 percent dissenting.

The following evening, we appeared at another sold-out show in London, Ontario. Palladino did not appear, despite his previous vow to do so. A woman did appear in the front row with a tape recorder, however. After the promoter speculated the woman might be Courtney's entertainment attorney Rosemary Carroll, we confronted her and asked her who she was. Instead of answering, she hastily left before we could confirm her identity.

Our last appearance was scheduled for the next day in our hometown, Montreal. But as we were flying back, the legal threats were flying faster. The afternoon of our scheduled appearance at Montreal's Rialto Theatre, the promoter and the Rialto manager each received a very nasty lawyer's letter from Rosemary Carroll threatening a lawsuit if our appearance that night proceeded as scheduled. In the letter, she called Harrison "pathetic" and accused us of "fabricating evidence." After contacting his own lawyer, the promoter decided that he couldn't afford a legal battle and he decided to pull the plug on that evening's show and refund all the tickets already purchased. He did agree, however, to join us in a press conference on the stage of the theatre to discuss the cancellation decision and give us the opportunity to outline our case for free.

At the appointed time, we joined Harrison and took turns expressing our thoughts and then answered questions from the crowd of assembled media. This set the stage for perhaps the most bizarre incident of this case.

When Harrison addressed the crowd, there was a sudden commotion from the audience. Moments later, two figures stumbled up to the stage and grabbed the microphone from Harrison's hand. One of the intruders was a former music columnist named Juan Rodriguez, the other was a prominent local journalist and former Montreal city councillor, Nick Auf der Maur, who just happened to be the father of Hole bassist Melissa Auf der Maur. Nick had grown close to Courtney Love, who often spoke fondly of Melissa's dad and even introduced him from the stage of Lollapalooza two years earlier.

Now he started to hurl insults at Harrison and asked what kind of father would say these things about his own daughter. "She's a wonderful girl" Nick said about Courtney. Somebody yelled from the crowd "Who are you?" to which he responded, "I'm Melissa's mother..." (laughter from the audience) .... . er, I mean father." Finally, two bouncers came and removed him from the stage when he looked like he was about to get violent. He later told *Shift* magazine that he "really wanted to poke [Harrison] in the nose, I was so pissed. But there were so many people on the stage I couldn't figure out which one he was." The incident has since become known as the "Battle of the Rock Star Pops."

When Halperin returned to his Montreal apartment after the tour ended, it had been completely ransacked but nothing appeared to be missing. The police never discovered who was responsible.

Only a month after our tour ended, *The People vs. Larry Flynt* was finally released, and to the surprise of many, Courtney turned in a brilliant performance as Flynt's wife, Althea. Some critics, unwilling to concede that Courtney possessed any talent, charged that she was merely playing herself, but most reviewers were gushing in their praise. "Casting the Lady Cobain was not merely an art-imitates-death stunt," wrote *Time* magazine. "She's a real actress, rangy and sympathetic, with an instinct for just the right dose of excess." Many reviewers even speculated that Courtney's performance merited Oscar consideration.

But not everybody was enamoured of the movie's theme. Gloria Steinem, the well-known feminist, charged that the movie glorified pornography and romanticized the sleazy Flynt. She even took out ads in trade publications such as *Variety* urging Oscar voters to reject the movie. This prompted Courtney to go ballistic, repeatedly railing against that "dyke cunt," according to her friends.

"Courtney loved all the praise she was getting for Flynt," said one of her new Los Angeles buddies. "She was even talking about quitting music and devoting herself to acting full-time if she got an Oscar nomination. She really got into the Hollywood thing."

It seemed she was on the Oscar path when she received a Golden Globe nomination in January for Best Dramatic Performance by an Actress. At the awards ceremony, she lost out to Brenda Blethyn of *Secrets and Lies*, a defeat that she didn't mind so much as the fact that her arch rival Madonna won a Golden Globe for her own performance in *Evita*.

But the real surprise that evening was Courtney's startling transforma-tion. In her previous public appearances – even on formal occasions – she was known for her trademark grunge attire and baby doll thrift shop gowns. When she arrived at the ceremony, she stunned the paparazzi as she stepped out of her limo in a classic Valentino gown and Harry Winston diamond necklace. On her arm was the acclaimed actor Edward Norton, her costar in *The People vs. Larry Flynt*, whom she was rumoured to be dating.

For the next month before the Oscar nominations were scheduled to be announced, Courtney seemed to be everywhere with her new look, adorning magazine covers, *Entertainment Tonight*, and fashion shows in a carefully orchestrated campaign by her publicist Pat Kingsley to enhance her credibility.

"The real question we were asking ourselves," says a friend of Courtney's, "is whether her old image was the phony one or her new image. She seemed to fit in very well to her new glamorous lifestyle. Obviously, it was done with the Academy [of Motion Pictures Arts and Sciences, who give out the Oscars] in mind, but she was very comfortable with it. I was surprised."

In February, Courtney surprised everybody when she announced that she had become engaged to Ed Norton and that they would be married in June. Was this just another ploy to clean up her image?

When the fateful day arrived and the Oscar nominations were announced, Courtney's name was not on the list. By all accounts, she was devastated. She could not blame Gloria Steinem and her crusade against the film, because Woody Harrelson, who played Larry Flynt himself, did receive a nomination. Still, it seems obvious that she was denied the nomination because of her reputation rather than because she was undeserving.

Soon after the bad news, several media reports had Courtney checking into another drug rehab center, although her publicity agency denied the reports and said she was merely "on vacation."

Several months later, Courtney appeared at the Hard Rock Cafe in New York City to participate in an antidrug campaign with the Partnership for a Drug-Free America, announcing to the assembled media, "Drugs are dumb and senseless like sucking your thumb." It reminded many of Kurt Cobain's attempt five years earlier to convince the world he had changed his ways.

In March, Courtney was asked to present a minor award at the Oscar ceremony in Los Angeles. In front of a billion viewers, she arrived wearing a stunning Versace gown, suggesting that her new image is here to stay. Her fiancé Ed Norton, however, arrived separately, fueling speculation that their relationship was in trouble. Months later, media reports emerged that Norton had dumped Courtney and she was stalking him with repeated phone calls and letters.

Perhaps the oddest evidence that Courtney has changed is a report that she has made up with her old nemesis Madonna and that the two are studying the Jewish Kaballah together.

Around the time of the Oscars, we received a call from respected BBC documentary filmmaker Nick Broomfield, who is often referred to as Britain's Michael Moore, director of the quirky Roger & Me. Among Broomfield's many award-winning documentaries are *Heidi Fleiss: Hollywood Madam* and *Aileen Wuornos: The Selling of a Serial Killer*.

Now, Broomfield had decided to turn his camera on the subject of Courtney Love and the death of Kurt Cobain. In April, he flew us to Seattle to introduce him and his crew to the case.

While we were there, Broomfield got a firsthand taste of the way Courtney deals with negative publicity. His production company had already verbally arranged to sell the American TV rights of his upcoming film to the cable network Showtime, which had aired a number of his previous films. But while he was in Seattle, he received a phone call from a Showtime executive explaining a major obstacle in their deal. Showtime is owned by Viacom, which also owns the cable music channel MTV. The executive told Broomfield that Courtney's camp called MTV and threatened to withhold all of Hole's and, more importantly, Nirvana's videos if Showtime went ahead and aired the documentary. Broomfield taped the conversation with the Showtime executive and is considering using it in the film, which will air on another U.S. channel as well as have a limited theatrical release and video distribution.

The trip to Seattle presented a golden opportunity for us to see the homicide detective Sergeant Cameron and bring him the additional evidence which had surfaced since our last trip, including the results of the handwriting analysis commissioned by *Unsolved Mysteries* as well as El Duce's revelation and subsequent polygraph test. Cameron had frequently said he would be glad to reopen the case if he saw any credible evidence.

So, with Broomfield's camera crew following us, we headed to Cameron's office at the downtown Homicide Division. When we arrived, we told the receptionist who we were and that we had some important information for Sergeant Cameron. We could see Cameron behind his cubicle, sitting at his desk seemingly unoccupied. She went to deliver the message. A few minutes later, another detective came out and told us Cameron was busy. We told him we had come three thousand miles to deliver some new evidence in the Kurt Cobain case and we just needed a few minutes of his time.

"That case is closed," said the officer. "Now leave!"

We explained that Cameron had promised to consider reopening the case if he saw any evidence.

"I told you to get out," he responded angrily, then threatened to arrest us if we didn't leave. We hastily complied. When we viewed the exchange on film later, Cameron could be clearly seen peeking out from behind his cubicle.

Two weeks after we flew back to Montreal, Broomfield interviewed Eldon Hoke about his claim that Courtney had offered him $50,000 to kill Kurt. A few days after this interview, as already discussed, Hoke was mysteriously killed by a train.

On May 21, Courtney was invited to present an award to Flynt director Milos Forman at a Los Angeles fund-raiser for the American Civil liberties Union (ACLU), which champions the cause of free speech. Her old friend Danny Goldberg is the president of the Southern California chapter of the ACLU.

Shortly after Courtney presented the award, Broomfield jumped up on the podium and announced, "I don't mean to be a party poop but I have some questions about Hollywood having a problem distinguishing reality from myth or image and unless it was now considered appropriate to threaten to kill members of the press who had written unflattering articles about you, I consider it extremely poor judgment to have Courtney Love as a special guest."

As he was speaking, Goldberg jumped up on stage and dragged Broomfield away, shouting, "You can't talk, you weren't invited to speak."

Broomfield later told the press, "I thought that was extremely interesting coming from the president of the ACLU." The film is scheduled to run on the BBC's *Storyville* series in August 1998.

As the murder theory continues to gain wider circulation, it is time to put to rest the rumours and innuendo. The truth will only emerge from the facts. In December 1994, Sergeant Cameron told the *Seattle Post-Intelligencer* that the forensic evidence in the case makes murder nearly impossible. But he couldn't reveal that evidence because of Courtney's wishes.

The circumstantial evidence, at least, seems to indicate that Kurt Cobain may have been murdered and that Courtney Love possibly knows who did it. If there is concrete evidence which proves otherwise, it is in her best interests to authorize its release.

It is impossible to ignore the lack of fingerprints on the gun; the use of Kurt's credit card after his death; the level of heroin in his blood – triple the lethal dose; the second set of handwriting on the so-called suicide note; a troubling conflict of interest on the part of the coroner; an unfinished will disowning Courtney. Alarm bells must at least be raised by reports of an impending divorce; Kurt's alleged affair; a man claiming that he was offered $50,000 to kill Kurt and twice passing a credible polygraph exam "beyond possibility of deception." None of these by themselves prove a murder took place but certainly offer a compelling justification for a new investigation or, more accurately, a first investigation.

Courtney Love owes it to the families of sixty-eight dead teenagers. She owes it to thousands more who still suffer acute depression over the death of their hero. But most of all, she owes it to a five-year-old girl named Frances Bean, who will one day hear some ugly stories and deserves to know how her father really died.

14
A Final Word

Between the time we turned in our manuscript for this book in the Fall of 1997 and the book's publication in April, there were enough new developments to almost fill another book.

First, our old friend Jack Palladino — the San Francisco private investigator hired by Courtney to keep tabs on us two years earlier— turned up in the news in a case involving another one of his celebrity clients *The New Yorker* reported that Palladino had gone underground to evade a subpoena from Paula Jones in her sexual harassment case against President Clinton. The article quotes Palladino's wife and investigative partner, Sandra Sutherland, describing their approach as "the honest con", noting that they believe it is acceptable to use subterfuge and outright lies in the service of a client. It seems that Palladino had been hired by the Clinton presidential campaign in 1992 to suppress the so-called "bimbo eruptions" — women in Arkansas who claimed to have had affairs with Clinton. In a bizarre coincidence, the person attempting to serve the subpoena was none other than Tom Grant, who had been hired as an investigator by Paula Jones' lawyers in her ongoing lawsuit against Clinton. Grant turned out to be instrumental in discovering the existence of Monica Lewinsky. Among the other new revelations about Palladino was the fact that he used to represent the infamous Hells Angels motorcycle gang.

In March, 1998 — with the Jones legal team and half the American media attempting to locate him — Palladino mysteriously appeared at the offices of our publishing company, Carol Publishing, demanding to see the head of the company about the impending publication of our book. When he was told to leave because he didn't have an appointment, he refused and insisted that he be allowed to correct the falsehoods in the book, which he had presumably not yet seen. He was told the book had already been shipped to bookstores and, after a couple of hours, he finally left.

Six weeks earlier, Courtney's camp had been a little more successful at suppressing discussion of the murder theory when they managed to get Nick Broomfield's film *Kurt & Courtney* withdrawn from Robert Redford's Sundance Film Festival, the world's largest independent film festival which takes place in Utah. For months, Courtney's lawyers had been threatening the festival with a lawsuit if it went ahead and screened the controversial documentary. Sundance refused to bow to these threats and vowed to show it anyway, standing by Broomfield, whose film *Heidi Fleiss: Hollywood Madam* had won the "Best Documentary" prize two years earlier. Then, three days before the festival was scheduled to open, Sundance announced that it was pulling *Kurt & Courtney* from its lineup because of a dispute over music rights. The film included two songs controlled by Courtney Love, Nirvana's "Smells Like Teen Spirit" and Hole's "Doll Parts". Broomfield insisted that the BBC, for whom he had made the documentary, had already obtained clearance for the songs but Love's lawyers insisted that he did not have permission to use them and they would sue the festival if the film was presented.

In a press conference on the opening day of the festival, Robert Redford issued a blistering attack on Courtney and her efforts to stop the film but insisted that his "hands were tied" because of the legal issues involved.

"As an artist who's benefited so much from freedom of speech in her career," he told the media, "I find it highly ironic that she chose to prevent another artist from showing his work." He went on to express his hope that the film would be shown elsewhere, saying, "Nick deserves a voice". Redford's attack reportedly infuriated Courtney because her publicity company, PMK, also represents Redford.

The Sundance withdrawal, however, did not faze Broomfield, who organized a secret invitation — only midnight showing of the film for selected media. The ensuing coverage, including worldwide newspaper headlines, gave the film publicity no money could buy; Courtney's attempt to silence Broomfield had backfired.

The film itself turned out to be more of a study of control and censorship than a serious look at the murder theory, although Broomfield did interview many of the central characters, including Tom Grant and Eldon Hoke (who, of course, was mysteriously killed by a train eight days after he talked to Broomfield). The most interesting revelation was an interview with a 22-year-old nanny who had worked for Kurt and Courtney until shortly before Kurt's death and then quit because "Courtney was always talking about Kurt's will. What a thing to talk about! She totally controlled him every second she could. I couldn't stand it up there. If he wasn't murdered, then he was driven to murder himself." As we discussed in the book, Kurt had approached his lawyer shortly before the death about drawing up a will and excluding Courtney but when he died, this will had not yet been signed so the nanny's account may be significant.

One of the most serious flaws in the film is a passage where Broomfield explores the theory which says suicide was impossible because Kurt had a triple lethal dose of heroin in his body at the time of his death, making it impossible for him to roll down his sleeves, put away the drug kit, pick up a shotgun and shoot himself. Tom Grant had challenged him to find a case in medical history where somebody had ingested a similar dose and lived long enough to shoot themselves.

Taking up this challenge, Broomfield located a doctor who insisted he had a patient who took "twice the dose" that Cobain did and lived. The doctor shows a slide of this patient balancing on one leg after taking this dose. On the basis of this finding, Broomfield announces that he "no longer believes the murder theory".

Indeed, if true, this would be a serious blow to the murder theory because the heroin study is by far the strongest evidence supporting Tom Grant's position. After seeing the film, Grant contacted the doctor about his findings to determine his methodology and received a detailed letter explaining his conclusions.

"I was prepared to concede a hole in the murder theory if there was anything to this doctor's findings," Grant insists. "But as I suspected, Broomfield made a serious mistake."

It turned out that the patient shown in the film had in fact taken methadone, not heroin, and had swallowed his dose rather than injected it, as Cobain had done. The doctor conceded that he was not even licensed to administer heroin so he could not have duplicated Cobain's dose even if he wanted to.

Grant turned over the doctor's letter to Roger Lewis, a Canadian expert on toxicity whose essay, *Dead Men Don't Pull Triggers* (see chapter 8) argues that Cobain couldn't have shot himself with a triple lethal dose of heroin in his system. When Lewis read the doctor's methodology, he immediately dismissed his study.

"Heroin is much stronger, much more toxic, and much faster acting than methadone," Lewis explained.

"Intravenously administered heroin is up to five times stronger than orally administered heroin. Furthermore, even a large oral dose of methadone would take approximately thirty minutes to produce effects due to the fact that the drugs must first pass through the stomach, whereas the effects produced by an intravenous large dose of heroin are immediate. The medical evidence which indicates Cobain was murdered is based strongly on well established facts regarding the extreme toxicity and rapid action of such a large overdose of intravenous heroin, therefore Broomfield's comparison bears no relevance to the Cobain case."

Grant says he doesn't blame Broomfield for the error even

though it is very damaging to the credibility of the murder theory.

"This is very complicated science," he says. "It is easy to get confused. That's why the police weren't able to pick up on it. You need somebody looking at this evidence who has experience with heroin toxicity. Nick thought he was on to something but he was wrong. I hope he'll try to correct the error somehow."

In Spring, 1998, an independent cinema in San Francisco, called the Roxie, announced that they would show Kurt & Courtney for three weeks, prompting an immediate threat by Courtney's lawyer Michael Chodos, who wrote a vaguely threatenening letter to the Roxie claiming the charges by Hank Harrison and others in the film are "false and defamatory, nothing more. They are extremely damaging to Ms. Love and very hurtful." The letter concluded by warning that "By choosing to displaying the film, or provide a forum for them to speak, you are endorsing and participating in their actions and statements, and are liable along with them for any resulting damage."

The Roxie chose to ignore this letter and opened to sell-out crowds. By the end of the 3-week run, the film had broken the theatre's box office record. They never again heard from Courtney or her lawyers. Inspired by the success of their San Francisco screening, the Roxie decided to distribute the film around the country with similar success. By July 1998, the film was showing in more than 40 American cities.

Media reaction to the film was mixed. Most film critics, including Janet Maislin of the New York Times, praised Broomfield's effort. Gene Siskel, one of the US TV duo *Siskel & Ebert*, gave it a thumbs down, complaining that the film didn't go far enough in pursuing the murder theory.

"I don't think the film proves anything," he said on the weekly television show, "so that's why I fault it and can't really recommend it; I think if you're going to raise these issues, then just stick with them, and pursue it the way a journalist really would; I don't feel the film was hard enough on the issue of the murder — I think there are leads there that should have been pursued a lot tougher." His partner, Roger Ebert, gave it a thumbs up. In England, Channel Four film critic Victor Olliver named *Kurt & Courtney* "Film of the Year", advising people to "go see it before she gets an injunction". The majority of music critics panned the film. "The American music media are extremely sycophantic," explained Broomfield. "They can not afford to alienate the music industry as I was told time and again while making this film. Geffen is very powerful. They control the most important commodity in the music media — access. They can prevent interviews, junkets, backstage passes, all the things music journalists crave."

The Roxie discovered how far this power extends when they attempted to place advertising for *Kurt & Courtney*. According to Roxie Manager Bill Banning, two Southern California radio stations told him they had been informed by Geffen that if they took advertising for the movie, they would never receive advertising again from the record company. A spokesperson for Geffen, however, denies the company engaged in this kind of censorship.

Around the time *Kurt & Courtney* received widespread release, our book was launched on April 8, 1998 — the fourth anniversary of the discovery of Kurt's body. When Courtney's publicist, Pat Kingsley, was asked by the *Houston Chronicle* whether her client intended to pursue legal action against our book or Broomfield's film, Kingsley replied, "She's totally lost interest in this. It's all history to her."

Three weeks later, we would have a chance to gauge Courtney's reaction directly. directly when her bassist's father, Nick Auf der Maur, died of cancer. This was the same guy who jumped up on stage during our lecture tour the year before and threatened to assault Courtney's father.

Now Courtney and the rest of the band flew to Montreal, our hometown, for the funeral. At the memorial service, although we came face to face with her, the solemnity of the occasion dictated that there would be no confrontation of any sort. The strangest incident, in fact did not involve Courtney at all but rather a local journalist for the *Montreal Mirror*. As the mourners headed for the wake, this reporter revealed that Auf der Maur had commissioned him two years earlier to "dig up dirt" on us on behalf of Courtney after it was first revealed that we were investigating the murder theory. It was this dossier that

Jack Palladino was carrying when he showed up in Ian Halperin's backyard in 1996. Auf der Maur's reward for gathering the information? "Courtney sent him flowers and a thank you note," our new friend revealed.

The death of Melissa Auf der Maur's father marked the beginning of a nightmare period for Courtney and her bandmates, which would lead one of them to speculate that "somebody must have put a curse on us."

Shortly after Courtney returned to L.A., she attended a fashion show when celebrity photographer Belissa Cohen tried to take her picture. According to witnesses, Courtney went ballistic, charging Cohen, grabbing her hair, kneeing her in the groin and whacking her in the face.

"Don't be taking pictures of me! Do you think I'm not still punk rock?" she reportedly yelled during the attack, then allegedly boasted to friends, "I just hit Belissa Cohen, and it felt good."

On May 28, Cohen filed a lawsuit against Courtney in Los Angeles Superior Court for undisclosed damages. At a press conference, she told reporters, "I was extremely frightened by the violence and viciousness of Ms. Love's physical attack upon me in front of others at a crowded fashion show... Ms. Love's conduct sends the message that celebrities are somehow above the law... For her own sake and that of the community with whom she will have future contact, I'd like to see Ms. Love get some help."

Love's previous physical altercations include a 1995 assault on Bikini Kill singer Kathleen Hanna during that year's Lollapalooza tour. Love pled guilty to the attack and was sentenced to anger management classes for the incident.

Courtney's spokesperson Heidi Schaeffer responded, "Basically, this is another out-of-control paparazzi targeting a celebrity."

Was this a return to the old Courtney? Sceptics speculated that her behavior was a conscious attempt to shed her Versace image in time for the release of her new album, which by coincidence was scheduled for the Fall, Geffen had just announced. Already, Courtney was going around bragging about the quality of the recording, which had just been completed.

Selected friendly media were granted interviews and even a sneak listen to some of the tracks. Courtney and her bandmates seemed to be everywhere getting the hype machine in overdrive, talking about "how proud" they were of the album — tentatively titled *Celebrity Skin* — which had been four years in the making. They failed to explain why the album took so long to emerge, especially since Courtney bragged three years earlier that they had written all the tracks in less than two weeks.

Our own sources had revealed that the original music was awful and that Billy Corgan of the Smashing Pumpkins had been brought in as producer to salvage the album but complained he "couldn't work miracles with mediocrity". At this point, we reported, he stepped down as producer to write new material for the album.

Now, Courtney was downplaying Corgan's involvement, at one point claiming, "Billy's not really involved and he doesn't have any writing credits." She was obviously still haunted by the charges which refuse to go away, that Kurt wrote most of the music on *Live Through This*. This was the last straw for Corgan who finally went public to refute Courtney's claims.

"Let's get one thing straight," he told Britain's *Select* magazine. "There wouldn't be a new Hole album if it wasn't for me. She invited me to be the Svengali producer. She claimed I just produced it and that's just rubbish. She is trying to have her cake and eat it, but I've got writing credit on seven songs."

Addressing the persistent rumors, he said, "I warned her upfront that everyone thought the last album was written by Kurt and asked if she was willing to accept my help, in light of what people are going to say. People around her asked me before we went into the studio not to get involved in the writing process but she encouraged me to write somgs, with and for them, so I did."

Corgan wasn't the only outsider brought in rescue the album. More than a year earlier, it was reported that Canadian musician Jordon Zadorozny, leader of the alternative group Blinker the Star, had been flown to Los Angeles by Courtney to write material for the new album. Geffen Records vehemently denied these reports, insisting that Zadorozny was in fact collaborating with Stevie Nicks. An advance track list we obtained in June, however, reveals that Zadorozny is indeed given a writing credit on two songs, "Reasons to be Beautiful", which allegedly makes reference to Kurt's suicide note, and "Northern Star".

This lack of honesty ensures that, no matter how good the album turns out to be, doubts will always persist about Courtney's musical talent.

Corgan wasn't the only long-time Courtney suppporter to turn on her. Two years ago, a university student named David Perle — considered by some to be the world's foremost expert on Nirvana — was Tom Grant's harshest critic and a strong supporter of Courtney. She even e-mailed him thanking him for his support. He had his own web page refuting the murder theory titled "Why Tom Grant Should Not Be Believed". About a year ago, he started slowly to change his mind, admitting that not all of what Grant says can be dismissed out of hand and calling on the authorities to investigate Kurt's death. At the time our book went to press, he was still sceptical. Now, Perle has carefully studied *Dead Men Don't Pull Triggers* and he has become one of Tom Grant's most ardent defenders. On his web page, he writes, "For at least a year and a half as of this notice, I have been seriously, and painfully, questioning what I believe; did Kurt Cobain kill himself, or might he actually have been killed by someone? I have learned things the past couple of years that, if believed, definitely do not show Courtney Love in a very positive light, and even more relevant to this matter, show that Kurt Cobain apparently could not have shot himself."

Limited to the internet however, people like Perle can't do Courtney significant damage in her ongoing quest to gain respectability and bury the rumours. But the steady drumbeat of accusation has now reached its way to the mainstream media whose acceptance she covets. Twice this year the *New York Times* has referred to Kurt's death as an "alleged suicide" and hundreds of newspapers and magazines have now reported the inconsistencies in Kurt's death without the sarcasm and conspiracy-bashing which used to accompany such articles.

One newspaper article even noted an interesting piece of trivia; it seems that Courtney Love and O.J. Simpson both share the same birthday, July 9.

One of the most damaging these articles quotes Palladino's wife and investigative partner, Sandra Sutherland, describing their approach as "the honest con", noting that they believe it is acceptable to use subterfuge and outright lies in the service of a client. of these was a June profile in the *New Yorker* titled "Endless Love", which analyzed Courtney's new image at length and discussed Broomfield's film, calling it "unnerving", and our book, which it called a "judicious presentation of explosive material". The piece was by no means a hatchet job of Courtney but did recycle many of the old stories and quotes from her bad girl days. This was precisely the kind of thing Courtney was paying her very expensive public relations machine to keep out of the media and they had managed very successfully for the past two years, keeping her on the cover of *Vogue, Harpers Bazaar*, honing her new Versace image. Now, it was all coming back to haunt her in one of America's most influential magazines.

Soon after, Courtney went to Europe to drum up publicity for her new album. Anxious to avoid a repeat of the *New Yorker* coverage, her publicists came up with a new strategy. Anybody who wanted a TV or radio interview with Courtney was forced to sign an agreement prohibiting them from asking "questions about Love's late husband, Kurt Cobain, or director Nick Broomfield's documentary *Kurt & Courtney* or any band member's personal life, or Love's estranged father Hank Harrison, or any half-truths/rumours relating to the use of illegal substances, et cetera." Many broadcasters refused to sign this document, instead reporting on her attempts at censorship. Articles about the murder theory have been appearing widely in England and Europe including an eight-page cover story in the British music magazine *Mojo* titled "Who Killed Kurt Cobain?"

Tom Grant believes this is an omen of things to come. "She can't escape her past," he says. "It's taken a long time but the truth is finally getting out there. I firmly believe justice will be done."

As he continues his elusive quest and we await Courtney's next incarnation, how many out there must be looking beyond images of justice, conspiracies and movie stars and asking themselves one fundamental question: When will Kurt get to rest in peace?

Appendix

To: Tom Grant.
From Courtney Cobain

I, Courtney Cobain, authorize The Grant Co., Los Angeles CA to release any records relating to the use of ~~card No.~~ Seafirst Bank Card No. [redacted] between April 1, 1974 to the present to the Seattle Police Department.

C. L. Cobain

Courtney Love Cobain

A note from Courtney authorizing financial information to be released to Tom Grant.

SEATTLE POLICE DEPARTMENT
INCIDENT REPORT

☒ INCIDENT ☐ INCIDENT AND ARREST ☐ ARREST ONLY

INCIDENT NUMBER: 93-89169

☐ DO NOT DISCLOSE ☒ NOT DISCUSSED ☐ DISCLOSE ☐ HAZARD ☐ DOMESTI

I HEREBY DECLARE THE FACTS HEREIN REPORTED BY ME ARE TRUE AND CORRECT. I UNDERSTAND THAT BY FILING A FALSE REPORT, I MAY BE SUBJECT TO CRIMINAL PROSECUTION.

INCIDENT CLASSIFICATION	TOOL/WEAPON USED	METHOD OF TOOL/WEAPON USE
DRUG OVERDOSE	HYPODERMIC SYRINGE	INJECTION

LOCATION	FIRM NAME	CENSUS
11301 LAKESIDE AVE. N.E.		C09

TYPE OF PREMISE (FOR VEHICLES STATE TYPE AND WHERE PARKED)	POINT OF ENTRY
PRIVATE RESIDENCE	

DATE/TIME REPORTED	DAY OF WEEK	DATE/TIME OCCURRED
05-02-93/2111 HRS	SUN	05-02-93/2110 HRS

☐ EVIDENCE SUBMITTED ☐ FINGERPRINT SEARCH MADE ☐ FINGERPRINTS FOUND ☐ LAB EXAM REQUESTED

PERSONS/BUSINESS INVOLVED — CODE: C (PERSON REPORTING, COMPLAINANT) V (VICTIM) W (WITNESS)

CODE	NAME (LAST, FIRST, MIDDLE)	ZIP CODE	RACE/SEX/D.O.B. (OPTIONAL) / OCCUPATION (OPTIONAL)	INJURED	HOME PHONE / WORK PHONE	HOU
V	COBAIN, KURT DONALD		W/M/02-20-67	X	448-7554	
	ADDRESS: 11301 LAKESIDE AVE. N.E.	98125	MUSICIAN			
C/W	COBAIN, COURTNEY L.		W/F/07-09-64		448-7554	
	ADDRESS: 11301 LAKESIDE AVE. N.E.	98125	MUSICIAN			

SUSPECT NUMBER 1

NAME (LAST, FIRST, MIDDLE)	RACE/SEX/D.O.B.	HEIGHT	WEIGHT	HAIR	EYES	SKIN

ADDRESS	HOME PHONE	WORK PHONE	WORK HOURS	OCCUPATION	EMPLOYER

CLOTHING, SCARS, MARKS, TATTOOS, PECULIARITIES, A.K.A. — RELATIONSHIP TO

0 2256 [illegible]

BA/CIT. NO. — CHARGE DETAILS (INCLUDE ORDINANCE OR R.C.W. NUMBER AND CHARGE NARRATIVES) — ☐ BOOKED ☐ Y.S.C. ☐ CITED ☐ K.C.J. #1

5/12/93

☐ ADDITIONAL PROPERTY (PROPERTY FORM 5.37.1 MUST BE ATTACHED) ☐ NOTHING TAKEN ☐ UNKNOWN AT TIME OF REPORT ☐ VICTIM FOLLOW-U

PROPERTY

ARTICLE TYPE	BRAND NAME	VALUE
☐ STOLEN ☐ RECOVERED — SERIAL NUMBER	OWNER APPLIED NUMBER	MODEL NUMBER
COLOR, SIZE, DESCRIPTION, CALIBER, BARREL LENGTH, ETC.		

1. ADDITIONAL PERSONS - CODE, NAME, RACE, SEX, D.O.B., ADDRESS, INJURY, HOSPITALIZATION, HOME AND WORK PHONES, HOURS, AND IF DISCLOSURE OF NAME IS PERMITTED.
2. ADDITIONAL SUSPECTS - DETAIL INFORMATION IN SAME ORDER AS SUSPECT BLOCK.
3. VICTIM'S INJURIES - DETAILS AND WHERE MEDICAL EXAM OCCURRED.
4. PROPERTY DAMAGED - DESCRIBE AND INDICATE AMOUNT OF LOSS.
5. PHYSICAL EVIDENCE - DETAIL WHAT AND WHERE FOUND, BY WHOM, AND DISPOSITION.
6. VEHICLE USED BY SUSPECT AND DISPOSITION.
7. NAME, ADDRESS, PHONE NUMBER OF JUVENILE'S PARENT(S)/GUARDIA CONTACTED AND IF INCIDENT ADJUSTED.
8. LIST STATEMENTS TAKEN AND DISPOSITION.
9. RECONSTRUCT INCIDENT AND DESCRIBE INVESTIGATION.
10. OUTLINE TESTIMONY OF PERSONS MARKED "HAS USABLE TESTIMONY"

ITEM NO.	
1	W1/COBAIN, KIM D, W/F/04-24-70, 1210 E. 1ST, ABERDEE
	98520, HM 533-2306, UNEMPLOYED, NOT DISCUSSED.
	W2/O'CONNOR, WENDY E, W/F/04-24-47, 1210 E. 1ST, A
	WA 98520, HM 533-2306, UNEMPLOYED, NOT DISCUSSED.
3	V/COBAIN SUFFERED SYMPTOMS ASSOCIATED WITH AN OVER
	OF A NARCOTIC ACCORDING TO MEDICAL PERSONNEL ON

PRIMARY OFFICER — SERIAL — UNIT — SECONDARY OFFICER — SERIAL — UNIT — APPROVING OFFICER

Police report of Cobain's 1993 drug overdose.

DO NOT DISCLOSE

SEATTLE POLICE DEPARTMENT
MISSING PERSON REPORT

'94 APR -4 7 09

CENSUS 078 | BEAT C4 | SIN 94-149669

ENDANGERED / [DIS]ABLED (REVERSE SIDE FOR DEFINITIONS) | INVOLUNTARY / JUVENILE | MISSING / RUNAWAY / OTHER | DATE REPORTED 4/4/94 | TIME REPORTED

NAME OF MISSING PERSON: COBAIN, KURT D -9/LERENA | SEX: MALE / FEMALE | RACE: BLACK / ASIAN/PAC. ISLANDER / UNKNOWN / WHITE / NATIVE AMERICAN | D.O.B./AGE 0220[6]

ADDRESS OF MISSING PERSON: 171 LAKE WASH BV E | ZIP CODE | HEIGHT 5'10 | WEIGHT 135 | EYE COLOR: BLUE / BROWN / HAZEL / BLACK / GREEN / MULTICOLORED / UNKNOWN | HAIR COLOR DIRTY

BUILD: VERY THIN / THIN / MEDIUM / MUSCULAR / STOCKY / OBESE | SKIN TONE FAIR | MARITAL STATUS MARRIED | MISSING PERSON'S BANK SEAFIRST/BROADWAY BRAN[CH] | BANK PHONE

PLACE OF BIRTH: MONTESANO, WA | OCCUPATION MUSICIAN | HOME PHONE | WORK HOURS — | DATE OF LAST CONTACT 040294

SOCIAL SECURITY NUMBER UNK | DRIVER'S LICENSE NO. UNK | LICENSE ST. WA | OTHER IDENTIFICATION NO. UNK.

SCARS, MARKS, TATTOOS, MISSING OR ARTIFICIAL BODY PARTS (DESCRIPTION AND LOCATION): "K" ON RIGHT FOREARM

MENTAL/PHYSICAL CONDITION: UNK

ARMED OR DANGEROUS (EXPLAIN): NOT DANGEROUS/ARMED W/SHOT GUN | MILITARY EXPERIENCE (ACTIVE OR RESERVE) YES / NO | FINGERPRINTS AVAILABLE: YES / NO / UNKNOWN

WORK/SCHOOL ADDRESS N/A | WORK/SCHOOL PHONE N/A | DOCTOR'S NAME UNK | DOCTOR'S PHONE UNK | DENTIST'S NAME UNK | DENTIST'S PHONE UNK

CLOTHING AND PERSONAL ITEMS — CHECK THIS BOX IF CLOTHING UNKNOWN

ITEM	STYLE/TYPE	SIZE	COLOR	ITEM	STYLE/TYPE	SIZE	COLOR
HEADWEAR				FOOTWEAR			
SCARF TIE, GLOVES				UNDERWEAR			
COAT/JACKET				WALLET/PURSE			
SWEATER				MONEY			
SHIRT/BLOUSE				JEWELRY			
SKIRT				OTHER			
BELT/SUSPENDERS				OTHER			
STOCKINGS/HOSE				OTHER			
EYEWEAR				OTHER			

VEHICLE INFORMATION — DID MISSING PERSON TAKE A VEHICLE? YES / NO / UNKNOWN

LICENSE NO. | LICENSE ST. | LICENSE YR. | V.I.N. | CONDITION OF VEHICLE

VEHICLE YEAR | VEHICLE MAKE | VEHICLE MODEL | VEHICLE STYLE | EXTERIOR COLOR | INTERIOR COLOR

CODE: C—COMPANION F—FRIEND P—PARENT/GUARDIAN R—RELATIVE W—WITNESS O—OTHER

NAME | CODE | ADDRESS | ZIP CODE | HOME PHONE | WORK PHONE

NAME OF PERSON REPORTING | ZIP CODE

POSSIBLE [DESTINATION] OF MISSING PERSON | HAS PERSON BEEN MISSING ON PRIOR OCCASIONS? YES / NO / UNKNOWN — LA

SUMMARY OF INCIDENT—INVESTIGATIVE ACTIONS TAKEN—OTHER INFORMATION

MR COBAIN RAN AWAY FROM CALIFORNIA FACILITY AND FLEW BACK TO SEATTLE. HE ALSO BOUGHT A SHOT GUN AND MAYBE SUICIDAL. MR COBAIN MAYBE AT [redacted] LOCATION FOR NARCOTICS. DET TERRY SPD/NARCOTICS HAS FURTHER INFO

DATA CENTER USE ONLY

WAC # | NIC # | D.O.E.: | T.O.E.: | SERIAL:

PRIMARY OFFICER | SERIAL 5344 | UNIT 532 | SECONDARY OFFICER | SERIAL | UNIT | SUPERVISOR'S SIGNATURE | SERIAL

FORM 5.12 — CRIMES AGAINST PERSONS / JUVENILE / COURT UNIT / K-9 UNIT

Missing person's report filed by Courtney, claiming to be Kurt's mother. Note the mention of Detective Terry, who was later murdered.

Seattle Police Department
HOMICIDE UNIT
M. .JOR INVESTIGATION SUMMARY

SUBJECT:	Suicide	SIN:	94-156500
DATE/TIME:	4-8-94 0856 hours the body was found	H #:	N/A at this time
LOCATION:	171-Lake washington Blvd. East	PREMISES:	Garage
VICTIM(S): (Race, sex & age)	COBAIN, Kurt Donald White male 27 DOB 2-20-67	# VICTIMS:	One
SUSPECT(S): (Race, sex & age)	N/A	# SUSPECTS:	None
CAUSE OF DEATH:	GSW to the head	WEAPON:	20 ga. shotgun
MOTIVE:	Unknown at this time		
CASE DETECTIVES:	Jim Yoshida & Steve Kirkland	ARREST (Y/N):	N/A

INCIDENT DESCRIPTION:

On 4-8-94 at approximately 0845 hours the body of Kurt Donald Cobain was found in the garage loft of the residence at 171-Lake Washington Blvd. East. Cobain (the lead singer or the rock group Nirvana) was observed lying on the floor of the loft with a shotgun on his chest by electricians working on the property. The electricians summoned police fire who forced entry into the loft.

Cobain suffered a single GSW to the head. The shotgun had been placed in Cobains mouth and discharged. There were marks on Cobains hands consistant with the firing of this we Cobain has been dead for several days.

Cobain has been positively identified through fingerprints.

The 20 ga. shotgun found on Cobains chest has been traced to a gun shop in the North En and sale to Cobain and a friend has been confirmed.

A lengthy suicide note was found in the loft near the body.

At this point in the investigation it appears the fatal wound to Cobain is self-inflict

The residence at 171-Lake Washington Blvd. East is owned by Kurt Cobain and his wife Courtney who is enroute to Seattle from Calif.

Captain Larry Farrar responded to the crime scene.

SCENE SUPERVISOR:	SCENE DETECTIVES:
Lts. George Marberg, Al Ge es and Sgt. Don Cameron	Jim Yoshida & Steve Kirkland

DISTRIBUTION: ☐ ALL BELOW:

☐ CHIEF OF POLICE ☐ ASST. CHIEF INVESTIGATIONS ☐ ASST CHIEF OPERATIONS
☐ MAJOR, C.I.D. ☐ MAJOR, VICE & NARCOTICS ☐ MAJOR, PATROL
☐ CAPTAIN, CRIMES/PERSONS ☐ SECTION LTS. (3) ☐ SECTION SGTS. (7)
☐ CLERICAL STAFF (2) ☐ Cr Ag Per DETS. (41) ☐ OTHER:

2/92

Police incident report describing the death scene.

FINGERPRINT ANALYSIS REPORT
SEATTLE POLICE DEPARTMENT

PRESS FIRMLY—USE BALLPOINT PEN

INCIDENT NUMBER: 94-15650[illegible]

VICTIM		SUSPECT (S)
Cobain, Kurt Donald		1
TYPE OF PREMISE: Green house	TYPE OF OFFENSE: Suicide	2
TIME DATE OF OFFENSE: 4/08/94	SECTOR: C	INDICATE FINAL DISPOSITION OF EVIDENCE IF RESULTS NEGATIVE: ☐ DESTROY ☐ RETURN TO OWNER ☐ EVIDENCE NEEDED FOR PROSECUTION REGARDLESS OF RE

LIST OF ITEMS TO BE EXAMINED (LIST IN ORDER OF PRIORITY)

EVIDENCE UNIT ITEM NUMBER	DESCRIPTION
Item #8	Remington M-11 20 guage shotgun Sar # 1088925.
	PLEASE DO NOT PROCESS [redacted] AS THIS WEAPON IS TO BE EXAMINED B
	THE WASHINGTON STATE PATROL CRIME LAB AFTER IT IS PROCESSED BY THE SPD I
	UNIT.
	HIGH PROFILE CASE.

REQUESTED BY	SERIAL	UNIT	DATE	APPROVED BY	SERIAL	SIGNATURE
S. Kirkland	3356	321.	5/6/94	CAPT L. Fa[illegible]	[illegible]	[signature]

FINGERPRINT ANALYSIS REPORT

The above item was processed for prints on 05/06/94 by Sr ID Technician T. Geronimo, #4466. Four cards of latent prints were lifted.

The four cards of lifted latent prints contain no legible prints.

FINGERPRINT EXAMINER NAME	SERIAL	SIGNATURE	DATE OF EXAMINATION
T. Geronimo	4466	[signature] 4466	05/09/94

Fingerprint analysis report on the shotgun found by Kurt's body.

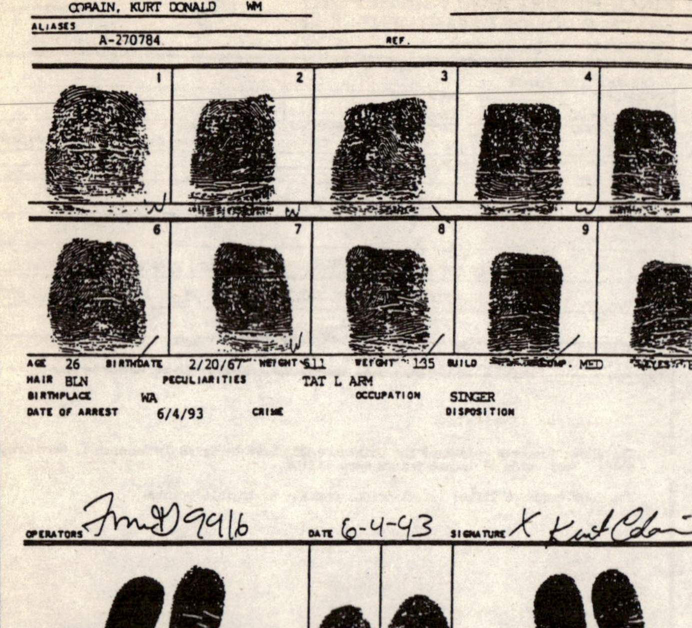

COBAIN, KURT DONALD WM

ALIASES

A-270784 REF.

1 2 3 4

6 7 8 9

AGE 26 BIRTHDATE 2/20/67 HEIGHT 511 WEIGHT 135 BUILD COMP. MED EYES

HAIR BLN PECULIARITIES TAT L ARM

BIRTHPLACE WA OCCUPATION SINGER

DATE OF ARREST 6/4/93 CRIME DISPOSITION

OPERATORS 9916 DATE 6-4-93 SIGNATURE X Kurt Cobain

Kurt's fingerprints, none of which were found on the shotgun.

STATE OF WASHINGTON

WASHINGTON STATE PATROL

930 Tacoma Avenue South, #8-70 (County/City Building) • Tacoma, Washington 98402-2102 • (206) 593-2006 • (SCAN) 462-.

CRIME LABORATORY REPORT

Agency: Seattle Police Department **Laboratory No.** 394-1785
Officer: Detective Stephen Kirkland
Suspect: N/A **Agency No.** 94-156500
Victim: Cobain, Kurt Donald

I received for examination the following items:

8. One Remington, model M-11 Sportsman, 20 gauge, self-loading (semiautomatic) shotgun bearing serial number 1088925.
10. One fired Winchester, AA, 20 gauge, 2-1/2 inch shotshell.

Results of Examination:

The item 8 Remington shotgun was empty (not loaded) when received. The shotgun was successfully test fired and found to be functioning in a normal manner. The trigger pull was determined to be approximately 3.6 to 3.8 pounds.

The shotgun's two-round magazine, plus one round in the chamber, give it a total capacity of three rounds. A functional crossbolt safety is located to the rear of the trigger. This safety was in the "OFF" position when the shotgun was received.

The shotgun's barrel is 22 inches in length, and is fitted with a compensator at the muzzle for a total overall firearm length of 45-5/8 inches.

The item 10 fired shotshell was determined to have been fired in the item 8 Remington shotgun bearing serial number 1088925. This shotshell has markings indicating its original load consisted of 7/8 ounce of number 8 shot.

Larry D. Hebert, Forensic Scientist May 18, 1994

Page 1 of 1

State of Washington crime laboratory report.

Boddah pro[illegible]

GP171

-ing from the tongue of an experienced simpleton who obviously
-ther be an emasculated, infantile complainee. This note should
easy to understand. All the warnings from the punk rock 101
the years. since my first introduction to the, shall we say, ethic
-th independence and the embracement of your community has proven
-ue. I havent felt the excitement of listening to as well as creating m
-lling and writing for too many years now. I feel [illegible]
[illegible] and the lights go out and the manic roar of the
is it doesnt affect me the way in which it did for Freddy Mercury who
love, relish in the love and adoration from the crowd. which is something
admire and envy. The fact is I cant fool you. Any one of you.
isnt fair to you or me. The worst crime I can think of would be to
by faking it and pretending as if im having 100% fun. Sometimes I feel
have a punch in time clock before I walk out on stage. Ive tried everything
-wer to to appreciate it (and I do. God, believe me I do. but its not enough
the fact that I and we have affected and entertained a lot of people.
be one of those [illegible] narcissists who only appreciate things when they
too sensitive. I need to be slightly numb in order to regain the enthusia
-ad as a child. On our last 3 tours Ive had a much better apprecati
people Ive known personally and as fans of our music, but I still cant get o
-stian, the jurth and [illegible] I have for everyone. Theres good in all of us and
-ly love people too much. so much that it makes me feel too fucking sad. The s
-tive, unappreciative, pisces, Jesus man! why dont you just enjoy it? I dont
-ddess of a wife who sweats ambition and empathy and a daughter who re
-h of what I used to be. full of love and joy, kissing every person she meets
-ne is good and will do her no harm. And that terrifies me to the point to where I
in. I cant stand the thought of Frances becoming the miserable self destructive,
that Ive become. I have it good, very good. and Im grateful, but
seven Ive become hateful towards all humans in general. Only because it seems
-eople to get along and have empathy. Empathy! Only because I love and feel
too much I guess. Thank you all from the pit of my burning nause
-r your letters and concern during the past years. Im too much of an erratic, moo
passion anymore and so remember, its better to burn out than to
[illegible]
-ay. peace love, Empathy. Kurt Cobain

-es and Courtney, Ill be at your altar.
-ease keep going Courtney (!)
for Frances
for her life which will be so much happier
without me. I LOVE YOU, I LOVE YOU

CAPT [illegible]

Copy of the suicide note which Tom Grant copied on Courtney's fax machine. The black lines are actually wrinkles in the fax paper. The marking 'GP171' in the top right corner and 'Capt ________' in the bottom right are police notations.